The Economics of Natural Resources in Latin America

T0384297

Revenues from commodities are extremely important for Latin America and the Caribbean, yet there is very little literature on the structure of these industries and on the various ways in which the state obtains commodity revenues. This book aims to understand the trade-off between the degree of taxation overall, the profitability of the relevant industry and the amount of investment and subsequent production in the region, as well as the relevance of institutions in the performance of the sector.

This volume focuses on economic efficiency: where Latin America stands in terms of the current tax system for the extractive sector; how policies have changed in this regard and how policies may be improved. *The Economics of Natural Resources in Latin America* is timely, since this new era of lower and volatile prices and possible reconfiguration of investment flows poses a challenge to natural resource tax systems in the world. The argument of the book will be made by a collection of papers around the issue of tax efficiency in the region and concludes with chapters on institutions and the role of transparency.

This book shows that there are varieties of experiences in resource taxation and management of revenues in Latin America that could be used to shape policy interventions in other regions. This variety is not only related to their diverse impact on welfare, but also on the policy challenges faced by the countries in the region. This volume is well suited for those who study and find interest in development economics, political economy and public finance, as well as policymakers who deal with resource economics in the region.

Osmel E. Manzano M is Regional Economic Advisor for the Country Department for Belize, Central America, Mexico, Panama and Dominican Republic at the Inter-American Development Bank, USA. He is responsible for the economic work and macroeconomic monitoring of the IADB in Central America, Mexico and the Dominican Republic.

Fernando H. Navajas is Professor of Economics at the Universities of Buenos Aires and La Plata and Chief Economist at FIEL, Argentina. He is currently President of the Argentine Association of Political Economy and Director of the Applied Economics Institute of the National Academy of Economic Science of Argentina.

Andrew Powell is Principal Advisor in the Research Department (RES) of the Inter-American Development Bank, USA. He has published numerous academic papers in leading economic journals in areas including commodity markets, risk management, the role of multilaterals, regulation, banking and international finance.

Routledge Studies in Development Economics

For a complete list of titles in this series, please visit www.routledge.com/series/SE0266

The Economics of Natural Resources in Latin America

Taxation and Regulation of
the Extractive Industries

**Edited by
Osmel E. Manzano M,
Fernando H. Navajas and
Andrew Powell**

Routledge
Taylor & Francis Group

LONDON AND NEW YORK

First published 2018 by Routledge

2 Park Square, Milton Park, Abingdon, Oxfordshire OX14 4RN

52 Vanderbilt Avenue, New York, NY 10017

Routledge is an imprint of the Taylor & Francis Group, an informa business

First issued in paperback 2019

Copyright © 2018 selection and editorial matter, Inter-American Development Bank; individual chapters, the contributors

The right of the Inter-American Development Bank to be identified as the authors of the editorial material, and of the authors for their individual chapters, has been asserted in accordance with sections 77 and 78 of the Copyright, Designs and Patents Act 1988.

All rights reserved. No part of this book may be reprinted or reproduced or utilised in any form or by any electronic, mechanical, or other means, now known or hereafter invented, including photocopying and recording, or in any information storage or retrieval system, without permission in writing from the publishers.

Notice:
Product or corporate names may be trademarks or registered trademarks, and are used only for identification and explanation without intent to infringe.

British Library Cataloguing-in-Publication Data
A catalogue record for this book is available from the British Library

Library of Congress Cataloging-in-Publication Data
A catalog record for this book has been requested

ISBN: 978-1-138-08536-7 (hbk)
ISBN: 978-0-367-88904-3 (pbk)

Typeset in Times New Roman
by Apex CoVantage, LLC

Contents

Figures

Tables

Contributors

Lenin H. Balza is an economist at the Infrastructure and Energy Department at the Inter-American Development Bank (IDB), USA. Previously, he worked as a research fellow at the Energy Division of the IDB, Santander Investment Group; and the Andean Development Corporation (CAF). He holds a Master's Degree in Economic Development (MPA/ID) from the John F. Kennedy School of Government at Harvard University. He also holds a Bachelor's Degree in Economics from Universidad Central de Venezuela, and studied Economics as a postgraduate student at Tercuato Di Tella University. His areas of interest and research include development strategies, energy economics and economic development in resource-rich countries.

Mauricio Calani is a Senior Economist at the Central Bank of Chile. His research interests include international macroeconomics, economic growth and macro-finance. Mr. Calani holds a Ph.D. from the University of Pennsylvania, USA (2016).

Atanas Christev is currently Assistant Professor of Economics at Heriot-Watt University, Edinburgh, UK. He received his Ph.D. in Economics from Kansas State University, USA. His research focuses on econometric models of firm adjustment in transition, including dynamic labor demand, asymmetric adjustment costs, employment and wage mobility; unemployment dynamics; and dynamic monopsony models.

Claudia Cooper currently works as Minister of Finance and Economics in Peru. She has previously been a member of the Peruvian Fiscal Board, Product Development and Institutional Relations Manager at Compass Group, Associate Researcher at Universidad del Pacifico, Chief Economist at the Ministry of Economics and Finance in Peru, and Treasury Manager and Chief Economist at Banco de Credito del Peru. She also has ample consultancy experience with multilateral institutions in the public and the private sector. She has taught at Universidad del Pacifico and New York University. She has undertaken doctoral studies in Economics at New York University and she holds a Bachelor's Degree in Economics from Universidad del Pacifico.

Akram Esanov is an expert on political economy of oil rent distribution, economic diversification of resource-rich countries, economic development and country risk analysis. Dr. Esanov has worked at such leading international financial and developmental institutions as the Asian Development Bank Institute, the European Bank for Reconstruction and Development, the World Bank and the Natural Resource Governance Institute. Trained as an economist, he is currently an Adjunct Professor at New York University, USA.

Ramón Espinasa is the General Coordinator of the Extractive Sector Initiative at the Infrastructure and Energy Sector of the Inter-American Development Bank (IDB), USA. For 20 years, up to 1999, he worked at Petróleos de Venezuela (PDVSA) where he was Chief Economist between 1992 and 1999. Dr. Espinasa is an Industrial Engineer from Universidad Católica Andrés Bello in Caracas (1974) and holds Ph.D. (1984) and M. Phil (1980) degrees in Energy Economics and Economic Development from the University of Cambridge and a Masters in Economic Development from the Institute of Social Studies in The Hague (1979). At present Dr. Espinasa is an Adjunct Professor at Georgetown University, USA, where he teaches two postgraduate seminars on World and Hemispheric Energy Security.

J. Rodrigo Fuentes is Professor of Economics at the Department of Economics in the Pontificia Universidad Católica de Chile. He worked as Senior Economist at the Research Department of the Central Bank of Chile. He was Dean of the Graduate School of Economics and Business and Assistant Professor in the School of Economics and Business at the University of Chile. He holds a Ph.D. and a Master of Arts in Economics, University of California Los Angeles (UCLA), and a BA in Economics and MSc in Finance from the University of Chile. He has published papers in domestic and international journals and he has been a consultant for the World Bank and Inter-American Development Bank, as well as for international and Chilean government agencies and the Chilean private sector.

Sui-Jade Ho's research interests are in international economics, public economics and macroeconomics. Her recent works include studies on the relationship between multinational corporations and firm employment, and on measuring misallocation in the manufacturing sector. She holds an MA in Economics from the University of Cambridge, UK, an MPA in International Development from Harvard University, USA, and a Ph.D. in Economics from the University of Michigan – Ann Arbor, USA.

Enrique Kawamura is Associate Professor of Economics and Director of the Master in Economics Program at Universidad de San Andrés, Argentina. His main fields include Macroeconomics and Finance. His main research interests include the political dimensions of fiscal policy, the analysis of political constraints and the dynamics of energy regulation in emerging markets. Professor Kawamura's research has been published in major academic journals such as the *Journal of Economic Theory*, the *Journal of Monetary Economics*, the *Journal of International Money and Finance,* the *Journal of Economic Behavior and Organization* and *Economía*, the journal of LACEA.

Osmel E. Manzano M is Regional Economic Advisor for the Country Department for Belize, Central America, Mexico, Panama and Dominican Republic at the Inter-American Development Bank, USA. He is responsible for the economic work and macroeconomic monitoring of the IADB in Central America, Mexico and the Dominican Republic.

Eduardo Morón is President of the Peruvian Association of Insurance Companies (APESEG, in Spanish). He is also Professor at the Faculty of Economics of Universidad del Pacifico, and member of the Fiscal Board in Peru. Previously, he was Chief Economist at the Latin American Reserve Fund (FLAR) from 2012–2014. He was Deputy Minister of Economics, Director at the Research Center of Universidad del Pacifico, and Director of the Master in Economics Program at the same university. He holds a Ph.D. in Economics from UCLA, USA, a Masters in Economics from Universidad del CEMA in Buenos Aires, Argentina, and he is Licentiate in Economics by Universidad del Pacifico in Lima, Peru.

Fernando H. Navajas is Professor of Economics at the Universities of Buenos Aires and La Plata and Chief Economist at FIEL, Argentina. He is currently President of the Argentine Association of Political Economy and Director of the Applied Economics Institute of the National Academy of Economic Science of Argentina.

Guillermo Perry is presently a Professor at the School of Economics at Universidad de Los Andes in Colombia, a Non-Resident Fellow at the Center for Global Development, Washington DC, USA, and a senior external advisor to the President of the Development Bank of Latin America (CAF). He was formerly the Chief Economist for Latin America and the Caribbean at the World Bank from 1996 to 2007, Minister of Finance and Public Credit (1994–1996) and of Mining and Energy (1986–1988) and Member of the Constitutional Assembly (1991) in his home country, Colombia. He was also Director of Colombia's two leading economic think-tanks, Fedesarrollo and the Center for Economic Development Studies (CEDE), a Visiting Fellow at St Antony's College at Oxford University, UK (1977–1978) and Robert F. Kennedy Visiting Professor at the MPA-ID program in the Kennedy School at Harvard University, USA (2010–2011). Mr. Perry attended the Ph.D. program in Economics and Operational Research at the Massachusetts Institute of Technology, USA (1968–1973).

Bernardita Piedrabuena Keymer has been the Director of Capital Markets and International Finance at the Ministry of Finance of Chile since April of 2014. Previously, Mrs. Piedrabuena was the Economic Specialist for Chile at the IDB (2010–2014); Economic Specialist for Uruguay at the IDB (2009–2010); and Macroeconomic Coordinator of the Ministry of Finance of Chile (2002–2006). She graduated in Economics from Pontificia Universidad Católica de Chile in 1994, where she was awarded the prize for the best student in her class. She holds a Master's Degree in Economic Science from Pontificia Universidad Católica de Chile, and a Ph.D. in Economics from Universidad de Chile.

Andrew Powell is Principal Advisor in the Research Department (RES) of the Inter-American Development Bank, USA. He has published numerous academic papers in leading economic journals in areas including commodity markets, risk management, the role of multilaterals, regulation, banking and international finance.

Foreword

Latin America is extremely fortunate in that it is one of the most commodity resource-rich regions of the world. As these natural assets are extracted, they can turbo-charge investment in other assets that are more productive. But this does not happen automatically: it requires smart and distinctive public policies. Good public policy is always demanding, and natural resource management is particularly so. Where governments have got it right, resource wealth has propelled development: diamond wealth enabled Botswana to become the fastest growing economy in the world. But conflicts over resource wealth can also create divisions and undermine governance to such a degree that the country collapses into poverty. The diamond wealth of Sierra Leone ignited violence and mis-governance that left the country at the bottom of the Human Development Index. As I wrote about in *The Bottom Billion*,[1] the natural resource trap is one of the mechanisms whereby the poor have stayed poor.

Latin America reflects this global pattern that some societies harness their resources for the public good and grow rapidly, while in others the resources inflame conflict and are dissipated. At the heart of these divergent outcomes are divergent policy decisions as to how the commodity sector is organized, how public companies are governed and how private ones are taxed. This book provides an excellent and detailed analysis of these topics. A point is how economic performance is dependent upon the quality of institutions: institutions really matter. Yet the easy money that resource extraction can bring tends to undermine institutions: resource-rich societies need strong institutions, yet often end up with weak ones.

So what can be done? Institutions are not just words on paper; they are teams of people organized around a mandate. When the institutions that will be needed for good management of natural resources are weak, complex new designs that look good on paper are likely to be unrealistic. It may be better to keep things simple and transparent, so that actions can readily be held to account. Only where institutions have gained a reasonable degree of sophistication can more complex systems of taxation be introduced. Latin America provides a natural laboratory to study these issues and this book does an excellent job in illuminating the various trade-offs. The chapters provide a balanced combination of the realism and contextual richness of country studies, with the analytic clarity that comes from transversal topics such as institutional development and transparency. Between them, they provide the reader with a compelling overall assessment of the topic.

For anyone interested in how to best to design and implement better fiscal regimes for commodity sectors in Latin America and beyond, this book will repay its value many times over.

Paul Collier

Note

1 Collier, Paul 2007. *The Bottom Billion*. Oxford University Press, Oxford.

1 The taxation of non-renewable resources in Latin America

Introduction and overview

Osmel E. Manzano M, Fernando H. Navajas and Andrew Powell

Latin America is an extremely resource-rich continent. From Mexico with its substantial oil and other commodity resources, through Venezuela, the country with the largest proven oil reserves in the world, and down to Chile, the world's largest copper producer, in the majority of countries in the region there is oil or gas to be extracted or metals and other minerals to be mined. At the same time, the prices of these commodities are very volatile. And not simply because there are many shocks around some easily identified trend. The shocks are large and persistent, making just identifying trends, if they exist at all, very difficult indeed. For substantial periods, prices have been well-above long-run extraction costs for many projects, implying that there are substantial excess economic profits, otherwise known as rents. This book is about how governments have shaped policies to facilitate the exploitation of these resources such that a significant part of those profits can be distributed to public revenues helping to boost investments such as roads and schools and in many cases to finance current expenditures as well.

The countries in the region have chosen a variety of economic structures to exploit their natural resource wealth. Some have maintained large public companies that not only search for oil and ore but also operate upstream extracting those resources. Some of the oil companies are vertically integrated so have downstream operations as well and some public mining companies may also own metal processing firms. In these cases, profits may be transferred directly to governments. Other countries have taken a very different approach relying almost exclusively on private firms to discover new deposits and reserves and also to exploit them. In these cases, tax and royalty systems aim to boost public revenues while maintaining sufficient incentives for firms to continue their activities.

To some extent these different structures reflect divergence in more general economic policies adopted by different countries in the region. Broadly speaking a set of countries (including Chile, Colombia, Mexico and Peru) have followed more open, pro-market policies designed to attract foreign investment while others (such as Argentina, Bolivia, Ecuador and Venezuela) shifted towards a greater degree of government intervention. But even in Chile, Colombia and Mexico state mining and oil companies continue to play critical roles. More recently the trend has been shifting to greater reliance on private firms in virtually all stages of the supply chain. Mexico has liberated energy markets, while in Chile and Colombia a greater share of recent investment has gone through private rather than public companies. The government of President Macri elected in late 2016 in Argentina is opening the economy and implementing more pro-market reforms once again. This implies that the importance of designing appropriate fiscal regimes including efficient tax systems is more important than ever.

This book provides a set of papers that highlight the many challenges involved in the taxation of natural resources in the Latin American region, looking in some detail at relevant country experiences. The chapters include a short history of the fiscal regime in the country and several chapters follow a common methodology to evaluate the most recent regime in place. Before providing a summary of the contributions of the chapters, this introductory chapter provides an overview of various related general topics to provide the context. The first topic is the behavior of commodity prices, including the recent "super-cycle" and the implications for public sector revenues. This sets the scene for why designing fiscal regimes may be such a challenge. The following section then considers recent literature on the design of those regimes highlighting several underlying problems including the behavior of prices. Reasonably sophisticated regimes and instruments may be required to effectively manage such a volatile revenue flow given the magnitude and the persistence of price shocks But the more sophisticated the regime, the more this then relies on there being a strong institutional setting. The next section then considers evidence regarding institutional strength in the region and attempts to gauge the gaps in the quality of institutions relative to best practices. The final section of the chapter considers the challenges for natural resource tax systems in Latin America in an era of lower prices and a possible reconfiguration of investment flows.

1   Commodity prices, the super-cycle and implications for fiscal revenues

Commodities are traded on forward-looking markets, focusing liquidity on specific, standardized contracts which then aggregate information regarding current and future supply, demand and other relevant conditions. This implies that current spot prices for commodities normally reflect all of the relevant information and so those prices represent a type of average expectation of where prices should be. In turn this means that prices will only change if new information comes to light meaning that price changes are inherently unpredictable. Spot prices can also be extremely volatile. One way to think about why this is the case is that as markets are forward looking, then in general the entire change in the future expected course of supply (or demand) is instantaneously reflected in the spot price today.

Indeed, sometimes commodity prices seem to depart from actual, current real supply and demand considerations. For example, if there is an increased probability of conflict in the Middle East, oil prices may rise substantially. But then hasty negotiations may reduce tensions once again bringing prices down, all without a single shot fired and without the supply of a single barrel of oil affected. Some analysts suggest that this reflects a type of financial speculation and that markets may then be playing a murky and de-stabilizing role. But most economists see this as markets performing efficiently and simply responding to information as to what might affect future supply and demand conditions.

As mentioned above the time from making new investments to seeing actual new production in many non-renewables can be very long, frequently several years and perhaps even a decade in the case of a large mine. This means that if there is unexpectedly higher demand it may take a long time for supply to catch up. In the meantime, stocks will dwindle and prices will rise. As stocks become very low, commodity price theory indicates prices will actually rise faster and faster for each marginal increase in demand.

High prices will stimulate new investment which is then generally sunk, meaning that it cannot be reversed or it's very costly to do so. And so, capacity then comes on stream many years later, and sometimes just when the original reasons for the boom, perhaps demand-related, have subsided. Over-capacity and over-production then hangs over the market and prices become depressed, producing countries suffer and new investment slumps. And it can take many years for either demand to pick up sufficiently or that over-capacity to fade and then the cycle begins again: the 20th century is littered with such boom-bust cycles.[1]

At the start of the 2000s there was much discussion as to whether this boom-bust cycle had changed. Commodity prices in general soared, oil pushed well beyond $100 per barrel, sophisticated investment banks predicted $200 per barrel, there was concern regarding a food crisis (and agricultural products were increasingly used for energy-related uses) and there were fears of under-supply and shortages in many commodity markets. Then came the global financial crisis, recession in most countries in the world and fears of deep financial dislocation and a prolonged economic downturn. Commodity prices slumped. But thankfully the financial crisis itself was relatively short lived and while growth in the US and Europe fell, with the integrity of the global financial system apparently secured, commodity prices shot back up again.

There are competing explanations for the 2002–2012 commodity super-boom. Some suggest the advent and growth of dedicated commodity investment funds and the idea that commodities formed a new "asset class" played a critical role. Some, particularly after the global financial crisis, blamed loose monetary policy in the US and Europe and the associated depreciation of the dollar – particularly as commodity prices are generally expressed in the US currency. But real factors surely played an important if not dominant role and, in particular, the spectacular growth of China is surely a central part of any explanation. Figure 1.1 illustrates commodity prices since 1990 and the massive China-led boom is clearly visible.

Chinese GDP grew at an average rate of more than 10% per annum for a decade between 2002 and 2012 such that China became the second largest economy in the world measured at market exchange rates and the largest by other measures. This is equivalent to adding an economy the size of Argentina or Sweden to the world every year for ten years! This level of growth in such a large economy is simply unprecedented. China demand outstrips its own supply in virtually every commodity and so this huge demand increase created correlated movements in pretty much all commodity prices, and stocks dwindled. As stocks become very low, commodity theory suggests each extra dollar (or Renminbi) of demand pushes prices further and further up, so prices become more and more sensitive to demand shocks. While commodity funds and monetary policy may play a role,

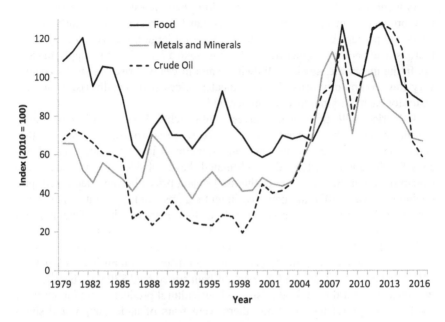

Figure 1.1 Real commodity prices since 1990

Source: IMF Commodity Price Indices and authors' estimates

those explanations are not actually needed to understand why the China boom became so large.

But history suggests that eventually supply does tend to catch up. More mines are dug, more wells are sunk, and more acres of land are planted and technology also improves, no doubt affected by the incentives provided by high prices to extract every last ton and barrel. Indeed, advances in technology were particularly important for oil. Horizontal drilling now allows a traditional well to extract oil from more than five miles away and deep down, and the technology to extract oil from shale (both shale-oil and oil-shale – confusingly these are different things) and tar sands has changed some of the economics of oil. Moreover, countries that had been out of the international oil market began to come back including Iran, Iraq and Libya. And just as supply appeared to be catching demand in most commodities, China started to slow and to rebalance away from an investment-led export economy more to one balanced between investment, exports and domestic consumption. At the time of writing, China is growing at around 6.5% and while there has been some rebalancing this did not progress as much as expected in the early to mid-2010s. Moreover, in the years following the global financial crisis, growth in the US, Europe and Japan has been very low. The impacts of lower world growth have been felt across many commodity markets.

An index of metals and minerals prices relevant for Latin America and the Caribbean fell by around 40% between 2011 and 2015. However, different commodities demonstrated differential trends. For example, bulk goods, such as iron ore and coal, suffered particularly heavily, falling by 61% and 51% respectively between 2011 and 2015. However, other commodities faired considerably better with zinc prices falling by only 6% and bauxite values increasing by a similar proportion over the period. Weaker demand growth in China has been a notable contributor to the collapse in prices. Annualized demand growth for copper, for example, fell from 12.4% in 2010 to 3.8% in 2015, reflecting the slowdown in Chinese investment expenditure. And then from 2014 to 2016 came the dramatic collapse in the price of oil.

While there is variation across different markets, lower demand coupled with the lagged but eventual supply response led to a change in the supply demand balance and rising stocks. Over-production then reigned in most markets. Only towards the end of 2016 did commodity prices stabilize and even start to rise in part as a response to expected stimulus and faster growth in the US. The behavior of commodity prices with deep and persistent boom and bust cycles implies particular challenges for fiscal regimes. This is reflected in the recent literature which is discussed in the next section.

The impacts on fiscal revenues has been quite dramatic for many commodity-producing countries. In Latin America and the Caribbean, some ten countries may be considered as dependent on non-renewables. On average, revenues from commodities in these countries accounted for more than 25% of total public sector revenues in the late 2000s. Figure 1.2 illustrates how public sector revenues from commodities then plunged as a percentage of total public sector revenues and as a percentage of GDP as commodity prices collapsed.

This has left several countries with significant fiscal problems implying larger deficits and rising debt. Many countries in the Latin America and the Caribbean are now pursuing fiscal consolidation programs and the fall in commodity revenues plays a large part in those decisions.

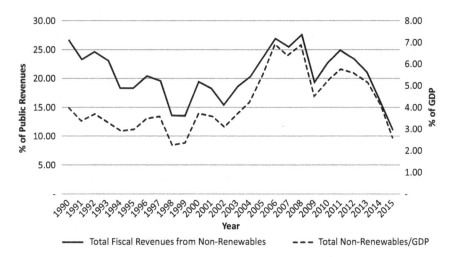

Figure 1.2 The importance of commodities in public revenues

Source: Powell (2017) and authors' estimates

After the next section considering the recent literature the discussion turns to institutions. Given the volatile nature of commodity prices and impacts on fiscal revenues, strong institutions may be required to manage the volatility inherent in these flows. The subsequent section details that for many countries in Latin America significant institutional gaps remain.

2   Recent literature on non-renewables

Non-renewable natural resource economics is a large area with many different streams of literature reflecting the underlying economic issues involved. The sector is characterized by very large required investments that are generally sunk and long production lags. Attempting to forecast where prices will be in the medium and longer term is then a paramount concern. Some countries are large enough producers to have some degree of market power or to act as so-called swing producers, and some private firms are very large, global, players. Private firms generally have much better information regarding their own cost-structures than governments that attempt to design tax systems so problems of asymmetric information abound. And as reviewed further below, prices are volatile with deep boom and bust cycles. Some countries have managed to construct fiscal regimes and spending rules and have performed relatively well while others have fared very poorly indeed, arguably because domestic institutions were not up the task of dealing with these complexities giving rise to what has been referred to as a natural resource curse. This set of fascinating issues has encouraged a growing literature considering different aspects of the issues involved and many such works then have relevance when considering the design of an appropriate fiscal regime.

Considering performance from a macroeconomic perspective, Humphreys et al. (2007) reviews how countries may be able to escape the "resource curse". The book provides a general overview of many issues related to the role on extractive industries (in particular oil) in development. Davis et al. (2003) gives greater details on the issues of macroeconomic volatility, country experiences and policy recommendations. Anderson (2012) considers the challenges of managing oil and gas in countries that have federal political systems where in general the gains from exploitations of natural resources is shared between a federal government and local or state authorities. The book discusses not only pertinent macroeconomic issues, but also institutional and social concerns. Argentina and Venezuela are discussed as two case studies providing useful background to the more detailed analysis presented in the relevant chapters of this volume.

There has also been more specific work on exactly how to design an appropriate fiscal regime for extractive industries. Johnston (2007), Radon (2007) and Cramton (2007) discuss tax regimes, contract negotiation and oil rights, respectively. Similarly, Tordo (2007) discusses some issues that need to be taken into consideration when designing a fiscal system for hydrocarbons. This paper looks more into the details of instruments and their impact of the life cycle of an oil project. In that context, the paper focuses on issues to achieve an efficient fiscal system. More recently, Calder (2014), discusses the main issues on administering the fiscal regime for extractive industries. Since the focus is on administration, the book mostly covers institutional, legal and procedural matters.

There is less literature that considers and attempts to draw lessons from specific country experiences in relation to managing tax regimes. Nakhle (2008) presents an interesting historical perspective on the issue. The paper focusses largely on the United Kingdom and attempts a type of evaluation of the tax regime in place over time. Hogan and Sturzenegger (2010) review country cases, including focusing on some Latin American nations. Their analysis is centered on oil and specifically they address the question as to why contracts in that industry have not favored a stable commercial framework for the sector. The role played by taxation is discussed to some extent but it is not the focus of the book. Daniel et al. (2010) discusses institutional choices in extractives taxation with some reference to country cases. In particular, the book discusses experiences in oil, gas and mineral taxations. However, the perspective is a broad historical discussion on how systems have evolved rather than a specific analysis regarding design and implementation issues as outlined in the book.

The existing literature makes clear that designing tax systems implies a complex set of trade-offs and taking into account constraints that may vary across countries. Different instruments may be employed and so there is also an interesting mapping from the alternative instruments that might be used and the expected outcomes. In general terms fiscal regimes may wish to capture as large a portion of the excessive profits as possible but at the same time minimize the volatility of fiscal revenue flows and yet these two objectives frequently imply quite different designs. Moreover, systems may wish to be flexible to respond to unforeseen circumstances but at the same time provide credibility to firms and to investors, again objectives that may imply divergent needs in terms of design and instrument selection. Finally, fiscal systems may wish to allocate risks in a fair fashion but also be efficient which may also provoke a complex design problem. The set of instruments that governments have used has grown over time and now includes common taxes, royalties, taxes specifically designed to capture rents (rent or R-taxation), various types of progressive schemes, flexible contracts, sector-specific profit taxes and incentive schemes introduced within tax systems plus other indirect or consumption taxes and export and import duties or subsidies.

3 Institutions and instruments: gaps in relation to best practices

Fundamental differences in the type and quality of institutions and regulatory frameworks imply a varied landscape in country fiscal regimes for commodities. In turn this may then provoke differences in the choice of instruments and influence not only company investment strategy but also operational behavior.

In the natural resource sector, Latin American economies display marked difference in terms of institutional gaps and instrumental policy gaps in relation to best practices around the world. These aspects are captured in the various chapters of this book. There are countries where institutional gaps with best practices worldwide are very significant while in others the gap is observed more at the level of instruments. These differences can be predicted in a simple screening of issues detected in global surveys leading to quite different cases in the region and pointing to different governance environments and different directions of reform agendas. One such type of screening is recurrently done by global surveys of policy perceptions (such as that performed by the Fraser Institute, 2015) which is used to depict in Figures 1.3 and 1.4 a simple benchmarking of the relative position of the region and the countries in both oil and gas and mining policies.

Figure 1.3 shows that Latin America scores poorly against other regions in the perception survey of policy in the hydrocarbons upstream sector. Only Trinidad and Tobago, Colombia and Brazil's offshore policies (and Uruguay which is only a prospective not developed case) have acceptable comparable levels of policy perception. Some important South American natural gas producers in both conventional (Argentina and Bolivia) and prospectively non-conventional natural gas (Neuquen-Argentina) have average, i.e. relatively poor perception positions, with Argentina now moving into a new scenario. Finally large producers such as Venezuela have worldwide minimum levels of performance at the perception level of policies while Ecuador closely follows this.

Figure 1.4 shows a similar picture in the case of the benchmarking of the policy perception in the mining sector. Here the region performs on average better than Asia. This is partly due to the high performance of Chile, followed by Mexico and Peru. Above average there are the cases of Brazil, Colombia and the province of

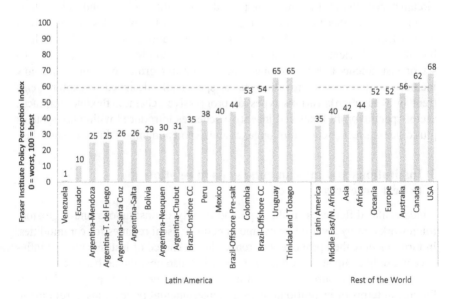

Figure 1.3 Benchmarking Latin American petroleum policy perceptions, 2015
Source: Fraser Institute Policy Perception Index

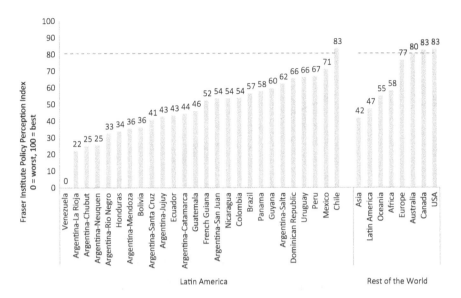

Figure 1.4 Benchmarking Latin American mining policy perceptions, 2015

Source: Fraser Institute (various years)

San Juan in Argentina. However, the rest shows poor policy perception in some important resource-abundant countries or regions such as Bolivia and many provinces of Argentina, which is again leveling up its outlook.

Do institutional factors embedded in policy perception correlate with tax systems in hydrocarbons and mining sectors in the region? The answer is positive and institutional gaps are correlated with instrumental gaps in the form of poor tax systems. Figures 1.5 and 1.6 show the scattered plot of the countries/regions shown in Figures 1.3 and 1.4 against their performance in terms of fiscal terms (for petroleum) or tax regimes (for mining), showing that countries/regions with low policy perception have also low ranked tax systems and that the region has bad as well as relatively good performers even though on average performance is poor relatively to other regions of the world.

These institutional gaps will have significant impacts on efficiency. As the chapters in this book shows, these impacts come from a mix of sector and general institutions. At the sector level, the chapter by Balza and Espinasa shows that there were dissimilar responses among Latin American oil producers to the significant increase in oil price levels over the last decade. They argue that this can be explained by the differences in the institutional framework governing the oil sector and thus on the set of incentives to invest in response to changing price signals.

However, general institutions also matter. The chapter by Ho and Perry shows that the expected negative response of oil and mineral production to an increase

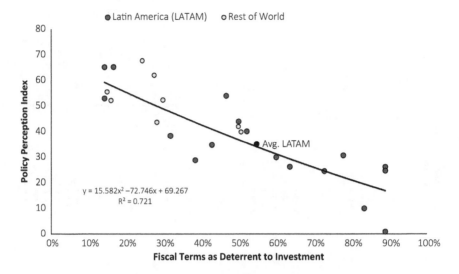

Figure 1.5 Petroleum Policy Perceptions Index and fiscal terms as deterrent to investment

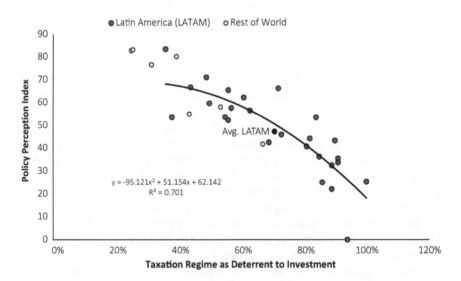

Figure 1.6 Mining Policy Perceptions Index and fiscal terms as deterrent to investment

in the tax rate is reduced when controls for quality of institutions are introduced. Therefore, in countries with better institutions the negative effect on efficiency of taxes could be smaller.

Furthermore, it is not only "general" institutions that could reflect a positive business environment that affect production decisions. Institutions related to revenue management might also impact these decisions. The chapter by Christev and Esanov finds that greater fiscal transparency, measured by membership in the Extractive Industries Transparency Initiative (EITI), tends to increase and might improve the country's business environment.

As we will explain later, to achieve efficiency, tax instruments should be neutral, flexible and predictable. It could be argued that these positive impacts of the institutional setting on production decisions is related to predictability. Countries with better sector and general institutions could be less likely to modify the tax schemes.

The results and lessons of natural resource taxation in Latin America reflect the experience of a region particularly affected by a super-cycle of commodity prices which is embedded in many findings of the papers and have important lessons for the field of natural resource taxation. Results can teach us how tax systems have adapted and evolved in face of this super-cycle. What have been the major designs or practical issues faced or triggered by this super-cycle story? What inconsistencies or lack of adaptation to a new environment were also created by those changes? What lessons can be learned?

4 What next for resource tax systems in Latin America?

The previous sections have argued that the region is heterogeneous in terms of governance, with large and varied institutional and instrumental gaps relative to best practices and that given the inherent volatility and persistence of shocks to commodity prices, the challenge to design and implement appropriate fiscal regimes is very significant indeed. This final subsection reflects on these challenges and suggests directions in which reforms tax systems may be required in the future.

It is clear, that the region still uses a variety of tax instruments. Table 1.1 details some of the revenue systems for non-renewable sectors in select Latin American and Caribbean countries. There are significant differences both between countries producing the same product and in the same country across different products. In the case of minerals, the traditional instruments of royalties and income taxes continue to dominate, while there has been a shift toward taxing profits rather than production. The case of oil, however, has made greater use of contingent instruments, perhaps because of the size of the rents available in this sector.

There has also been a tendency to increase the complexity of instruments. In Peru, the design of royalties currently mimics taxes on net profits. The arrangement is similar in Chile, which has a "Specific Tax on Mining". Venezuela's windfall tax in the oil sector is a royalty contingent on the price. The mix of instruments further complicates the analysis of the tax burden.

Tordo (2007) lists certain desirable characteristics, including:

- Neutrality: A system is said to be neutral if it does not affect the decisions of private agents.
- Flexibility: A system is said to be flexible if it may adapt to changes in external conditions.
- Stability: A system is stable if there are no large changes, or if changes are predictable.

Table 1.1 Revenue instruments in Latin America and the Caribbean

Sector	Country	Royalty	Income Tax			Windfall taxes	Dividend	Other taxes	State participation
			Contract contingency	Income Tax	Different rate to corporate				
Oil	Argentina	Yes. Fixed rate of 12%	No	Yes	No	No	No	No	Yes
	Mexico	No	No	No	No	Yes. Right on hydrocarbons for the stabilization fund (paid when price exceeds a threshold)	No	Ordinary right on hydrocarbons: 73.5% of sales value; right for the Fund for Technological and Scientific Research, among others	Yes. National company only producer
	Trinidad and Tobago	Yes. 10% on onshore sales and 12.5% on offshore sales	No	Yes. 50% of gross revenues	No	No	No	Supplemental petroleum tax: 0% to 35% depending on oil prices	Yes
	Venezuela	Yes	Yes	Yes	Yes	Yes	No	Territorial tax	Yes. National company. 60% on joint ventures
Gas	Argentina	Yes. Fixed rate of 12%	No	Yes	No	No	No	Export tax	Yes
	Bolivia	Yes. 12%	No	Yes	No	No	No	Direct tax on hydrocarbons (IDH). 32% of gross output;	Yes

								additional 32% tax on megafields' production
Trinidad & Tobago	Yes. Fixed rate of 12.5%	No	Yes. 35% on profits	No	No	No	No	Yes
Peru	Yes. 37.24% for locally consumed gas; 30%–38% for gas exported	Yes	Yes, 30%	No	No	No	No	Yes
Copper — Argentina	Yes. 0% to 3% depending on the province	No	Yes	No	No	No	Sales tax	Yes
Chile	Yes	After 2006, 0–5% depending on scale	Yes	Yes (mining income tax, depends on scale)	No	Yes (4.1% on non domiciled)	No	Yes
Peru	Yes	1% – 12% (paid if no stabilization agreement)	Yes	Yes (special mining tax, paid if no stabilization agreement)	No	Yes (4.1% on non–domiciled)	Workers profit sharing	Yes
Mexico	No	No	Yes	No	No	No	Workers profit sharing and special mining duty	No
Gold — Peru	Yes	Yes	Yes, fixed rate of 30%	No	No	Yes (4.1% on non domiciled)	No	No

Source: Corbacho et al. (2013)
See Tordo (2007) for further elaboration.

Traditional systems of royalties and income taxes score poorly on neutrality and stability. Profit or net income taxes may be more efficient and may display a greater deal of stability. However, they increase the complexity of the system and the administrative burden.

The challenge in Latin America is to move towards systems that are neutral but at the same time that are more efficient. In the next chapters we will see that indeed countries are moving in that direction. However, there is still a mix of instruments and there could be gains in continuing this trend.

The chapter by Cooper and Morón for Peru explains a law which modified the mining royalty regime. This law established that the royalty is no longer based on sales, instead it is determined according to a quarterly operational profits-to-sales ratio, with progressive marginal rates. They estimated that when the existing royalty based on gross income is replaced by an extra levy on the income tax – as it was approved for the mining sector – the distortion is kept to a minimum while the tax collection could be higher.

However, in the case of Peru, for oil and gas, taxes continue to be more "traditional". In both cases royalties are based on sales or gross production, with certain contingencies for price and production volumes. They show that, in both cases, taxes based on profits could generate more revenue.

Furthermore, tax systems based on "pure profit" will have to take into account how to deal with depreciation. In the case of Chile, the chapter of Fuentes et al. shows that until 2005, the only tax paid by private companies was the income tax. In 2006, the government put in place a specific tax on mining activities (SMT) based on taxable operating income of the mine operator. There were two important adjustments to the operating income worth mentioning: (1) SMT payment was considered as spending necessary to produce income, which implies that it can be subtracted from incomes in order to calculate the income tax and (2) it does not allow accelerated depreciation of fixed assets, accelerated amortizations of organizational and start-up costs, and losses carried from one year to the next are to be deducted from operating incomes so as to calculate the tax base on which to apply the SMT.

Their estimation shows that, given the nature of the SMT tax, which is applied to operating income tax, it is less distortive than a gross revenue tax (royalty), but it introduces a distortion since it does not allow for 100% deduction of exploration costs as in the case of income tax. They compare the untaxed case with the actual tax regime applied in Chile, finding that exploration effort does not change its pattern over time much, but output follows a smoother path under the scenario with taxes than without taxes. Therefore, in net present value there is a loss of revenue and a deadweight loss.

Furthermore, these deadweight losses will be affected by the price. Their estimation shows that the deadweight loss as share of tax revenues could double if the price of copper falls by a third. In their chapter they show that there are better combinations of instruments that can keep tax revenues and reduce deadweight losses.

Related to this issue is the combination of instruments in countries where geological characteristics are different across operations in the same sector. In the chapter by Manzano, the case of the oil sector in Venezuela is presented. In Venezuela, there are different geological areas for oil. After applying the same tax structure to all of them, in the 1990s reforms were introduced to take into account these differences. However, as the chapter shows, it's less clear that reforms based on profitability of marginal areas might not have the best impact in terms of efficiency.

In particular, areas that the state oil company kept (Petroleos de Venezuela S.A. or PDVSA) were not subject to tax changes. However, the paper shows that those areas are the ones with the highest marginal social value. Furthermore, the paper calculates what would happen if the PDVSA tax regime was modified so as to match those of the different special agreements. It shows that the extra-surplus generated in PDVSA areas is generally greater. In addition, the level of government revenue increases under the "easing" of the tax rules, which means that the sector is in a point where the marginal change in the tax rate would be more than offset by the marginal change in production.

Finally, an important issue is the role of federal institutions. As we mentioned, this has been widely discussed in the literature, but the impact on efficiency not. The chapter by Kawamura looks into the issues of production, investment and, especially, government regulation of the Argentinian oil and gas sectors. The chapter uses a model to argue why the incentives in the political system could lead to low enough resource-regulated prices. This would explain the decline in exploration investment seen in Argentina.

In summary, governments in the region have adapted the instruments used for revenue collection towards more neutral and flexible ones, with positive impacts on efficiency. However, three main challenges remain. In most cases, they still coexist with more inefficient instruments. Second, in some countries not all extractive sectors have moved towards these instruments. Finally, even with the use of new instruments their adaptation to different geological conditions is still an area that needs improvement.

Besides these challenges in neutrality and flexibility, the other great challenge in the region will be stability. As shown in the chapter by Fuentes and coauthors, in Chile in 2010, the table of tax rates was modified to generate additional resources. Though in principle the argument could be considered as valid – the government needed revenue to reconstruct infrastructure damaged by the 2010 earthquake – it raised the issue of time commitment.

Similarly, in the chapter by Manzano it shows that in the first decade in this century Venezuela reversed some of the earlier tax reforms. Because of that, some marginal areas were no longer profitable and will not produce. The reform was reversed towards more revenue from royalties which would generate more revenue in the short run.

5 Conclusions

Designing efficient fiscal regimes for non-renewables that transfer a large portion of excess profits (or rents) but that are stable while retaining some flexibility given inevitable unforeseen events remains an enormous challenge, especially given the very volatile nature of commodity prices.

The region has made some notable advances and has been moving towards more neutral and flexible instruments, using some forms of pure profit of cash flow taxes. Nevertheless, this transition is still incomplete.

Given the varied quality of institutions the credibility and stability of regimes and instruments may continue to be questioned and a new era of low prices may provoke a new examination of fiscal regimes.

The chapters that follow provide a more detailed explanation of fiscal regimes, how they have adapted and how they have performed. As new reforms are considered it is hoped that the arguments presented and the interesting and varied experiences will assist policymakers and others to reflect on how to design appropriate regimes for the future.

Notes

1 See Mariscal and Powell (2014) for an analysis of booms and busts and discussion as to the magnitude and the likely end of the China-led commodity boom. See Powell (2015) for a summary of commodity price theory and why such booms and busts are such a feature of commodity prices.
2 Impuesto Directo a los Hidrocarburos (Hydrocarbons Direct Tax).

References

Anderson, George, ed. 2012. *Oil and Gas in Federal Systems*, Oxford University Press, Oxford.

Calder, Jack. 2014. *Administering Fiscal Regimes for Extractive Industries: A Handbook*, International Monetary Fund, Publication Services, Washington DC.

Cramton, Peter. 2007. "How Best to Auction Oil Rights", in Humphreys, Macartan, Jeffrey D. Sachs and Joseph E. Stiglitz, eds., *Escaping the Resource Curse*, pp. 114–151. Columbia University Press, New York.

Daniel, Philip, Michael Keen and Charles McPherson, eds. 2010. *The Taxation of Petroleum and Minerals: Principles, Problems and Practice,* Routledge Explorations in Environmental Economics, United Kingdom.

Davis, M., R. Ossowski and A. Fedelino, eds. 2003. *Fiscal Policy Formulation and Implementation in Oil-Producing Countries*, International Monetary Fund, Publication Services, Washington DC.

Fraser Institute. Various years. Fraser *Institute Annual Survey of Mining Companies*, Fraser Institute, Vancouver, Canada.

Humphreys, Macartan, Jeffrey D. Sachs and Joseph E. Stiglitz, eds. 2007. *Escaping the Resource Curse*, Columbia University Press, New York.

Johnston, David. 2007. "How to Evaluate the Fiscal Terms of Oil Contracts", in Humphreys, Macartan, Jeffrey D. Sachs and Joseph E. Stiglitz, eds., *Escaping the Resource Curse*, pp. 53–88. Columbia University Press, New York.

Mariscal, R. and A. Powell. 2014. *Commodity Price Booms and Busts: Detection, Magnitude and Implications for Developing Countries*. IDB Working Paper #444. January 2014.

Nakhle, Carole. 2008. *Petroleum Taxation: Sharing the Oil Wealth: A Study of Petroleum Taxation Yesterday, Today and Tomorrow*, Routledge, London.

Powell, A. 2015. "Commodity Prices: Over a Hundred Years of Booms and Busts", *VOXEU*, April, available here http://voxeu.org/article/commodity-booms-bust-evidence-1900-2010

Powell, A. 2017. "Routes to Growth in a New Trade World", IDB Latin American and Caribbean Macroeconomic Report, available here www.iadb.org/macroreport

Radon, Jenik. 2007. "How to Negotiate an Oil Agreement", in Humphreys, Macartan, Jeffrey D. Sachs and Joseph E. Stiglitz, eds., *Escaping the Resource Curse*, pp. 89–113. Columbia University Press, New York.

Tordo, S. 2007. *Fiscal Systems for Hydrocarbons: Design Issues*, World Bank Working Paper No. 123, World Bank, Washington DC.

2 The effects of commodity taxation on sector performance[1]

Guillermo Perry and
Sui-Jade Ho

Oil and mineral rich countries face a dilemma in taxing these activities. If the amount of fiscal revenues derived from oil and mineral exploitation is too low, the country may miss opportunities for socially productive investments in human capital and infrastructure. But, on the other hand, attempts to extract higher fiscal revenues may significantly discourage exploration and development investments and, hence, result in lower tax bases in the future.

The actual impact of oil and mineral taxation on sector performance will depend on a variety of factors related to the particular design of taxes and their enforcement, as well as on the governance and contractual structure in these sectors and on other country specific characteristics, such as their geological potential, infrastructure and overall quality of governance and institutions. It will also depend on global factors such as the level of interest rates and the expected oil and mineral prices and their volatility.

The technical literature highlights the effects of taxes on "high-grading" (rendering some otherwise profitable prospects to be unprofitable for exploration and development, as well as to prevent some low grading resources to be produced) and on "tilting" (changing the allocation of production over time). Generally, it finds that more neutral taxes (such as corporate income taxes, especially if they permit immediate expensing of exploration and development investments) lead to less high grading and tilting than taxes levied on the value of production (such as most royalties) or on the value of reserves.

As an example, Deacon (1993) simulated the effects of these three types of taxes in the US petroleum industry, using a simple model of a typical firm maximizing the present value of its profits under conditions of price taking and no uncertainty.[2] His results indicate that taxes on the value of production lead to higher overall production losses due to high grading, while taxes on the value of reserves lead to more tilting, accelerating production of proven reserves but delaying exploration (so as to maintain a low level of remaining proven reserves at any moment of time). As shown in the appendix, this could also be the case in Latin America not only for oil, but also for mining.

As a consequence, taxes on reserves tend to generate much higher tax revenues in the short run and significantly lower in the future, as compared to the other two types of taxes, for the same present value of taxes. Taxes on the value of production also generate higher tax revenues in the short run and lower in the future as compared to corporate income taxes, for the same present value of taxes. Corporate taxes with immediate expensing (or production sharing countries which give the host country an entitlement of a free-risk share of production after the investor has been reimbursed for exploration and development costs or has recovered them with the sales of initial production) will generate tax flows in new reservoirs or mines only after the initial investment has been recovered, which can take several years after initiating production, while royalty taxes would deliver tax flows once production starts. These examples illustrate well how the trade-offs between present and future tax revenues can depend significantly on the choice of taxes.

As a further example, another potential source of fiscal revenue in oil and gas are signature bonuses. If large, this type of "tax" could have very large impacts on "high grading", rendering uneconomic the exploration of expected low profitability deposits. Though it might be expected not to produce "tilting" in models of non-financially constrained firms and without uncertainty, as it would be a sunk cost at the moment of initiating drilling and production, if the bonus is large it may lead to front-loading production in order to guarantee prompt recovery of such an investment. Naturally, this tax could give significant cash resources upfront and at the expense of future tax revenues.

Introducing uncertainty and risk considerations would increase the expected impact of all taxes on investment and production decisions, as compared to theoretical cases without uncertainty. It also augment differences in the impact of different types of taxes on exploration, development and production decisions, given the large differences in the way in which they allocate risks between government and investors. A corporate income tax would, in principle, allocate production costs and market risks roughly proportionally between government and investors. However, the tax treatment of exploration and development costs will shift overall cost and market risks more against the government if immediate expensing is permitted (which is, on the other hand, the subtype of income tax with lower high grading and tilting effects) and it will shift cost and market risks against investors if exploration and development costs can only be deducted over long depreciation and amortization periods. A system based on "excess" profit taxes, which would be the tax that reduces the highest grading and production tilting, would however shift risks more against the government than any other type of tax. Royalties would shift risks even more against the investor than any type of income taxes and signature bonuses would allocate all risks to the companies.

Thus, risk allocation considerations increase the effects of "high grading" and "tilting" of most type of taxes, but even more for signature bonuses and royalties, in that order, than for corporate taxes. More important for our purposes, if actual tax parameters are determined by market conditions, for example through bidding or negotiation, those taxes that allocate more risks to the investors will lead to lower than expected present value of taxes, as investors will charge a higher "risk premium" on their proposals.

In the one extreme, signature bonuses that allocate all risks to investors would lead to the lowest expected present value of taxes, which is the reason why such bonuses are normally only a small proportion of the total government take, except in cases of badly "cash strapped" governments. Royalties would lead to lower present value of taxes than any form of corporate income taxes. In the other extreme, "excess" profit taxes with immediate expensing would give the highest expected present value of taxes, but would allocate more risk to the government than any other type of tax. The latter consideration, together with its higher complexity, explain why these are not widely used as the main form of oil and mineral taxation, even if economists would recommend them almost unanimously, as discussed below.

Given these differences in effects on risk allocation and investment, production and tax flows among different types of taxes, it would be desirable to disaggregate fiscal revenues from oil and minerals by type of tax in multiple country studies. On the other hand, as we will discuss below, there are significant differences within each type of taxes, as applied in each country. Further, there have been important changes over time in many countries[3] and there is a significant variety of regimes within countries at any given moment of time, depending both on the vintage of active contracts and on the degree of decentralization in tax decisions, as there are substantial differences in state and local oil and mineral taxes in several federal countries. This complexity can be properly considered in individual country studies, but would be impractical to attempt to introduce it in multiple-country studies, even if such detailed information were readily available on comparable terms across countries, which it is not.

Further, due to the trade-offs between risk allocation and expected present value of taxes, on the one hand, and between present tax flows and expected future tax flows, on the other, most countries use in practice combinations of royalty and income-based taxes, or their equivalents, which may differ less de facto than what appears to be the case de jure. Signature bonuses are also widely used, but, as mentioned, normally they represent a very small fraction of the total government take.

A recent study commissioned by the Independent Petroleum Association of America (Johnston et al. 2008) shows that countries that use Production Sharing Contracts in oil and gas (slightly more than half of producing countries) and those that use royalty plus income tax systems (slightly less than half), are quite similar in practice in their de facto financial effects, in spite of their apparent huge differences de jure. Thus, less than half of those using Production Sharing Contracts reimburse past costs at the moment of initiating production, which makes this system similar to an income-tax system with full immediate expensing. The rest of them permit total or partial recovery over time through a kind of depreciation schedule, which makes them akin to usual corporate tax systems without full expensing. In addition more than half of Production Sharing Contracts regimes put annual limits to the share of the "cost oil" or "recovery oil", which has the equivalent effect of a royalty plus income tax system.

The simulations performed by Johnston et al. show indeed that these two apparently opposing fiscal systems often lead to almost identical financial impacts. They also show that there are countries with high or low overall government takes using either type of system, though it is true that most of the highest government takes correspond either to service agreements or to Production Sharing Contracts regimes.[4]

To complicate matters further, countries frequently change contractual and fiscal provisions and on occasions shift from one regime to another.[5] As several studies have shown (e.g. Johnston 2008), the frequency of such changes increase in periods of booming prices. Normally the political pressures mount in such periods (or after large findings) in favor of renegotiating higher government takes or of shifting toward Production Sharing Contracts or outright nationalizations.[6] Changes in the opposite direction tend to happen in periods of low prices or when production is severely decaying.

Both Johnston and Rogers (2008) and Johnston (2008) warn that the "best" contracts and tax systems from the firm's financial point of view (those with lower expected government takes and risk allocation tilted against the government) are precisely those that carry the larger political risks and thus may often turn out not to be in the best interest of companies. Further, firms that know this may engage in high grading and front loading of production, given the high political risk of such contracts, contrary to what would be predicted from economic considerations that disregard political risks. In other words, considerations of political risks tend to mitigate the theoretical differences in effects between different types of taxes discussed above.

Similar conclusions emerge from Otto et al. (2006), a comprehensive analysis of mining royalties commissioned by the World Bank. This study shows, first, that royalty systems vary widely across countries: some are specific per ton while others are ad valorem; some have the same rates across minerals and some do not; some are profit based (the royalty varies with indicators of profitability) and some are hybrids.[7] Though most regimes are ad valorem, within them most permit significant cost deductions – e.g. transport, handling, inventory and insurance costs – so rates vary with international prices or with size, ore grade or oil quality and location.[8] In all such cases the actual effects of such a system may be more similar to that of an actual corporate income tax with slow depreciation and amortization clauses, than to the effects of a "pure" fixed rate royalty on the value of production. In the Chilean case, the royalty rate increases with the level of operational profits, approximating the effect of a resource rent tax (a combination of an income tax and an excess profit tax).

Second, the study shows that most countries use royalty systems in combination with income taxes, in order to "guarantee" a minimum tax proceed per year. They generally apply ad valorem rates not higher than 3% for small or low profitability mines that do not lead to significant high grading or tilting effects according to different simulations. Such a mixed regime reduces significantly political risk and it may in the end be in the interest of the investors, contrary to the conclusions of pure economic analysis that do not contemplate political risk. At the time of the World Bank study, only Chile, Mexico, South Africa, Sweden and some Argentine provinces did not impose any form of royalty tax, though three of these countries were actively considering to introduce one (Chile, South Africa and Zimbabwe). Chile and South Africa has since established a profit-based royalty system.

If the conclusions of these comprehensive studies are true, the large differences of effects by type of taxes expected from theoretical or simulation studies may actually be quite blurred in practice when political risks are considered. In addition, as mentioned, there is great variety within types of taxes, and some royalty regimes have elements that approximate their incidence to that of a common income tax, without immediate expensing. Even more important, most countries have a combined low-rate royalty and income tax type regime and, due to frequent changes, at any moment in time the "tax system" in many countries is really a collection of different tax regimes that were in place when each of the actual producing contracts were awarded or negotiated, or because in some federal countries tax regimes vary by state or province (as is the case in the US, Canada, Australia and Argentina).

Thus it may be less important and less practical to attempt to differentiate between types of taxes in multiple-country studies and it may enough to concentrate in comparing overall tax ratios or government takes, as most studies end up doing. Further, as normally those countries with more tax stability and better designs of royalty and income tax systems are those with better overall institutions, the interaction of the aggregate tax ratio and adequate indexes of quality of institutions appear to be a reasonable way to capture differences in tax regimes' quality and stability. For all these reasons, this is the approach followed in the present chapter.

1 Methodological approach

Using panel data estimations for a large number of resource-rich countries in order to answer the question posed in this paper (the effects of oil and mineral taxation on sector performance) has pros and cons with respect to detailed individual country or individual mine studies. While the latter can simulate well much of the complexity usually found in oil and mineral taxation and many country specificities, they lack external validity. The former can overcome this problem at the cost of excessive simplifications about the tax regime.

Two limitations on the availability of comparable data impose significant restrictions to panel data estimations. The first one, as already mentioned, refers to the lack of disaggregated fiscal revenues from oil and minerals by tax categories (signature bonuses, royalties, income taxes, resource rent taxes, etc.) that may have in theory significant differential effects on sector investment and production. However, the arguments presented in the last section suggest that using effective total sectoral tax ratios and their interaction with indexes of quality of institutions is a practical and perhaps not too bad approximation.

Total fiscal revenues from hydrocarbons come from the database constructed by Villafuerte et al. (2010). Total fiscal revenues was constructed by us from mining activities were collected from published IMF's Article IV consultations for the same period (1992–2009). As we don't have these data for all countries for all these years we used unbalanced panel estimations.

On the other hand, comparable oil and mineral investment data across countries is not available. This limitation led us to use data on changes of active rigs as a proxy for investment in oil- and gas-rich countries (given that either exploration or development investment require increasing the number of active rigs) and to estimate reduced form equations, using oil and mineral production, GDP or rents as the dependent variable, for the whole sample of oil- and mineral-rich countries. The data on crude oil and gas rigs were obtained from Baker Hughes Inc. From their monthly data, the average numbers of active rigs per year were calculated to be consistent with our other data which are in annual intervals.

Baker Hughes has data on rigs only for 22 of the 30 countries on which we had data on fiscal revenues from oil and gas from the IMF. Thus models are run on unbalanced panels on 22 countries (in some particular cases just on 20 due to non-availability of some of the other data).

The basic equation for active rigs that we estimated for oil- and gas-rich countries is as (1) below.

(1) $RIGSit = \alpha + \beta RIGSi, t-1 + \gamma Pit + \omega \sigma Pit + \phi \delta RESit$
$+ \Omega Rit + \pi NRTAXit + n\mu i + wt + \epsilon it$

where *Pit* are present, expected (futures) prices (or alternatively lagged prices to account for adaptive expectations); *σPit* is a measure of volatility of prices; *δRESit* are recent reserves findings; *Rit* is the relevant interest rate and *NRT AXit* is the tax ratio. The latter was estimated, alternatively, as the ratio of fiscal revenues from oil and minerals (from the sources discussed above) to oil and mineral production, GDP or rents.

Therefore, additional variables were added to this basic equation. On the one hand, we included an interaction of future prices and expected future rigs with an OPEC dummy to test if the response of countries with collective market power is somewhat different. We also included interactions of tax ratios with indexes of institutional quality (from the World Bank and OECD) to attempt to capture the effect of the quality of the contractual environment and fiscal provisions.

After doing that we estimated the basic equation (2) below for changes in oil and gas production given the observed or estimated changes in active rigs, current prices and tax ratios.

(2) $\partial Zit = \alpha + \beta \partial RIGSit + \gamma Pit + \theta NRTAX it + \mu i + wt + \epsilon it$

For model (2), the data for oil production and rigs were detrended, as recommended in Espinasa et al. (2012). First, a level equation was estimated using ordinary least squares (OLS, with the pooled sample) and country and year fixed effects (FE). Then, a difference equation was estimated using the above methodology. The three different measures of natural resource taxes were used to investigate if there is any different effect on the model.

Then, we estimated a reduced form of (1) and (2) above for the whole sample including oil- and mineral-rich countries:

(3) $Zit = \alpha + \gamma Pit + \omega \sigma Pit + \pi NRTAXit + \mu i + wt + \epsilon it$

We also included institutional variables in this equation as self-standing variables and we interacted with prices and tax ratios.

Finally, we benchmarked the efficiency of oil tax and institutional systems in oil-rich Latin American countries against their peers, by comparing the country fixed effects coefficients in our different specifications of equation (1). We also computed DEA (Data Envelopment Analysis) scores for all oil-rich countries, using as inputs the average level of reserves and/or net addition of reserves during the period and the inverse of the tax ratio.

2 Results

Results for equation (1) (natural logs of number of active rigs) for the OLS and instrumental variables (IV) estimations with country and time fixed effects are shown in Tables 2.1 and 2.2 below. OLS estimations controlling by institutional quality and OPEC dummies are shown in Tables 2.3 and 2.4. The main conclusions from these results are:

•   All estimations give significant and consistent results for our main variable interest, the one year lagged tax ratio, whether we define it as the ratio of total fiscal revenues from oil and gas with respect to oil and gas GDP, and

Table 2.1 Equation (1): Level of active rigs, fixed effects

	Rigs	Rigs	Rigs
	(1)	(2)	(3)
Average oil prices	.	0.337***	0.236**
	.	(0.116)	(0.116)
Standard deviation of oil prices	0.115***	−0.011	0.05
	(0.028)	(0.065)	(0.066)
Δ in reserves	0.238**	0.238*	0.2
	(0.115)	(0.122)	(0.138)
Natural resource tax revenue/Natural resource GDP (−1)	−0.233***		
	(0.063)		
Natural resource tax revenue/Oil production (−1)		−0.224***	
		(0.059)	
Natural resource tax revenue/Hydrocarbon exports (−1)			−0.229***
			(0.061)
Constant	3.184***	−1.973**	1.327***
	(0.261)	(0.943)	(0.321)
r2	0.234	0.24	0.275
N	332	388	370
Year fixed effects	Yes	Yes	Yes
Country fixed effects	Yes	Yes	Yes

All variables are in logs
Standard errors in parentheses
*, **, *** significant at the 10, 5 and 1 % level

production or net exports. A 10% increase in the tax ratio reduces the number of active rigs in the following year around 2.25% to 2.29% according to the OLS estimates and between 2.66% and 4.14%, depending on the definition of the tax ratio, for the IV estimations (using as instrumental variables both lagged terms of the tax ratio and an index of quality of institutions – the Government Effectiveness Index from Kauffman and Kray, various years).

- We also obtained significant results when we interacted the tax ratio with a variable of institutional quality (the Kauffman and Kray World Bank index of Government Effectiveness Index): the higher the value of this index, the lower the negative effect of the tax ratio on future active rigs (Table 2.3). This interaction seems thus to capture the effect of the quality of the oil and gas tax system, as expected. Results using the Revenue Watch Index (RWI) instead of the Government Effectiveness Index did not give significant

Table 2.2 Equation (1): Level of active rigs, instrumental variables

	Rigs	*Rigs*	*Rigs*
	(1)	*(2)*	*(3)*
Average oil prices	−0.891	0.528**	0.339
	(0.618)	(0.220)	(0.221)
Standard deviation of oil prices	0.201	−0.121**	−0.134**
	(0.163)	(0.062)	(0.063)
Δ in reserves	0.131	0.099	0.108
	(0.135)	(0.143)	(0.143)
Natural resource tax revenues/Natural resource GDP (−1)	−0.411***		
	(0.119)		
Natural resource tax revenues/Oil production (−1)		−0.258***	
		(0.099)	
Natural resource tax revenues/ Hydrocarbon exports (−1)			−0.319***
			(0.118)
r2	0.168	0.208	0.218
N	262	305	293
Instrumental variables	*In column (1) for Natural resource tax revenues/Natural resource GDP (−1) we use the lag of the Government Effectiveness and the second lag of the variable*		
	In column (2) for Natural resource tax revenues/Oil production (−1) we use the lag of the Government Effectiveness and the second lag of the variable		
	In column(3) for Natural resource tax revenues/Hydrocarbon exports (−1) In column		

All variables are in logs
Standard errors in parentheses
*, **, *** significant at the 10, 5 and 1 % level

Table 2.3 Equation (1): Level of active rigs, with institutions and OPEC dummies (fixed effects)

	Rigs	Rigs	Rigs	Rigs
	(1)	*(2)*	*(3)*	*(4)*
Average oil prices	0.326***	.	.	.
	(0.115)	.	.	.
Standard deviation of oil prices	0.005	0.062*	0.077**	0.093**
	(0.064)	(0.034)	(0.036)	(0.036)
Reserves	−0.176***	−0.179**	−0.139*	−0.107
	(0.063)	(0.079)	(0.083)	(0.083)
Δ in reserves	0.325***	0.270*	0.266*	0.278*
	(0.124)	(0.150)	(0.149)	(0.148)
Natural resource tax revenues/Oil production (−1)	−0.212***	−0.143**	−0.154**	−0.154**
	(0.059)	(0.067)	(0.067)	(0.067)
WBGI–Government Effectiveness × Natural resource tax revenues/Oil production		0.015*	0.015*	0.01
		(0.009)	(0.008)	(0.009)
OPEC × Future oil prices			−0.065	−0.246***
			(0.042)	(0.081)
OPEC × Future rigs				0.148***
				(0.057)
Constant	−1.414	0.79	0.614	0.378
	(0.955)	(1.001)	(1.005)	(0.998)
r2	0.257	0.198	0.205	0.225
N	388	306	306	306
Year fixed effects	Yes	Yes	Yes	Yes
Country fixed effects	Yes	Yes	Yes	Yes

All variables are in logs
Standard errors in parentheses
*, **, *** significant at the 10, 5 and 1 % level

results, probably because of the significantly fewer number of observations (Table 2.4).

- Results (not shown) were not significant when we defined the tax ratio as the ratio of fiscal revenues from oil and gas to the WB estimate of oil and gas rents (World Bank 2011). Thus, we decided not to use this variable in further estimations.
- The coefficients of the control variables used in the basic equation came out as significant and with the expected signs in some, but not in all, specifications:

    (1) The coefficient on the level of international prices is positive and significant in most cases. The coefficient on volatility of prices is negative and significant, as expected, only in IV estimations. In some cases the estimation procedure drops the price level variable and gives a positive and significant coefficient on price volatility. It may be that in these cases

Table 2.4 Equation (1): Level of active rigs, with RWI and OPEC dummies (fixed effects)

	Rigs	Rigs	Rigs	Rigs
	(1)	(2)	(3)	(4)
Average oil prices	0.326***	.	.	.
	(0.115)	.		
Standard deviation of oil prices	0.005	0.151***	0.169***	0.204***
	(0.064)	(0.036)	(0.037)	(0.037)
Reserves	−0.176***	−0.321***	−0.302***	−0.210**
	(0.063)	(0.082)	(0.082)	(0.082)
Δ in reserves	0.325***	0.404***	0.410***	0.462***
	(0.124)	(0.150)	(0.150)	(0.144)
Natural resource tax revenues/Oil production (−1)	−0.212***	−0.188*	−0.204**	−0.201**
	(0.059)	(0.098)	(0.097)	(0.094)
Revenue Watch Index × Natural resource tax revenues/Oil production		−0.001	−0.001	−0.001
		(0.002)	(0.001)	(0.001)
OPEC × Future oil prices			−0.072*	−0.390***
			(0.037)	(0.082)
OPEC × Future rigs				0.219***
				(0.051)
Constant	−1.414	−0.131	−0.398	−0.987
	(0.955)	(1.121)	(1.123)	(1.088)
r2	0.257	0.28	0.292	0.349
N	388	253	253	253
Year fixed effects	Yes	Yes	Yes	Yes
Country fixed effects	Yes	Yes	Yes	Yes

All variables are in logs
Standard errors in parentheses
*, **, *** significant at the 10, 5 and 1 % level

the measure of volatility is capturing the effect of price levels, as these two variables show a high correlation.

(2) The coefficients on level of reserves are negative and significant in some equations, while the coefficient of the recent addition to reserves is often positive and significant. A plausible interpretation is that recent addition of reserves requires development, and thus increases in active rigs, while older reserves may already have declining production and require less active rigs.

(3) The coefficients on interest rates (not shown) never came out as significant. A plausible interpretation is that its effect is dominated by the more important effect of the level of oil prices, and it does not show as significant given the high correlation among these two variables.

• The OPEC dummy gave significant results when interacted with future prices and expected number of rigs (column 4, Tables 2.3 and 2.4). OPEC countries seem thus to behave differently from the rest. A plausible interpretation of these results is the following: OPEC countries invest somewhat less than the others when expecting higher prices because they often have some spare capacity, but, at the same time, they invest more when expecting a higher number of total future rigs in order to keep an edge on their market power by increasing their production capabilities more than the others.

We ran several other specifications of these equations, which are not shown but can be obtained from the authors on demand. We used lagged or future international prices obtaining very similar results than those shown below. We estimated random effect models also obtaining very similar results to those with fixed effects. On the other hand, estimations using as dependent variables differences in log of rigs and changes in logs of tax ratios as independent variables gave less significant results than the ones shown below.

Results for equation (2) (changes in production) are shown below, estimated for variations around trend (Table 2.5) and differences (Table 2.6) of both the dependent variable and the level of active rigs. We also estimated a reduced form (Table 2.7) linking directly tax ratios, prices, price volatility reserves and recent net additions to reserves to oil and gas production (without the intermediate step of available rigs). We observe that:

- Most estimates give positive and significant results for the key control variable: variations around trend or changes in the number of active rigs.
- We do not get significant results in any of the estimations for the independent effect of our variables of interest (alternative measures of tax ratios) on changes in oil production, in addition to their indirect effect through changes in the number of active rigs (as obtained above in Tables 2.1 to 2.4).
- Only the pooled data estimates give significant independent effects of prices, in addition to their indirect effect through the number of active rigs (as obtained above in Tables 2.1 to 2.4).
- The coefficients on price volatility are positive, and often significant, contrary to what was expected.
- Table 2.7 below shows estimates of a reduced form relating changes in production (variations over trend) to lagged tax ratios, without including rigs in the equation. Results show that the lagged effect of increasing tax ratios by 10% reduce detrended production between 3.7% and 4.4%, depending on how we define the tax ratio, in both difference and systems generalized method of moments (GMM) estimations. The effect of price levels on changes in production are positive and significant in both difference and systems GMM estimations. Negative effects of price volatility are significant only in the difference GMM estimations. Coefficients on reserves, or on recent additions of reserves, are seldom significant in these reduced form estimations.

Results for equation (3) (the reduced form for changes in production of oil and minerals) are shown in Tables 2.7 to 2.10 below. Main conclusions are:

- We get negative and significant coefficients for our variable of interest (the tax ratio defined as fiscal revenues over GDP) in OLS estimations when we

Table 2.5 Equation (2): Changes in oil production, variations around trend (pooled OLS and country and year fixed effects)

	Pooled			Country and year fixed effects		
	Oil production (cycle)	Oil production (cycle)	Oil production (cycle)	Oil production (cycle)	Oil production (cycle)	Oil production (cycle)
	(1)	(2)	(3)	(4)	(5)	(6)
Rigs cycle	0.058	0.119*	0.049	0.110**	0.091**	0.033
	(0.076)	(0.065)	(0.048)	(0.046)	(0.040)	(0.031)
Average oil prices	0.192***	0.228***	0.233***	.	.	.
	(0.028)	(0.028)	(0.024)			
Standard deviation of oil prices	−0.055***	−0.106***	−0.109***	0.068***	0.068***	0.067***
	(0.015)	(0.018)	(0.017)	(0.013)	(0.012)	(0.010)
OPEC × Oil prices	0.001	0	0.001	0.014	0.003	−0.005
	(0.005)	(0.005)	(0.004)	(0.015)	(0.012)	(0.009)
Natural resource tax revenues/Natural resource GDP	0.032			0.027		
	(0.021)			(0.028)		
Natural resource tax revenues/Oil production		0.006			0.005	
		(0.023)			(0.025)	
Natural resource tax revenues/Hydrocarbon exports			0.01			−0.01
			(0.018)			(0.019)
Constant	−0.707***	−0.559*	−0.659***	−0.144	0.067	0.013
	(0.106)	(0.334)	(0.069)	(0.119)	(0.357)	(0.028)
r2	0.142	0.105	0.134	0.574	0.601	0.726
N	335	389	353	335	389	353

All variables are in logs
Standard errors in parentheses
*, **, *** significant at the 10, 5 and 1 % level

Table 2.6 Equation (2): Changes in oil production, differences (pooled OLS and country and year fixed effects)

	Pooled			Country and year fixed effects		
	Δ in oil production (cycle)	Δ in oil production (cycle)	Δ in oil production (cycle)	Δ in oil production (cycle)	Δ in oil production (cycle)	Δ in oil production (cycle)
	(1)	(2)	(3)	(4)	(5)	(6)
Δ in rigs (cycle)	0.039	0.122*	0.048	0.108**	0.119**	0.059
	(0.071)	(0.070)	(0.064)	(0.052)	(0.047)	(0.037)
Average oil prices	0.054	0.126**	0.116**	.	.	.
	(0.055)	(0.061)	(0.058)			
Standard deviation of oil prices	0.034	-0.062	-0.056	0.054***	0.045***	0.052***
	(0.033)	(0.040)	(0.040)	(0.018)	(0.017)	(0.014)
OPEC × Oil prices	0.007	0.005	0.005	0.016	0.001	-0.006
	(0.007)	(0.008)	(0.007)	(0.024)	(0.018)	(0.014)
Natural resource tax revenues/Natural resource GDP	-0.005			0.011		
	(0.031)			(0.040)		
Natural resource tax revenues/Oil production		-0.04			-0.016	
		(0.034)			(0.035)	
Natural resource tax revenues/Hydrocarbon exports			-0.019			-0.007
			(0.028)			(0.028)
Constant	-0.207	-0.953*	-0.353**	-0.024	-0.152	0.073*
	(0.189)	(0.502)	(0.160)	(0.169)	(0.502)	(0.041)
r2	0.051	0.028	0.021	0.567	0.63	0.737
N	319	368	335	319	368	335

All variables are in logs
Standard errors in parentheses
*, **, *** significant at the 10, 5 and 1 % level

Table 2.7 Equation (2): Changes in oil production reduced form (GMM)

	Oil production (cycle)	Oil production (cycle)	Oil production (cycle)	Oil production (cycle)	Oil production (cycle)	Oil production (cycle)
	Difference GMM			System GMM		
	(1)	(2)	(3)	(4)	(5)	(6)
Oil production (cycle) (−1)	0.100**	−0.071	−0.062	0.065	−0.067	−0.07
	(0.048)	(0.055)	(0.072)	(0.052)	(0.048)	(0.071)
Future oil prices	0.119***	0.168***	0.176***	0.265***	0.341***	0.378***
	(0.025)	(0.041)	(0.036)	(0.059)	(0.083)	(0.099)
Standard deviation of oil prices	−0.007	−0.089***	−0.085**	−0.002	−0.034	−0.031
	(0.023)	(0.027)	(0.033)	(0.037)	(0.050)	(0.054)
Reserves	−0.004	−0.002	0	−0.222*	−0.478	−0.689
	(0.006)	(0.012)	(0.010)	(0.116)	(0.354)	(0.485)
Δ in reserves			−0.087			0.207
			(0.118)			(0.252)
Natural resource tax revenues/Natural resource GDP (cycle) (−1)	−0.369**			−0.437*		
	(0.178)			(0.227)		
Natural resource tax revenues/Oil production (cycle) (−1)		−0.373*			−0.433**	
		(0.188)			(0.178)	
Natural resource tax revenues/Hydrocarbon exports (cycle) (−1)			−0.404			−0.404**
			(0.256)			(0.190)
Constant	−0.378***	−0.446***	−0.483***			
	(0.071)	(0.114)	(0.083)			
r2						
N	343	386	362	315	357	334

All variables are in logs
Standard errors in parentheses
*, **, *** significant at the 10, 5 and 1 % level

Table 2.8 Equation (3): Effect of tax ratios on oil and mining GDP (OLS, fixed effects)

Dependent variable	Contribution of oil and mining to GDP (%)	Contribution of oil and mining to GDP (%)	Contribution of oil and mining to GDP (%)
	(1)	*(2)*	*(3)*
Natural resource tax revenue/ Natural resource GDP	−0.018	−0.018	−0.003
	(0.022)	(0.022)	(0.022)
Average oil prices × oil–rich	12.752***	11.365***	
	(3.128)	(2.142)	
Standard deviation of oil prices × oil–rich	−1.232		
	(1.894)		
Gold prices × gold–rich	10.207	11.116***	
	(7.682)	(3.966)	
Standard deviation of gold prices × gold–rich	0.315		
	(3.868)		
Copper prices × copper–rich	11.585**	9.436***	
	(4.5)	(2.281)	
Standard deviation of copper prices × copper–rich	−1.235		
	(2.396)		
Diamond prices × diamond–rich	−3.52	−4.038	
	(5.291)	(5.204)	
Silver prices × silver–rich	−13.927**	−10.782***	
	(5.896)	(3.132)	
Standard deviation of silver prices × silver–rich	1.661		
	(2.647)		
Alumina prices × alumina–rich	8.874	6.199	
	(11.984)	(9.765)	
Standard deviation of alumina prices × alumina–rich	−1.097		
	(4.430)		

(Continued)

Table 2.8 (Continued)

Dependent variable	Contribution of oil and mining to GDP (%) (1)	Contribution of oil and mining to GDP (%) (2)	Contribution of oil and mining to GDP (%) (3)
Average oil prices			11.253***
			(1.476)
Gold prices			.
Copper prices			−4.446***
			(1.645)
Diamond prices			.
Silver prices			.
Alumina prices			.
Constant	−15.164	−10.137*	22.772**
	(9.294)	(5.847)	(9.326)
r2	0.496	0.494	0.441
N	492	492	492

All prices are in logs
Standard errors in parentheses
*, **, *** significant at the 10, 5 and 1 % level

Table 2.9 Equation (3): Effect of tax ratios and institutions on oil and mining GDP (OLS, fixed effects)

Dependent variable	Contribution of oil and mining to GDP (%) (1)	Contribution of oil and mining to GDP (%) (2)
Natural resource tax revenue/Natural resource GDP	−0.049*	−0.052**
	(0.026)	(0.026)
Average oil prices × oil–rich	15.163***	13.461***
	(3.088)	(2.328)
Standard deviation of oil prices × oil–rich	−1.681	
	(1.884)	
Gold prices × gold–rich	8.873	7.384*
	(6.937)	(4.388)
Standard deviation of gold prices × gold–rich	−1.668	
	(3.629)	
Copper prices × copper–rich	10.711**	11.873***
	(4.827)	(2.476)
Standard deviation of copper prices × copper–rich	0.602	
	(2.424)	

Dependent variable	Contribution of oil and mining to GDP (%)	Contribution of oil and mining to GDP (%)
	(1)	*(2)*
Diamond prices × diamond–rich	−6.944	−7.386
	(5.357)	(5.318)
Silver prices × silver–rich	−11.242**	−9.097***
	(5.337)	(2.892)
Standard deviation of silver prices × silver–rich	1.187	
	(2.350)	
Alumina prices × alumina–rich	11.969	9.714
	(15.162)	(14.414)
Standard deviation of alumina prices × alumina–rich	−1.339	
	(4.002)	
WBGI–Government Effectiveness	2.055	2.349
	(4.237)	(4.202)
WBGI–Government Effectiveness × Natural resource tax revenues/ Natural resource GDP	−1.611	−1.742
	(1.109)	(1.096)
WBGI–Government Effectiveness × Oil prices	0.793	0.843
	(0.659)	(0.654)
WBGI–Government Effectiveness × Gold prices	−3.307**	−3.038*
	(1.619)	(1.557)
WBGI–Government Effectiveness × Copper prices	2.814***	2.911***
	(1.072)	(1.055)
WBGI–Government Effectiveness × Diamond prices	0.982	1.053
	(0.952)	(0.945)
WBGI–Government Effectiveness × Silver prices	−0.113	−0.034
	(0.942)	(0.933)
WBGI–Government Effectiveness × Alumina prices	0.343	0.455
	(2.068)	(2.045)
Constant	−22.521**	−20.867**
	(10.941)	(10.348)
r2	0.546	0.545
N	466	466

All prices are in logs
Standard errors in parentheses
*, **, *** significant at the 10, 5 and 1 % level

Table 2.10 Equation (3): Effect of tax ratios on oil and mining GDP (GMM estimations)

Dependent variable	Contribution of mining to GDP (%)	Contribution of mining to GDP (%)
	(1)	(2)
Instrumental variable	Difference GMM	System GMM
	WBGI–Government Effectiveness	WBGI–Government Effectiveness
Contribution of mining to GDP (%) (–1)	0.137	0.857***
	(0.130)	(0.093)
Natural resource tax revenues/Natural resource GDP	–0.038	–0.154**
	(0.054)	(0.063)
Average oil prices oil–rich	12.348***	3.483***
	(1.758)	(1.077)
Gold prices gold–rich	–124.65	–0.307
	(107.512)	(1.680)
Copper prices copper–rich	3.868	0.484
	(14.555)	(0.663)
Diamond prices diamond–rich	–9.05	0.245
	(27.587)	(1.142)
Silver prices silver–rich	–38.424	–2.437*
	(36.531)	(1.371)
Alumina prices alumina–rich	14.139	–1.442
	(53.001)	(3.633)
Constant		3.832
		(4.468)
r2		
N	424	466

All prices are in logs
Standard errors in parentheses
*, **, *** significant at the 10, 5 and 1 % level

include institutional variables as controls and in GMM systems estimations. A 10% increase in the tax ratio would reduce oil or mining GDP by about 0.5%, according to OLS estimates, or 1.5%, according to GMM systems estimates. We also interacted the tax ratio with separate dummies for oil- and for mineral-rich countries (not shown) but results were weaker.

• The coefficients on control variables have expected signs and are significant in some, though not in all cases:

    • Price level effects appear to be positive high and significant in basic OLS estimations for oil and copper, but not for other mineral prices. However, only oil price effects appear as positive and significant in GMM estimations. Silver prices appear to have negative and significant effects. These non-significant or unexpected results of some mineral prices may be a consequence of the small number of countries exporting each type of mineral.

- Coefficients on price volatility are never significant.
- Interactions of prices with indexes of quality of institutions give positive significant results in the case of copper-rich countries (and, strangely, negative significant effects in the case of gold-rich countries).

Finally, Tables 2.11 and 2.12 rank countries in two different ways. First, by retrieving the coefficients in country fixed effects in the different specifications used for equation (1). Second, by estimating DEA scores for number of active rigs using as inputs levels of reserves (or recent reserve findings) and the inverse of the tax ratio.

Table 2.11 shows high country specific coefficients across different specifications of equation (1) for Mexico and Venezuela and quite low for Trinidad and Tobago, Ecuador and Bolivia. Saudi Arabia, Iran, Indonesia and Oman also appear with high scores (higher than Norway!), while most African countries appear with very low scores. These results should be interpreted with caution, as they may be influenced by two factors. First, in countries with a dominant public oil enterprise (with an asterisk in Table 2.11) the response of investment to tax ratios may be more muted than in countries with high private sector participation. Thus, while a very high tax ratio may cause a dramatic effect on private investment, the effect on public sector companies might be less as they will in any case invest a high fraction of their remaining profits (especially as otherwise they risk having them also transferred to the budget). Second, country specific fixed effects may be affected by differential geological and sector infrastructure attractiveness that are not fully captured by the level of remaining or new reserves.

Table 2.12 shows the DEA scores considering as inputs the inverse of tax ratios and, alternatively, average outstanding reserves, net additions to reserves and net additions to reserves and reserves in 2000 as inputs. They are higher for Mexico, Indonesia and Oman in all three estimations. They are also high for Vietnam in two estimations and for Venezuela and Colombia in one. Bolivia and Trinidad and Tobago appear now in an intermediate situation in two estimations, and very low in another one, while Ecuador and most African countries are still down the list in all estimations. Gulf countries appear in general ranked much lower than in Table 2.11.

Countries with high reserves are punished more in DEA efficiency estimates than when assessing efficiency through country fixed effects, as in Table 2.11, where more controls are being used in the equations. Given that production from old reserves may be naturally declining (unless secondary recovery is generalized) while production from recent reserve additions may in contrast be naturally increasing, changes across columns are important for countries that either have had very low or very high net additions of reserves during the period. Those with low net additions of reserves (such as Venezuela, Saudi Arabia and Iran) have lower ranks in estimations 1 and 3 (where old reserves have significant weight), while the contrary happens in countries with high net additions of reserves during the period (such as Vietnam).

Table 2.11 Benchmarking oil tax systems efficiency, coefficients of fixed effect terms

	Estimation 1 in Table 2.3		Estimation 2 in Table 2.3		Estimation 4 in Table 2.3	
	Explanatory variables are oil prices, standard deviation of oil prices, reserves, change in reserves and natural resource tax revenue/oil production (−1)		Explanatory variables are standard deviation of oil prices, reserves, change in reserves and natural resource tax revenue/ oil production (− lagged), Government Effectiveness Index times natural resource tax revenue/oil production		Explanatory variables are standard deviation of oil prices, reserves, change in reserves and natural resource tax revenue/oil production (lagged), Government Effectiveness Index times natural resource tax revenue/oil production, OPEC X future oil prices, OPEC X future rigs	
Countries	FE Term 1	Rank	FE Term 2	Rank	FE Term 4	Rank
AGO*	−1.057	19	−1.246	19	−1.210	19
ARE*	0.544	8	0.733	8	0.444	9
BOL[1]	−1.886	21	−2.038	21	−1.795	21
COG	−2.223	23	−2.421	23	−2.178	23
COL	−0.043	13	−0.084	13	0.063	11
DZA*	0.723	7	0.549	9	0.520	8
ECU	−0.904	18	−0.940	18	−0.787	18
GAB	−2.050	22	−2.101	22	−1.937	22
IDN	1.237	5	1.185	5	1.189	4
IRN*	1.338	4	1.273	4	1.038	6
KWT*	0.202	10	0.260	10	0.006	12
LBY*	0.123	11	−0.060	12	−0.164	13
MEX*	1.969	2	2.111	1	2.066	1
NGA*	−0.103	14	−0.268	15	−0.342	15
NOR	0.331	9	0.896	7	0.781	7
OMN*	0.807	6	1.023	6	1.059	5
QAT*	−0.454	15	−0.106	14	−0.212	14
SAU*	1.576	3	1.683	3	1.476	3
SYR*	0.053	12	−0.003	11	0.168	10
TTO [2]	−1.696	20	−1.528	20	−1.339	20
VEN*	2.037	1	1.939	2	1.765	2
VNM [3]	−0.902	17	−0.929	17	−0.700	17
YEM [4]	−0.724	16	−0.795	16	−0.652	16

Source: http://iisdb.stanford.edu/res/2251/NOC_study_prospectus.pdf

*Countries with a dominant public oil enterprise.
1 http://en.wikipedia.org/wiki/YPFB
2 http://en.wikipedia.org/wiki/Petrotrin
3 http://en.wikipedia.org/wiki/Petrovietnam 4/ www.eia.gov/cabs/Yemen/Full.html

Table 2.12 Benchmarking. DEA scores and ranks. Inverse tax ratios, average outstanding reserves, net additions to reserves and reserves in 2000 as inputs

Sample	2000–2008		2000–2008		2000–2008	
Input	(1) Average reserves (2) Natural resource tax revenues/Natural resource production (inverse)		(1) Δ reserves (2) Natural resource tax revenues/Natural resource production (inverse)		(1) Δ reserves (2) Natural resource tax revenues/Natural resource production (inverse) (3) Reserves in 2000	
Output	Rigs		Rigs		Rigs	
Countries	Rank	Theta	Rank	Theta	Rank	Theta
AGO	20	0.092	20	0.025	21	0.099
ARE	17	0.125	9	0.125	17	0.125
BOL	7	0.560	21	0.025	7	0.566
COG	19	0.095	22	0.011	22	0.097
COL	5	0.799	12	0.090	1	1.000
DZA	10	0.377	6	0.226	9	0.468
ECU	14	0.236	19	0.032	11	0.379
GAB	23	0.079	23	0.010	23	0.089
IDN	1	1.000	7	0.204	1	1.000
IRN	15	0.229	5	0.229	16	0.229
KWT	18	0.108	10	0.108	19	0.108
LBY	21	0.092	11	0.092	20	0.107
MEX	1	1.000	1	1.000	1	1.000
NGA	22	0.082	14	0.082	18	0.117
NOR	11	0.361	8	0.177	12	0.364
OMN	1	1.000	3	0.401	1	1.000
QAT	16	0.135	16	0.075	15	0.314
SAU	12	0.348	4	0.348	14	0.348
SYR	6	0.729	13	0.083	6	0.752
TTO	9	0.422	18	0.034	8	0.512
VEN	8	0.457	2	0.457	10	0.457
VNM	1	1.000	17	0.066	1	1.000
YEM	13	0.328	15	0.081	13	0.351

Δ reserves was calculated for the period between 2000–2007 for all countries except for Bolivia (2002–2007) and Iran (2000–2005).
Reserves in 2000 was calculated for all countries except for Bolivia (2002).

Once again, ranks may be partially explained by differences in responses between private and public enterprises to tax ratios.

3 Concluding remarks

This chapter used panel data on 41 oil and mineral-rich countries (defined as such according to IMF criteria)[9] to estimate the potential effects of total tax ratios on oil and mineral activities. To capture potential effects of the quality of oil and mineral taxes, we also estimate the interaction of total sectoral tax ratios with indexes of the quality of oil tax regimes and of the overall quality of country institutions.

Using these results, we then attempt to benchmark the efficiency of oil and mineral taxation and institutional regimes in Latin America.

We found that on average an increase in the tax ratio of about 10% reduces in around 2.2% the number of active rigs in OLS estimations. These turn out to be very robust results across different specifications. The reduction appears higher in estimations in which the tax ratio is defined in alternative ways (fiscal revenues related to oil production divided alternatively by oil GDP, oil production and net oil exports per capita) and is instrumented with an index of institutions and its own lagged value: an increase in the tax ratio of about 10% leads to a reduction of active rigs between 2.6% and 4% depending on how we define the tax ratio.

We then include different indexes of quality of institutions and find that a higher value of such an index reduces the negative effect of the total sectoral tax ratio. We interpret this result as an indication that the quality of taxes matter, assuming that their quality (a combination of a better mix, design and enforcement of oil and gas taxes and higher perceived stability of the tax regime) improves with improvements in the quality of overall institutions.

Finally, we test if OPEC countries have different reactions to increases in prices: we find, indeed, that the level of active rigs in OPEC countries reacts less to future price changes than in other countries, though it also increases with overall expected *increases* in rigs, suggesting that that OPEC countries act as rational price setters.

We then use both OLS and IV estimates for equations in which changes in the level of production are explained by changes in active rigs, the level of international prices and their volatility, the total sectoral tax ratio, an OPEC dummy multiplied by the level of expected prices, and country and time fixed effects. We do not find a direct effect of tax ratios on production in addition to their indirect effect through the level of active rigs. We then included mineral-rich countries in the sample and estimated reduced forms in which changes in oil and mineral GDP are explained by the level of international prices and their volatility, the total sectoral tax ratio and country and time fixed effects. The coefficient on tax ratios was negative in all cases, but significant only in some. The latter suggests that a 10% increase in the tax ratio eventually reduces production by about 0.5% (in OLS estimations) and 0.75% in IV (using systems GMM and also instrumenting the tax ratio with an index of institutions).

Finally we attempt to benchmark the efficiency of Latin American oil tax and institutional systems, by inspecting the fixed effects coefficients in the equations for rigs and producing Data Envelopment Analysis (DEA) estimates using remaining proven reserves and the inverse of tax ratios as inputs and active rigs as outputs. In both cases Mexico ranks relatively high. Venezuela ranks high according to fixed effects coefficients, but its ranking according to DEA scores depends on the use as inputs of either average reserves or net additions to reserves during the period (reflecting the fact that most of its reserves are relatively old). Colombia always ranks in an intermediate position. Trinidad and Tobago rank poorly according to its fixed effects coefficients, but better (moderately) according to DEA scores. Ecuador and, especially, Bolivia rank low according to both estimates. A reason why Mexico and Venezuela (as well as most Gulf countries) may rank relatively high in these estimates could be related to the dominance of a public state company. In fact, increasing tax ratios may have a more detrimental effect in countries with dominance of private investment, as a sharp increase in tax ratios may cause a huge drop in investment in such cases, while state oil companies may reduce their investment to a lower extent (they either invest their remaining net profits or maybe asked to transfer them to the budget).

Appendix

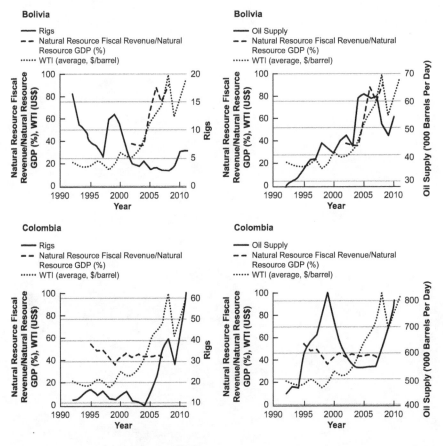

Figure 2.1 Active rigs, production and tax ratios in oil-rich Latin American countries

Source: IMF, EIA, UNDP, Baker Hughes

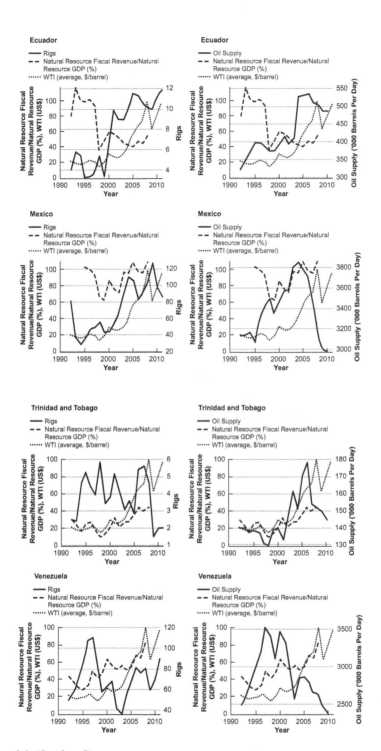

Figure 2.1 (Continued)

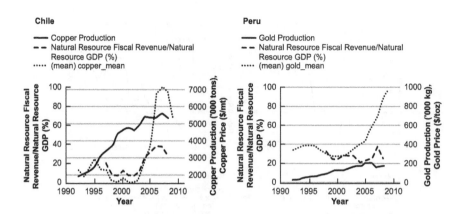

Figure 2.2 Production and tax ratios in mineral-rich Latin American countries

Source: IMF, UNDP, Economic Commission for Latin America and the Caribbean (ECLAC)

Notes

1 Prepared for the IADB Research Network Project "The Future of Taxation in Latin America and the Caribbean", (RG-K1198), Sub Project (2) Fiscal Revenues and Efficiency in LAC Non-Renewable Natural Resource Sectors.
2 The comparisons are made for tax rates in each tax that render the same present value of tax flows among them.
3 See, for example, Johnston 2008.
4 See figure 3 in Johnston and Rogers 2008.
5 Though in some cases a regime change may leave the underlying tax system essentially unchanged, as happened in Colombia in 2003 from Production Sharing Contracts to royalty plus income tax concessions.
6 See also Perry et al. 2010, comparing the cases of Colombia and Nigeria.
7 See Table 3.3.
8 See Tables 3.4 to 3.8.
9 Guide on Resource Revenue Transparency (2007), IMF www.imf.org/external/np/pp/2007/eng/051507g.pdf.

References

Alesina, A., F. R. Campante and G. Tabellini. 2008. "Why Is Fiscal Policy Often Procyclical?" *Journal of the European Economic Association*, 6(5), September, 1006–1036.

Arellano-Yanguas, Javier. 2008. *A Thoroughly Modern Resource Curse? The New Natural Resource Policy Agenda and the Mining Revival in Peru*, IDS Working Paper 300, IDS, Brighton.

Deacon, Robert. 1993. "Taxation, Depletion and Welfare: A Simulation Study of the U.S. Petroleum Resource", *Journal of Environmental Economics and Management*, 24(2), 159–187.

Espinasa, Ramon, Sergio Guerra Reyes, Enrique ter Horst, Osmel Manzano, German Molina and Roberto Rigobon. 2017. "A Micro-Based Model for World Oil Market", *Energy Economics*, Accepted Manuscript.

Johnston, Daniel. 2008. "Changing Fiscal Landscape", *Journal of World Energy Law & Business*, 1(1), 31–54.

Johnston, Johnston and Tony Rogers. 2008. *International Petroleum Taxation*, Independent Petroleum Association of America Study, Washington DC.

Kaufmann, Daniel and Aart Kraay. Various years. *Worldwide Governance Indicators*, The World Bank, Washington DC.

Otto, James, Craig Andrews, Fred Cawood, Michael Doggett, Pietro Guj, Frank Stermole, John Stermole and John Tilton. 2006. *Mining Royalties, A Global Study of Their Impact on Investors, Government, and Civil Society*, The World Bank, Washington DC.

Perry, Guillermo, Olawale Ogunkola, Mauricio Olivera and Babajide Fowowe. 2010. "Oil and Institutions: Tale of Two Cities: Nigeria and Colombia", *Reporte de Investigación Fedesarrollo 10-05*, Fedesarollo Colombia.

Sinnott, Emily, John Nash and Augusto de la Torre. 2011. *Natural Resources in Latin America and the Caribbean: Beyond Booms and Busts?* World Bank Latin American and Caribbean Studies, World Bank.

Villafuerte, Mauricio, Pablo Lopez-Murphy and Rolando Ossowski. 2010. *Riding the Roller Coaster: Fiscal Policies of Nonrenewable Resource Exporters in Latin America and the Caribbean*, IMF Working Paper, WP/10/251, November, International Monetary Fund, Washington DC.

World Bank. 2011. *The Changing Wealth of Nations: Measuring Sustainable Development in the New Millennium*, The World Bank, Washington DC.

Wright, G. and J. Czelusta. 2004. "The Myth of the Resource Curse", *Challenge*, 47(2), March/April, 6–38.

3 Towards efficient taxation of minerals

The case of copper in Chile[1]

J. Rodrigo Fuentes[2],
Bernardita Piedrabuena Keymer[3] and
Mauricio Calani[4]

Countries endowed with non-renewable natural resources face the challenge of capturing fair rents from their resources. Some states choose to exploit their resource by themselves, while others prefer to grant concessions. The former group obtains revenues from profits; the latter receives rents through taxation. In any case, the key question is how to establish the most efficient way to collect revenues from this natural wealth without distorting production and investment decisions. Given that this endowment belongs to current and future generations, the way that rents are collected and spent may induce undesirable intergenerational transfers.

The recent commodity price windfall has renewed the interest of the profession on how to collect revenues and how much to consume and save for future generations. This research focuses on the first issue which is to determine the most efficient way to collect rents given the property structure of the resources.

Chile provides an interesting case to study. This economy is the main copper producer in the world, supplying 43% of world copper exports. In the copper sector, private property and one state-owned firm coexist. In 2010, one third of copper production was produced by the state-owned company, CODELCO. That same year, copper revenues accounted for around 21% of total government revenues, mainly because of its high price.

Despite its importance, little attention has been paid to whether the tax structure is efficient for the amount collected. Current legislation implies that private companies pay a corporate income tax and a specific mining tax (SMT) that depends on operating income of the firm. This project critically analyzes the Chilean tax structure on copper mining activities. In particular, it will address the deadweight loss of the actual tax structure and will shed light on the efficiency of this structure.

The plan of the chapter is as follows. Section 1 provides a brief history of the role of copper in the Chilean development, and a discussion on the effect of copper price on the Chilean economy. Section 2 describes the industrial organization of the copper mining sector nowadays, and the role of the state in the sector as well as the importance of the sector for public finances. In Section 3 we present Deacon's (1993) model. Section 4 describes the data used for estimation and calibration of the key parameters of the model. Section 5 defines the tax scenarios to be analyzed, taking into account the characteristics of the Chilean tax system. Section 6 displays the simulation of the different scenarios and a sensibility analysis. Finally, Section 7 gives our concluding remarks. An appendix contains more details about data and parameters calibration.

1 The role of copper in Chilean development

1.1 The history of copper mining

The history of the mining sector is closely related to the country's economic development since the early stages of the republic. The discovery of important silver reserves in 1832 and the introduction of technological innovations in the processing of copper in 1831 triggered the development of the mining sector in Chile (Cariola and Sunkel 1982). This mining development based on copper and silver lasted until 1880. Later, these minerals were replaced by nitrate as the main export commodity, for which Chile was the main world producer. According to Wagner (2005), Chile produced between 30% to 40% of the total world supply of copper during the "golden period of copper". This amount diminished to less than 15% in the 1890–1910 time period. The main conjecture to explain this production shrinking was the lack of technological progress to exploit low-grade reservoirs.

It was not until the beginning of the 20th century, after important innovation in the industry, that the copper industry became an important part of the national economy again. During the previous century, copper mining was selective; only reservoirs with high-grade were exploited. Starting in 1910, innovations allowed exploiting minerals of low ore (less than 2%); this is the so-called bulk mining (Radetzki 2010). The innovations in the sector reduced the production cost in a way that mines were re-opened. This is the case of "El Teniente", one of the largest mines in Chile and in the world, which ceased operations in 1897 and resumed in 1912 (Radetzki 2010).

This revival of the copper mining was led by foreign capital, in particular from the US, which arrived in Chile in the early years of the 20th century. Given the magnitude of the projects, this event created the so-called Large-Scale Mining Industry of Copper (*La Gran Minería del Cobre*), which was privately owned. All this happened in a context of no income tax or specific tax to this activity, which is one of the reasons why Chile was attractive to foreign investors. There exist records that the first tax paid by the industry occurred in 1924 (Wagner, 2005), when Chile introduced the income tax. The state collected taxes from the Large-Scale Mining Industry of Copper using income tax and a system of multiple exchange rates. The implicit plus the explicit tax rate on profit was 29% in 1940 and it rose as high as 77% in 1954, becoming almost 71% in the first half of the '60s (Wagner 2005 and the references therein).

In the mid-1950s, the so called "new deal" started, which consisted in gradually changing the tax system in place, abandoning the use of multiple exchange rates, and favoring direct taxes to profit with some exemptions to new investment in the sector. This continuous change in the rules of the game created a favorable environment for an arranged *Chileanization* of Large Copper Mining. In 1966 the Law 16,245 created joint venture corporations between the Chilean state and the foreign companies that operated the Large Copper Mining. The law established a 25% minimum participation of the state in such companies.

In 1971 the Parliament unanimously approved the complete nationalization of the large copper mines. The sector was managed by the Copper Corporation (95%) and the National Enterprise of Mining (*Empresa Nacional de Minería*, 5%).

In 1976, the Decree Law 1,350 created Codelco Chile (*Corporación Nacional del Cobre de Chile*), a company that took control over the mines nationalized in the early '70s. Before that, in 1974, the Decree Law 600 was enacted with the goal of attracting foreign investment to the country in any sector. This decree was aimed at eliminating suspicions of foreign investors, who had seen their assets seized in 1971. Later, in 1982, the government enacted the Organic Constitutional Law of Mining Concessions, which set the rules for adequate compensations in case of future expropriation. The Chilean Mining Code, enacted in 1983, provided additional support to the law of mining concessions.

This new legislation became the cornerstone to attract private foreign capital to the Large-Scale Mining Industry of Copper. Even though these laws were approved in the late '70s and early '80s, it was not until the early '90s that foreign direct investment (FDI) came massively to the copper sector.[5]

1.2 Chilean macroeconomy and copper

The importance of the terms of trade on the performance of the Chilean economy has been documented in several studies. For instance, Fuentes (2011) analyzes 200 years of growth of the Chilean economy using a neoclassical growth model. As expected over such a long time period, Fuentes found two structural breaks in the long-run growth performance. He argues that the performance of the Chilean economy is closely associated to government behavior, openness and external conditions. The inclusion of fiscal expenditures, terms of trade, and a measure of openness in the empirical model dissipate the structural breaks found in the data.[6] On a different venue, De Gregorio and Labbe (2011) analyze the effect of copper price on macroeconomic fluctuations of the Chilean economy. They found that there is a close relationship between the cycle of copper price and the business cycle in Chile. What is most interesting is that the relationship becomes weaker in the last two decades. They attribute this latter finding to the fact that Chile implemented a fully flexible exchange rate system in 1999. The real exchange rate becomes a natural shock absorber, which helped isolate the economy from external shocks. A complementary vision about the weaker effect of copper price on Chilean activity is in Borensztein et al. (2010a). The authors suggest that, in general terms, the different mechanisms that government has established to smooth the copper price effects on fiscal spending worked well. While before 1987 the correlation between both variables was positive and significant, between 1987 and 2009 it turned to be negative and non-significant.

The construction of a business cycle model for the Chilean economy is beyond the scope of this paper. However, we will illustrate the relationship of the GDP cycle and copper cycle. Instead of using growth rate over rolling windows as

De Gregorio and Labbe (2011) do, we apply the Hodrick–Prescott filter to both series (in logs) to obtain the cyclical component. Figure 3.1 exhibits the evolution of both cyclical components from 1850 to 2010. The volatility of the cyclical component is much larger for copper price than for GDP. The synchronization of the series is relatively high until 1880; after that and until the First World War, copper was not the main export product as described in section 2.1, and therefore the cycle of GDP does not follow the cycle of copper. From 1915 on, both series move together again, especially between the two world wars and in the 1970s and 1980s. As documented by De Gregorio and Labbe (2011), the relationship becomes weaker over the last 20 years.

To formally check the correlation between the cyclical component (CC) of copper price and GDP series we run a regression using the latter as dependent variable. We include lags of the cyclical component of GDP, the cyclical component of the copper price and dummy variables for the periods 1881–1910 (D8110) and 1990–2010 (D9010): The first dummy captures the effect of the period when copper stopped being important as an export product. The second dummy allows us to check the idea that after 1990 the relationship between both cycles becomes weaker. Table 3.1 shows the regression results. The first column shows that the long-run coefficient of copper cycle is 0.126, which means that a deviation of 10% from the trend of the copper price generates a deviation of 1.3% from the trend of GDP. The second column shows that the effect of copper cycle on GDP

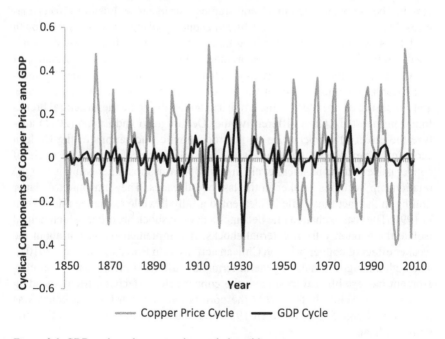

Figure 3.1 GDP cycle and copper price cycle logarithm

Source: Own estimations based on data of Braun et al. (2000) and Central Bank

Table 3.1 GDP cycle and copper price cycle

Dependent variable: GDP (CC)	[1]	[2]
GDP (CC) in t-1	**0.613****	**0.603****
	(0.113)	**(0.107)**
GDP (CC) in t-2	**−0.297****	**−0.308****
	(0.123)	**(0.120)**
Copper price (CC) in t	**0.086****	**0.123****
	(0.026)	**(0.037)**
D8110		0.005
		(0.009)
D8110*Copper price (CC) in t-1		**−0.160****
		(0.057)
D9010		0.006
		(0.008)
D9010*Copper price (CC) in t-1		**−0.075***
		(0.041)
Constant	0.000	−0.002
	(0.004)	(0.005)
Adjusted R-squared	0.384	0.399

HAC standard errors in parentheses
*, ** Significance at 10% and 5%, respectively

cycle is much smaller for the periods 1881–1910 and 1990–2010. In the latter period the long-run effect is 0.067 which is lower compared to 0.174, which is the long-run effect for the period 1911–1989.

2 Mining sector today

2.1 Industrial organization

Chilean copper production in 2010 added up to 5,419 thousand metric tons, of which 31.2% was produced by Codelco, and 68.8% by private companies. The biggest 14 private companies produced almost 61% out of the total Chilean production. The main fields are Escondida (20.1%), Collahuasi (9.3%), Los Pelambres (7.3%) and Anglo American Sur (4.8%). The controlling shareholders of these sites are foreign companies (Table 3.2). Also, all of them pay the specific mining tax not only because of their size of production, but also because they had recourse to the SMT laws enacted in 2005 and 2010 (more details in the next section).

Costs of copper mining industry have been increasing since 2005. In 2011 the average net cathode cost (C3) amounted to 1.74 dollars per pound, 149% higher than in 2004, ranging from 1.0 to 2.2 dollars per pound depending on the company. In particular, Codelco was located in the 69th percentile of the Chilean copper mining cost distribution, after being in the lowest cost quartile in the period 2000–2008.

Table 3.2 Who is who in the Chilean copper industry?

	Production 2010 kTM %		Ownership
Codelco	1,689	31.2%	100% Chilean government
Escondida	1,087	20.1%	57.5% BHP Billinton, 30% Rio Tinto, 12.5% JECO Corporation
Collahuasi	504	9.3%	44% Anglo American plc., 44% Xtrata plc., 7% Mitsui & Co. Ltd., 5% Nippon Mining & Metals Co. Ltd.
Los Pelambres	398	7.3%	60% Antofagasta Minerals, 25% Nippon LP Inv., 15% Mitsubishi Holding
Anglo American Sur	258	4.8%	100% Anglo American plc.
Spence	178	3.3%	100% BHP Billinton
El Abra	145	2.7%	51% Freeport McMoRan Copper & Gold, 49% Codelco
Zaldfvar	144	2.7%	100% Barrik Gold Co.
Anglo American Norte	140	2.6%	99.98% Anglo American plc., 0.02% others
Candelaria	136	2.5%	80% Freeport McMoRan Copper & Gold, 20% Sumitomo Co.
El Tesoro	95	1.8%	70% Antofagasta Minerals SA, 30% Marubeni Co.
Cerro Colorado	89	1.6%	100% BHP Billinton
Quebrada Blanca	86	1.6%	76.5% Aur QB Inc. Agencia Chile, 13.5% Inv. Mineras SA, 10% Enami
Lomas Bayas	72	1.3%	100% Xstrata plc.
Michilla	41	0.8%	74.2% Antofagasta Minerals, 26.8% others
Others	356	6.6%	
TOTAL	5,419	100%	

Source: Cesco, Companies, and Securities and Insurance Supervisor

Energy costs, labor costs, and ore grade explain the upward trend observed in cost figures during the 2005–2011 time period. According to Cochilco (2008), between 27% and 35% of the copper production costs are explained by labor costs, 20% by energy, between 30% and 32% by others' inputs and 15% by capital depreciation. At the same time, costs depend negatively and significantly on ore grade.[7] Considering that from 2005 to 2010 oil prices rose 125%, salaries increased 84% (in dollars),[8] and ore grade decreased from 1.11% to 0.89%, we could explain the large surge of copper mining costs in this period.

Despite the high copper prices of the last seven years, profitability has decreased since 2006. While in 2006 average profitability, measured by the return on equity (ROE), was 112%, in 2010 it diminished to 70%. The aforementioned cost increase between 2005 and 2010, followed by the specific tax rises (which will be discussed in the next section), explain the large reduction in profitability.

Despite the lower profitability of the recent years, copper mining business is still very attractive for private companies, considering the perspectives of high copper prices in the medium term. The legal dispute that nowadays is having CODELCO and Anglo American it is an example of the attractiveness of the sector. In October of 2011, Codelco informed Anglo American that it will exercise its option of buying 49% of Anglo American Sur (AAS)'s mining assets in Chile. Anglo American defied the move, arguing that it was not obliged to sell any of its shares to Codelco, and announced in November that it had sold 24.5% of its assets to Mitsubishi Co. The option described to buy 49% of AAS's mining assets is attractive to Codelco for two reasons: (1) There is a huge difference between the option price and the market value of the 49% of the firm (US$6,000 millions versus US$10,700 millions) and (2) AAS (Los Bronces) is neighbor of the Andina division of Codelco, which is in expansion and had planned to buy AAS so as to become the main deposit of Codelco in the coming years.

2.2 The role of the state in the copper mining today

As documented in the previous section, the state participates in the copper industry through a large state-owned company, Codelco. This company accounted for 31.2% of total production in 2010. It has developed joint ventures with six private companies to explore and produce in Chile, besides the activities developed in Brazil and Ecuador.

Besides the role as a main producer, the state regulates the mining activity. There are three types of legal frameworks that are relevant for private companies that want to operate in this sector: the law that regulates foreign direct investment and the specific body of rules applied to exploration, concessions and exploitation of ore deposits.

In 1974 the military government enacted the Law – Ranking Decree 600 (DL600) in order to protect and promote FDI. This decree assures foreign investors the right to transfer their principal and net profits thereon to other countries. The spirit of the law is to apply non-discriminatory treatment to foreign over domestic investors. However, foreign companies could choose to be subject to, for a ten-year period, an invariable effective fixed -tax rate of 42% on taxable income. Accelerated depreciation and cumulative losses could be deducted from profits to calculate taxable income.[9] Investments above US$50 million may request an extension of up to 20 years of this special treatment. Alternatively, foreign companies can waive (only once) this right and ask for application of the ordinary tax law, which is the one applied to national investors; this tax can be subject to changes over time.

Two specific rules to the mining sector were passed in 1982 and 1983. The Organic Constitutional Law of Mining Concessions, enacted in 1982, establishes economic compensations in case of future expropriations. These compensations are based on the net present value of the verified reserves at the time of expropriation. Moreover, the constitutional status of the law makes it difficult to be modified. The second law was the Chilean Mining Code, enacted in 1983, which provides additional property right protection to the investors and sets the rules for

Table 3.3 Law 20,026: SMT according to annual sales of mine operator

Annual sales of the mine operator	Rate
1 Mine operator with annual sales < 12,000 MFT[12]	0.0%
2 12,000 MFT ≤ Annual sales ≤ 50,000 MFT,	
2.1 Regarding that portion in excess of 12,000 and no no greater no greater than 15,000 MFT	0.5%
2.2 Regarding that portion in excess of 15,000 and no greater no greater than 20,000 MFT	1.0%
2.3 Regarding that portion in excess of 20,000 and no greater no greater than 25,000 MFT	1.5%
2.4 Regarding that portion in excess of 25,000 and no greater no greater than 30,000 MFT	2.0%
2.5 Regarding that portion in excess of 30,000 and no greater no greater than 35,000 MFT	2.5%
2.6 Regarding that portion in excess of 35,000 and no greater no greater than 40,000 MFT	3.0%
2.7 Regarding that portion in excess of 40,000 MFT	4.5%
3 Mine operator with annual sales greater than 50,000 MFT	5.0%

Source: Law 20,026

concessions, exploration and exploitation. It also establishes boundaries for the action of the state in the sector. According to this law, the state is the absolute, exclusive and inalienable owner of all mines, but it can grant the concession to explore and exploit them through state-owned companies.

In the early 2000s, a debate emerged about the benefits received by the foreign investors compared to their contribution to the state. One of the consequences of this debate was the Elusion Law, enacted in 2002, which primarily sought to eliminate loopholes in the legislation that reduced tax collection. But the debate around mining activities continued until the approval in May 2005 of a Specific Tax on Mining (SMT) activities (Law 20,026) to be charged starting January 1, 2006. Before this date there was no specific tax on these activities. The SMT was levied on the taxable operating income of the mine operator[10] based on annual sales, according to the categories shown in Table 3.3.

Two operational issues need to be emphasized: (1) SMT payment was considered as spending necessary to produce income, which implies that it can be subtracted from incomes in order to calculate the income tax;[11] and (2) Law 20,026 does not allow accelerated depreciation of fixed assets, accelerated amortizations of organizational and start-up costs, and losses carried from one year to the next to be deducted from operating incomes so as to calculate the tax base on which to apply the SMT (Cochilco 2006).

The Law 20,026 was not applicable to foreign investors who signed a DL600 contract before December 1, 2004, but they could opt to voluntarily relinquish the previous contract signed with the Chilean state, and sign a new one. In this case, foreign investors could claim an invariable SMT regime for 12 years with a maximum SMT rate of 4%, while fulfilling additional requirement of information.[13] Nonetheless, they could not apply again to other invariable tax regime and would not be able to deduct accelerated depreciation spending for personnel income tax purposes.[14] Those who were not operating under the DL600 could opt for this new regime as long as they fulfilled the same requirements of those operating under DL600 (Cochilco, 2006). Foreign investors who after December 1, 2004 invested under the protection of DL600 more than 50 million dollars in mining activities could opt for an invariable SMT regime for 15 years with a rate of 5%.

In February of 2010 an earthquake hit Chile causing huge human and capital losses. In order to get resources to finance the reconstruction of the country, a new law was enacted, Law 20,469 that introduced changes in the Law 20,026 of 2005. The SMT, as in the previous law of 2005, was to be levied on the taxable operating income of the mine operator based on annual sales, but, this time, the tax would depend on production and operating margin according to Table 3.4. Nonetheless, those investors having an invariable SMT regime according to Law 20,026 opted to adopt the regime of Law 20,469, which allowed a special SMT regime from 2010 to 2012 with lower tax rates. Starting from 2013 they would pay tax rates according to the Law 20,026. Also, they would extend their invariable SMT regime for six more years according to the tax rates established in Law 20,469.

Table 3.4 Law 20,469: SMT according to annual sales of mine operator

Annual sales of the mine operator	*Rate*
1 Mine operator with annual sales ≤ 12,000 MFT	0.0%
2 12,000 MFT ≤ Annual sales ≤ 50,000 MFT,	0.5%
2.1 Regarding that portion in excess of 12,000 and no greater than 15,000 MFT	1.0%
2.2 Regarding that portion in excess of 15,000 and no greater than 20,000 MFT	1.5%
2.3 Regarding that portion in excess of 20,000 and no greater than 25,000 MFT	2.0%
2.4 Regarding that portion in excess of 25,000 and no greater than 30,000 MFT	2.5%
2.5 Regarding that portion in excess of 30,000 and no greater than 35,000 MFT	3.0%
2.6 Regarding that portion in excess of 35,000 and no greater than 40,000 MFT	4.5%
2.7 Regarding that portion in excess of 40,000 MFT	5.0%
3 Mine operator with annual sales greater than 50,000 MFT,	
3.1 If operating margin is no greater than 35	8.0%
3.2 Regarding that portion of operating margin that excess 35 and no greater than 40	10.5%
3.3 Regarding that portion of operating margin that excess 40 and no greater than 45	13.0%
3.4 Regarding that portion of operating margin that excess 45 and no greater than 50	15.5%
3.5 Regarding that portion of operating margin that excess 50 and no greater than 55	18.0%
3.6 Regarding that portion of operating margin that excess 55 and no greater than 60	

(*Continued*)

Table 3.4 (Continued)

Annual sales of the mine operator	Rate
3.7 Regarding that portion of operating margin that excess 60 and no greater than 65	21.0% 24.0%
3.8 Regarding that portion of operating margin that excess 65 and no greater than 70	27.5%
3.9 Regarding that portion of operating margin that excess 70 and no greater than 75	31.0%
3.10 Regarding that portion of operating margin that excess 75 and no greater than 80	34.5%
3.11 Regarding that portion of operating margin that excess 80 and no greater than 85	14.0%
3.12 If operating margin is greater than 85	

Source: Law 20,469

2.3 Public finances and copper revenues[15]

Since the beginning of the 1930s fiscal revenues from copper have been a very important source of resources to finance Chilean public spending. While from 1930 to 2011 they represented on average 12% of total fiscal spending, in the last six years fiscal revenues from copper averaged 24% of the total annual fiscal revenues. This increase is explained by high copper prices and the new taxes enacted.

During 2006–2011, transfers from Codelco represented almost 60% of the fiscal revenues from copper, while fiscal revenues from taxes to private mining companies reached 40% (Figure 3.2).

Transfers from Codelco to the treasury are the sum of income taxes – which include the standard profit tax,[16] the special profit tax of 40% to public enterprises[17] and the SMT[18] – of payments established in Law 13,196[19] and of dividends. On average, they represented 48.9%, 19.6% and 31.5% of the Codelco's transfers to the treasury during 2006–2011, respectively.[20]

Private mining companies contribute with resources to the treasury by income taxes, that is, the standard profit tax and the personal income tax to remittances,[21] and by SMT. Between 2006 and 2011 they represented 79% and 21% of fiscal revenues from private mining, respectively.

Nonetheless, the contribution of copper to finance fiscal spending has not been stable, ranging from a minimum of 0.1% in 1933 to a maximum of almost 50% in 2008, explained mainly by copper price volatility and tax regimes. In this context, government has established, starting from 1987, different mechanisms aimed to smooth copper price effects on fiscal revenues.[22]

In 1987 the Copper Compensation Fund (*Fondo de Estabilización del Cobre* [FEC]) started to operate. It was established to save in (or withdraw from) a treasury account the transitory higher (lower) fiscal revenues from Codelco (copper). In 2000, the government announced that fiscal policy would be led by a fiscal rule that stated that the central government should have a structural surplus of 1% of the GDP each year. The rule entailed that only 99% of permanent or structural fiscal revenues could be spent, and that transitory or cyclical higher (lower) fiscal

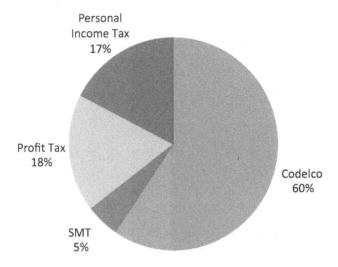

Figure 3.2 Fiscal revenues from copper, 2006–2011, as % of total revenues from copper
Source: Budget Office

resources from Codelco (copper) and taxes should be saved (financed). In 2008 the structural surplus goal was reduced to 0.5% of the GDP. The government has fulfilled the rule every year but in 2009. That year fiscal revenues decreased significantly due to the negative effects of the international financial crisis on copper price and domestic activity. At the same time, the government increased its spending in order to counteract the negative effects of the crisis on domestic activity and employment. Considering all this, the structural balance was in the range of –1.2% and –2.9%.[23] The new government that took office in 2010 announced that its goal would be to get a structural deficit of 1% of GDP by 2014.

FEC continued in operation until 2006. In 2007 the FEC was eliminated, and since then all cyclical revenues related to copper and GDP cycle are deposited in or withdrawn from, according to the case, the Social and Economic Stabilization Fund (*Fondo de Estabilización Económica y Social* [FEES]).[24]

The methodology used to calculate the cyclical component of the fiscal revenues from Codelco (copper) that should be saved in (withdrawn from) the FEC/FEES was based on the estimation of a reference copper price which is supposed to reflect the long-term price of this commodity. The difference between the spot price and the reference (long-term) price of copper (multiplied by the production) were deposited in or withdrawn from the FEC/FEES.[25] Between 1987 and 2001, the reference price of copper was calculated yearly by the Ministry of Finance. Since 2002, this price has been established yearly by a committee of experts called upon by the Ministry of Finance.

In 2005 fiscal revenues from molybdenum (Codelco) were included in the estimation of structural fiscal revenues using the same methodology as the fiscal

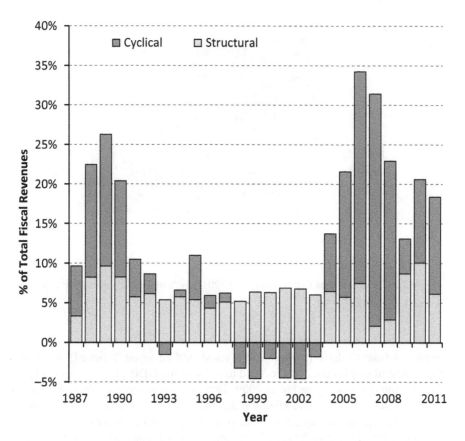

Figure 3.3 Component of fiscal revenues from copper and molybdenum, 1987–2011, as % of total fiscal revenues

Source: Own estimations, and Budget Office

revenues from copper. In the same year, the estimation of fiscal structural balance started including fiscal revenues (income taxes) from the largest private mining companies and, in 2007, fiscal revenues from SMT. Figure 3.3 and Figure 3.4 show the fiscal revenues from copper and molybdenum since 1987. In the case of fiscal revenues from Codelco (copper) between 1987 and 2001, they were calculated using the formula of structural balance. At the end of the '80s and beginnings of the '90s, government saved resources from copper. Due to the low copper prices prevailing during the period of the Asian, Russian, Brazilian and SARS crisis (1998–2003), the government had to withdraw resources from FEC. Since 2004 to the present, except for 2009, the government has saved a significant amount of fiscal revenues from copper in the FEES, which in 2011 had US$13 billion in assets (6% of the GDP).

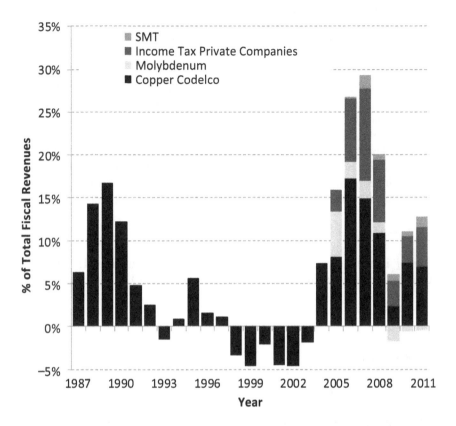

Figure 3.4 Source of fiscal revenues from copper and molybdenum, 1987–2011, as % of total fiscal revenues

Source: Own estimations, and Budget Office

3 Deacon's model

The conceptual framework is based on a dynamic model developed by Deacon (1993) for the oil industry in the US economy. Deacon considers three types of taxes: income tax, property tax on reserves and severance tax. The latter is what we call the royalty or SMT, which in the case of Chile has important differences in respect to the case considered by Deacon. Chile does not have property tax on reserves.[26] Regarding income tax, there are some differences in the Chilean law that need to be taken into account.

Following Deacon (1993), in an untaxed scenario the industry's net cash flow in any year is equal to its revenues from production, less production cost and exploration spending.[27]

$$\Pi_t = p_t y_t - C(y_t, R_t) - D(w_t), \tag{1}$$

where p is price of copper, y is output, w is "exploration effort", R is outstanding reserves, $C(.)$ is production cost, and $D(.)$ is exploration cost. Upper case variables denote stocks measured at the beginning of year t and lower case variables are flows during the year.

As in Deacon's model, we assume production cost depends positively on current output and negatively on the level of reserves, which is a fixed factor. C is also a function of the price vector of all variable factors, which will be calibrated as one parameter that summarizes this effect. In the case of exploration cost, it depends on the current "exploration effort".

The industry's reserves are changing over time as firms make exploration efforts. Further, we assume that the stock of reserves at the beginning of year t is a concave function of all cumulative exploration efforts up to that date less cumulative production. Then, the available reserves at the start of year t are:

$$R_t = F(W_t) - Y_t, \quad F'>0, F''<0 \tag{2}$$

where W_t is cumulative exploration effort, Y_t is cumulative output, and $F(.)$ is cumulative gross reserves additions. The state variables W_t and Y_t evolve according to:

$$W_t + w_t = W_{t+1}, \tag{3}$$

$$Y_t + y_t = Y_{t+1}, \tag{4}$$

for $t = 0, \ldots, T$.

The optimal behavior of the industry is characterized as the solution to the following problem:

$$\max_{\substack{\{w_0,\ldots,w_T\} \\ \{y_0,\ldots,y_T\} \\ \{W_1,\ldots,W_{T+1}\} \\ \{Y_1,\ldots,Y_{T+1}\}}} \sum_{t=0}^{T} \Pi_t (1+r)^{-t},$$

given $p_0, \ldots, p_T$, an interest rate r, a terminal date T, W_0, and Y_0; subject to (2), (3), (4), $w_t \geq 0$, $y_t \geq 0$.

The Lagrange equation for this problem is:

$$L = \sum_{t=0}^{T} \left\{ \Pi_t (1+r)^{-t} + \phi_t (W_t + w_t - W_{t+1}) + \lambda_t (Y_t + y_t - Y_{t+1}) \right\} \tag{5}$$

Note that the objective function $f : \Re^{2T} \to \Re$, is a continuous, real valued function on a non-empty, compact set $S = (W, Y) \in \Re^{2T}$ with respect to the usual topology (absolute value on the real line). Then by the Weierstrass Theorem, there exists a maximizer $(\{W\}, \{Y\}) \in \Re^{2T}$ of f, over S. Also, invoking concavity, by Berge's Theorem we know that there exists a unique maximum. Thus assuming interior solution we can use the first order conditions

$$\frac{\partial L}{\partial w_t} = \frac{\partial \Pi_t}{\partial w_t}(1+r)^{-t} + \phi_t \le 0, \quad w_t \ge 0, w_t \frac{\partial L}{\partial w_t} = 0 \tag{6a}$$

$$\frac{\partial L}{\partial y_t} = \frac{\partial \Pi_t}{\partial y_t}(1+r)^{-t} + \lambda_t \le 0, \quad y_t \ge 0, y_t \frac{\partial L}{\partial y_t} = 0 \tag{6b}$$

for $t = 0, \ldots, T$, plus equations (3) and (4) and the initial stocks W_0 and Y_0. Also, we require the terminal state restriction – which substitutes for the usual transversality condition in the infinite horizon problem.

$$\frac{\partial L}{\partial W_{T+1}} = -\phi_T = 0 \tag{6c}$$

$$\frac{\partial L}{\partial Y_{T+1}} = -\lambda_T = 0 \tag{6d}$$

As it is showed in Deacon (1993), $-\lambda_t$ is the present value cost decrease that results from a marginal addition to the reserve period t and $-\lambda_t \ge 0$; while ϕ_t is the present value benefit increase that results from a marginal "exploration effort" in period t and $\phi_t \ge 0$.

Deacon uses the sequential representation of this problem. Alternatively we can use the corresponding recursive representation. Thus the Bellman equation characterizing the problem of the firm is the given by

$$v(W,Y) = \max_{W' \ge W, K' \ge K} \{\Pi(W,Y,W',Y') + \frac{1}{1+r}v(W',Y'), \tag{7}$$

with $W' = W + w$ and $Y' = Y + y$. Then a recursive competitive outcome is a value function $v: \Re^2 \to \Re$, and policy functions W and Y: $\Re_+^2 \to \Re$ for the representative firm, an exogenously given price for the world market of copper, and an aggregate law of motion $H_W : \Re_+ \to \Re_+$ for cumulative exploration effort and $H_Y : \Re_+ \to \Re_+$ for cumulative production, such that: given the copper price and functions H_W and H_Y, the value function v solves the Bellman equation (7) and policy functions W and Y are the associated policy functions. Note that since we do not model the demand side of world copper but fix world price then we cannot talk about an equilibrium notion, nor do we require the *consistency* requirement or the *market clearing* requirement which are usual in the definition of the recursive competitive equilibrium.

4 Data and parameters

4.1 Data

Cumulative gross reserves additions $F(W)$ were estimated according equation (2) with time series on Chilean copper reserves and cumulative production for the period 1950–2010 (See Figure 3.7 in the Appendix). Chilean copper reserves for the period 1950–1994 were calculated from world copper reserves published by

US Geological Survey (USGS) assuming that Chilean reserves represent, on average, 25% of the total.[28] Reserves for the period 1995–2010 were obtained directly from Mineral Commodities Summary of USGS (Figure 3.8 in the Appendix).[2930]

Cumulative Chilean copper production for the period 1950–2010 was computed with annual time series flows of copper production. The starting date for forming the cumulative production was 1601. Data sources are from Sutulov (1976) for the period 1601 to 1859; from Braun et al. (2000) for the period 1860 to 1959, and for 1960 to 2010 from Comisión Chilena del Cobre (Cochilco) (Figure 3.9 in the Appendix).

One of the key decision variables is w, which we call "exploration effort". Deacon (1993) associated this variable to the number of drillings while exploring for oil. The data available in our case correspond to the total number of acres in concession for mining exploration of all minerals, which is a measure of the stock of potential acres to be explored in a given year. Given that the measured value added of copper in the total value added of the mining sector is 83%, we will assume that this also is the percentage of total acres for mining exploration that corresponds to copper exploration. Additionally, given that we have data for mining exploration spending in Chile, we check that both series are coherent between them. Series for the period 1984–2010 was obtained from the Annual Mining Reports of *Servicio Nacional de Geología y Minería* (Sernageomin). But we still need to estimate the exploration effort. Considering that exploration concessions are granted for four years, we will assume that the company made an exploration effort equivalent to one-fourth per year, i.e. they explore one-fourth of the total acres per each year of concession. Thus w_t corresponds to one-fourth of the total acres available for exploration in the previous year. Starting with the number of acres in concession for exploration in 1984 as W_0, we add the estimated w_t to obtain the cumulative exploration effort. These series are used to estimate $F(W)$ and the cost function of exploration $D(w)$ (Figure 3.10 in the Appendix).

Exploration cost series was obtained from Metals Economics Group, and corresponds to mining exploration spending in Chile for the period 1972–2010 (Figure 3.11 in Appendix).

4.2 Estimation and calibration of the parameters of the model

There are three functions required for the model to write the profit function: the cost function, the exploration cost function and the function of accumulative reserves, $F(W)$.

Parameters of cost function were calibrated for 2010 applying Deacon's[31] strategy to the weighted average cost of the copper mining industry located in Chile. We assume a Cobb–Douglas production function of copper given by $y_t = A k_t^\mu R_t^{1-\mu}$, where k is "non-reserve inputs" used in production (labor, fuel and equipment). Given R as a fixed factor, production cost is $C(y_t, R_t) = \theta y_t^\varepsilon R_t^{1-\varepsilon}$, where $\varepsilon = 1/\mu$ and θ is a function of A and the price of k. From the profit maximization we obtain the traditional first order condition $\dfrac{\sigma_t k_t}{\rho_t R_t} = \dfrac{\mu}{1-\mu}$, which shows that we can compute μ from the ratio of cost shares for k and R. Note that $\sigma_t k_t$ is the expenditure on non-reserve inputs, and $\rho_t R_t$ is the cost related to reserve input.

We assume that $\sigma_t k_t$ is equivalent to fully allocated cost (C3)[32] multiplied by total copper production of Chile. Based on information of Brook Hunt, in 2010 the C3 weighted average copper cost for the mining industry located in Chile was US$149.2 per pound of fine copper. In the same year, Chilean copper production reached 5.4 million of metric ton of fine copper. To obtain $\rho_t R_t$, we used the relation $\rho_t R_t = (r+\delta)q_t R_t$, where q_t is the asset price of R_t. We obtained q_t from the average price acquisition of private copper mining companies which were in the exploration or development stage held in 2011 and beginning of 2012. The copper price of reserves implied by those transactions was US$0.21 per pound.[33] Interest rate was set at 3% and δ corresponds to the average ratio of total production to reserves, for the years of the 2000s (3.8%). We obtained as final results $\mu = 0.79$ and $\theta = $ US$7,783.

The cost function for exploration is estimated using aggregate data on exploration cost since 1985 up to 2010. The exploration effort is measured as explained in section 5.1 (in thousands of acres). Following Deacon (1993) we estimate a quadratic function:

$$D(w_t) = \alpha_1 w_t + \alpha_2 w_t^2$$

The estimation results are presented in Table 3.5. Nevertheless, the coefficient of the linear term was not statistically significant, it was used in the model but it does not make any difference in the results.

The second function to be estimated is $F(W)$. It relates the stock of reserves with the number of acres under concession. This function is expected to be increasing and concave. The larger the concession area for exploration is, the more reserves will be accumulated, but at a decreasing rate. The proposed functional form by Deacon is

$$F(W) = \Gamma(1 - \exp[-\beta W_t]).$$

There is an endogeneity issue since W is a decision variable, therefore $F(W)$ was estimated using instrumental variables. The instruments were one lag of W, contemporaneous value and one lag of the price of copper. Table 3.6 presents the results of the estimation.

Initial values of state variables were $W_0=17,063$ thousands of acres, and $Y_0=127.3$ million metric tons. We assume an interest rate of 3%, and a copper

Table 3.5 Exploration cost function

	Coefficient	Standard deviation
α_1	0.0084	0.0300
α_2	0.0004	0.0001

Table 3.6 Estimation results of $F(W)$

	Coefficient	Standard deviation
Γ	249.1874	39.7617
B	0.00022	0.00012

price of 6,658 dollars per fine metric tons, which is the price of 3.0 dollars per pounds established by the Copper Committee as the long-term reference copper price for 2012.

5 Relevant tax regimes in the case of Chile

5.1 Base scenario

Profits in the untaxed scenario are:

$$\Pi_t = p_t y_t - C(y_t, R_t) - D(w_t) \tag{8}$$

The financial statements of companies report normal depreciation, so we will assume that $C(.)$ includes this type of depreciation.[34] This is going to be an important issue, since accelerated depreciation can be deduced to pay income tax, but not for the purpose of the SMT. In the latter case, companies can use only linear depreciation according to the tables provided by the Internal Revenue Service (SII). Likewise, firms will deduct exploration expenses from revenues for the purpose of the income tax but not for the SMT, where they use a more complicated formula explained later.

5.2 Income tax[35]

Every company operating in Chile has to pay a flat tax rate on profits or *Impuesto de Primera Categoria* (τ^E). Between 2004 and 2010 this rate was 17% and it was increased temporarily to 20% in 2011 and to 18.5% in 2012 in order to obtain higher revenues to finance the reconstruction of the country after the earthquake of February 2010. It should return to 17% in 2013.

Income Tax Law (*Ley de la Renta*) allows the use of accelerated depreciation of fixed assets for calculating taxable profits. According to the law normal depreciation is equivalent to one-third of accelerated depreciation. This is equivalent to multiplying the total cost $C(.)$ by a factor of $1+2d_N$, where d_N corresponds to the share of normal depreciation on total cost.[36] In 2010, average ratio of depreciation to total costs of the 12 largest companies in the copper industry was 12%.

With respect to exploration cost, we follow the same criterion as in the baseline case.

Considering all these factors, after-tax net revenues with τ^E is:

$$\Pi_t = p_t y_t - C(y_t, R_t) - D(w_t) - \tau^E (p_t y_t - C(y_t, R_t)(1 + 2d_N) - D(w_t)) \tag{9}$$

5.3 Specific mining tax

We are working with two scenarios. The first one uses the SMT established in Law 20,026 of 2005. The tax rate was applied to operating income but depended on annual production (see Section 3). Nonetheless, big firms had signed the DL600 contract which entailed an invariable tax regime for them. The Law 20,026 allowed firms to back out of the previous contract and sign a new one that stated an invariable SMT of 4% maximum for 12%. Given that almost every firm that pays SMT in Chile produces more than 50,000 metric tons, we suppose a scenario where firms pay a SMT rate of 4%.

The second scenario uses SMT set in Law 20,469 of 2010. This law kept the tax base of the previous SMT – operating income – but established a new rate scale for SMT that depends on annual production and operating margin (see Section 3).[37]

In both cases, there are three important technical issues to highlight about how to calculate operating income. First, law establishes that when calculating operational income, SMT payment has to be considered as spending necessary to produce income, which implies that it can be subtracted from operational income in order to calculate the proper income bracket and tax rate. As a consequence, the calculation of operating income is recursive, which explains why operating income is divided by $1 + \tau^R$ in equation (10), where τ^R is the SMT.[38]

Second, the law does not allow accelerated depreciation of fixed assets to be deducted from revenues to obtain taxable income, but what the law calls normal depreciation. Given that our cost function includes normal depreciation, we will not make any adjustments to it.

Third, SMT law does not allow accelerated amortizations of organizational and start-up costs (which includes exploration cost), but normal amortizations which should be done at least in six years. Income Tax Law (*Ley de la Renta*) establishes that exploration costs have to be capitalized and recovered through annual amortizations. Once exploration is considered successful, the law allows the company to amortize the capitalized exploration expenses within six years; nonetheless mining companies amortized exploration costs in one year (for purposes of income tax). On the contrary, if exploration is not successful, the total exploration expenses can be deducted from operating revenues in one year. In practice, under the untaxed scenario and income tax scenario, exploration outlays are considered costs for tax purposes in the year that investors declared whether exploration was successful or not.

The SMT law does not allow amortizing 100% of exploration costs in one year, but throughout six years. The Metal Economic Group provides exploration costs in base metals.[39] Therefore we need to estimate when and how much of the capitalized exploration outlays will be considered a cost to deduct from the operational income. In doing so, we need to know when the exploration effort is successful or not; according to specialists of the copper industry, it takes eight years for the investor to find out. The probability of success is 0.1% according to PDAC (2010). Assuming that firms amortize one-sixth of the capitalized exploration cost, in every year the expected amortization for a given year will be:

$$E(Amortization)_t = 0.999 * D(w)_{t-8} + \frac{1}{6} * 0.001 * \sum_{i=0}^{5} D(w)_{t-8-i}$$

The series obtained is expressed as percentage of total exploration costs in base metals of year t. The average ratio, which we will call f, for the 2000s was 70.5%.

Combining all the factors aforementioned, after-tax net revenues with SMT is:

$$\Pi_t = p_t y_t - C(y_t, R_t) - D(w_t) - \tau^R \left(\frac{p_t y_t - C(y_t, R_t) - D(w_t)f}{1 + \tau^R} \right) \tag{10}$$

6 Simulations of the scenarios

In this section, we present the simulations results obtained from solving the dynamic problem of the firm. Using backward induction and iterating over the Bellman equation (7) we obtain the evolution of the control variables over time, using the parameters estimated and calibrated in the previous section. The assumed time frame (*T*) is 60 years, which is arbitrary. There is no obvious time frame to choose, since if we choose a finite T, the optimal production level at T+1 will be positive and so the profit of the firm. Therefore, we should choose a time frame such that the production path is not affected by the election of T.[40]

There are two exercises that we will conduct in this section. First, we compare the actual Chilean tax system with an untaxed situation to compute the dead-weight loss of the whole system. Also, we set the tax rates to zero, separately to estimate the distortionary effect of the other tax. Second, keeping tax revenue constant, we play around with the tax rates to find a combination of taxes that generate the same tax collection but a minimum deadweight loss.

6.1 The deadweight loss of the actual system

The profit maximization under the actual tax system was described by equations (9) and (10), which are characterized by:

- Income tax is equal to 18.5% and the law allows for deducting accelerated depreciation and the SMT from the before-tax profit.
- SMT charged according to a table that was approximated by a function that depends on profit calculated using a normal depreciation rate.

When imposing an income tax the conditions of the maximization problem should not change with respect to an untaxed situation, but due to the effect of depreciation the optimal *y* and *w* do change. Figure 3.5 and 3.6 present the evolution of the flow of the exploration effort (*w*) and output (*y*), respectively, in the untaxed scenario versus the actual Chilean tax system scenario. The exploration effort rapidly decreases over time, in the first ten years. This could be due to the fact that the marginal effect on reserves is strongly decreasing. The difference between the untaxed and the current regime scenarios is almost nil, over the entire program. Note that part of the exploration costs are tax deductible and for that reason there is an incentive to spend more at the beginning to increase the benefit of tax deduction and to reduce the marginal cost. In general, the exploration effort is not very sensible to any type of tax, which could be due to the absence of uncertainty in the firm's problem.

Reserves will change accordingly to the exploration effort and so do marginal costs of production. Given that firms are price-takers in the international market, the change in marginal costs would change the optimal level of production. Figure 3.6 exhibits the evolution of output flow in the untaxed and current regime scenarios. Output is also decreasing since there are incentives to push production close to the initial period to maximize the cash flows; this effect is mitigated by

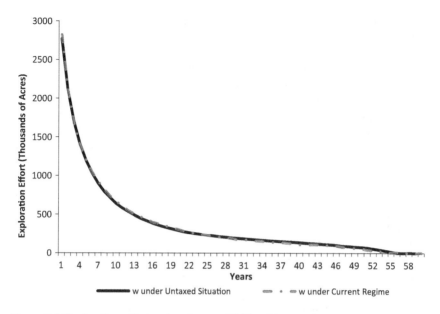

Figure 3.5 Exploration effort: untaxed versus SMT and income tax

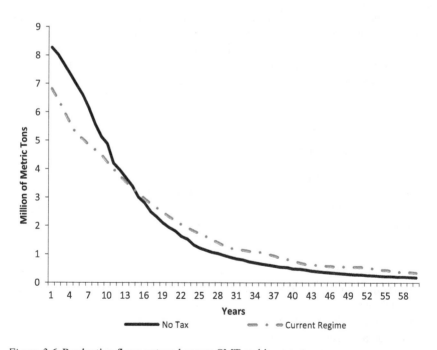

Figure 3.6 Production flow: untaxed versus SMT and income tax

the fact that the increasing Y has a negative effect on reserves. We found a measurable effect of the tax system. Output falls 18% during the first year comparing the taxed with the untaxed case and it follows a smoother path under the taxed scenarios. Since the trajectory of the exploration effort does not change much, both plans will accumulate reserves at the same pace.

Reserves have a negative effect on the marginal cost and a positive effect on output and profits; but considering that the SMT rate is increasing with the margin, the firm faces a trade-off between increasing output to increasing profit and the effect of taxes on profit. Therefore, it may be optimal not to raise output immediately, but to follow a smoother path to avoid increasing the tax rate to be paid.

Next we estimate the deadweight loss as the difference between the present value of profit flow in the untaxed scenario and the present value of profit flow in the corresponding taxed scenario and the present value of tax paid. Table 3.8 shows these calculations. The current tax regime collects 23.5% of undistorted profit, when the price of copper is US$3 per pound. The cost of this represents a deadweight loss of 22% of the tax revenue. From the total tax collection, SMT contributes with 42% while the other 58% comes from income tax. The dead weight losses (DWL) of each tax cannot be compared as percentage of total revenues, since the base will change with the tax; but looking at the third column, as percentage of undistorted profit, the SMT generates lower DWL.

Table 3.7 also shows a sensitivity check of our calculations. Assuming that the price of copper in the next 60 years becomes the long-term average of US$2 per pound (instead of $3), we estimate the deadweight loss as 50.2% of the total tax revenue. There is a large effect on tax revenue due to the reduction in the profit of the firm, therefore the DWL increases as percentage of this base. But if we take the DWL as a percentage of the undistorted profit, the increase in DWL is less dramatic. However, the reduction in copper price will induce a higher cost in collecting one extra dollar in taxes, since the DWL increased more than proportionally.

6.2 The minimum DWL

In this section we move the SMT rate and income tax rate to obtain the same tax revenue and to compute the DWL associated with each combination of both taxes. The SMT is a table or a function rather than a constant rate, so the assumption was that any modification will increase (or reduce) the whole function proportionally. Table 3.8 exhibits the results of this exercise. The number 1 in column SMT implies that the function is at the actual level; thus the combination 1 in the SMT column and 0.185 in the income tax column correspond to the actual regime. The 21.6% corresponds to the DWL calculated in the previous section, as a percentage of total revenue.

Starting from the actual regime and moving upward in the table, we increase the income tax and reduce the SMT tax, in a way that the tax revenue is constant and computing at each step the DWL. As shown in the table, the DWL as percentage

Table 3.7 Deadweight losses under different price scenarios and tax regimes

	Base scenario			Alternative scenario		
	Price = US$3 per pound			Price = US$2 per pound		
	Revenue (% of undistorted π)	DWL (% of tax revenue)	DWL (% of undistorted π)	Revenue (% of undistorted π)	DWL (% of tax revenue)	DWL (% of undistorted π)
Current system(*)	23.46%	−22.01%	−5.16%	18.06%	−50.17%	−9.06%
Pure SMT tax(**)	9.93%	−35.54%	−3.53%	6.15%	−96.55%	−5.94%
Pure income tax(**)	15.39%	−37.39%	−5.76%	13.03%	−78.17%	−10.19%

Note: (*) Current system sets income tax in 18.5% and SMT tax as the function we defined in footnote 36
(**) Total revenue is different from that in the current arrangement

Table 3.8 Deadweight losses keeping tax revenues

Income tax (%)	SMT (times)	DWL (% undistorted profit)	DWL (% of revenue)
0.281	0	5.6%	23.5%
0.27	0.112	5.6%	23.4%
0.26	0.219	5.4%	22.9%
0.25	0.323	5.4%	22.7%
0.24	0.431	5.4%	22.6%
0.23	0.535	5.4%	22.6%
0.22	0.642	5.3%	22.2%
0.2	0.848	5.2%	21.9%
0.185	**1**	**5.2%**	**21.6%**
0.17	1.151	5.0%	20.8%
0.15	1.351	4.4%	18.5%
0.1	1.843	3.4%	14.3%
0.05	2.328	2.5%	10.7%
0.04	2.424	2.3%	9.8%
0.03	2.52	2.1%	8.9%
0	2.807	1.8%	7.4%

of tax revenue increases from 21.6% to 23.5% when the SMT is equal to zero but we need to raise income tax to the level of 28.1% to keep tax revenue constant.

Moving in the opposite direction, increasing SMT and reducing income tax, the DWL decreases down to 7.4% when the income tax is zero and we increase SMT up to 2.8 times of its actual level. Therefore reducing income tax and increasing the SMT reduce the DWL. Of course, this exercise makes consideration neither to the political problem faced by the policymakers to change the tax structure nor to the general equilibrium situation, since an income tax reduction needs to be applied to the entire economy.

7 Concluding remarks

The mining sector has played an important role in the Chilean economic history. The main development of this industry started around 1910, after a process of innovation that permitted the exploitation of low-grade. Thus copper has been the main export product for Chile in the 20th century. The property of the copper mines has experienced many changes during that century. At the beginning, the owners were foreign producers; since the middle of the century the state become more involved in the activity, reaching a peak of intervention with the nationalization of all copper mines in 1971. After a new foreign direct investment law (1974) and a new concession law (1982) and mining code (1983), private companies began investing again in the copper sector. As of today around 70% of total production belongs to private companies and the rest belongs to Codelco, a large state-owned firm that operates in the sector.

Copper revenues are important for the fiscal budget through tax collection and Codelco's profit. Until 2005, the only tax paid by private companies was the income tax. In 2006, the government put in place a specific tax on mining activities based on the taxable operating income of the mine operator. There were two important adjustments to the operating income that are worth mentioning: (1) SMT payment was considered as spending necessary to produce income, which implies that it can be subtracted from incomes in order to calculate the income tax; and (2) Law 20,026 does not allow accelerated depreciation of fixed assets, accelerated amortizations of organizational and start-up costs, and losses carried from one year to the next can be deducted from operating incomes so as to calculate the tax base on which to apply the SMT. In 2010, the table of tax rates was modified to generate additional resources for the government to reconstruct infrastructure damaged by the 2010 earthquake.

Using the conceptual framework proposed by Deacon (1993), we assessed the impact of the SMT and income tax in the mining activity. We calibrated the parameters of the model according to the Chilean mining sector. Given the nature of the SMT tax, which is applied to operating income tax, it is less distortive than a gross revenue tax (royalty), but it introduces a distortion since it does not allow for 100% deduction of exploration costs as in the case of income tax. We compare the untaxed case with the actual tax regime applied in Chile, finding that exploration effort does not change its pattern much over time, but output follows a smoother path under the scenario with taxes than without taxes. Given that the level of the reserves is the same at the end of the period, the integral of both output series is about the same; output under the actual tax regimes is lower than output in the untaxed case during the early periods of the plan. The opposite is true in the late periods.

Our estimation is that the actual tax regime induces a deadweight loss equivalent to 22% of tax revenues if the price of copper remains constant at US$3 per pound over the entire program. This DWL increases dramatically; if the price is cut at US$2 per pound during the entire period of analysis, the DWL would be 50% of the tax revenue. Allowing for choosing the combination of tax rate that ensures the same government revenue from this activity and that minimizes the DWL, we found that a combination of zero income tax and a SMT that is 2.8 times the actual value may reduce the DWL down to 7.4%.

There are several important remarks that should be made regarding our estimations. First, the estimated deadweight loss corresponds to a firm that is already in the market; we are not estimating the effect on potential entrants to the market. Second, we are using a representative firm to calculate the effect of the tax; but it could be the case that for a marginal firm the SMT would be high enough to drive it out of the market. Hence, our work is not modeling the dynamic of the industry. Third, our model does not consider the effects on production and exploration decisions (neither on investment and enter/exit decisions) of the uncertainty regarding changes in copper price or in tax regime. Higher uncertainty should reduce the efforts of production and exploration, and could change the sensibility of the response of both variables to different taxes. Fourth, we assume that it is politically possible to modify the tax rate for the mining sector, without affecting the rest of the sectors in the economy. In summary, these caveats suggest that the projected deadweight loss here underestimate the one that will prevail in an environment with uncertainty and entry/exit of firms. Further research in this area should include a quantification of how and by how much these factors could affect the efficiency of the mining sector.

Appendix

This appendix contains more details about data, parameter calibration and estimations.

Data

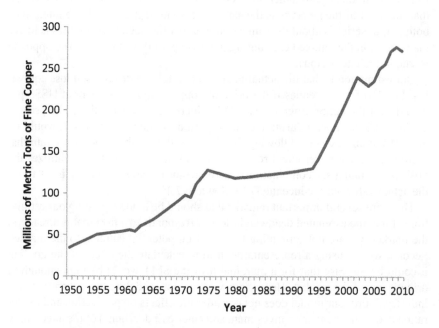

Figure 3.7 Cumulative reserve addition *F(W)*

Source: Own estimations

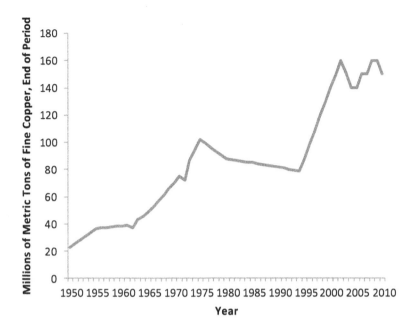

Figure 3.8 Chilean copper reserves

Source: Own estimation based on USGS data

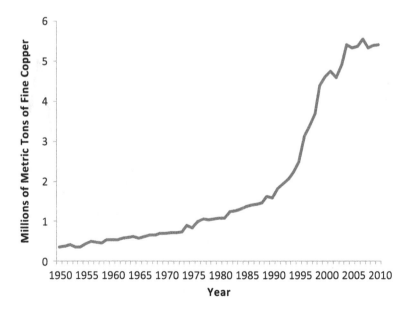

Figure 3.9 Chilean copper production

Source: Sutulov 1976; Braun et al. 2000; Cochilco 2011

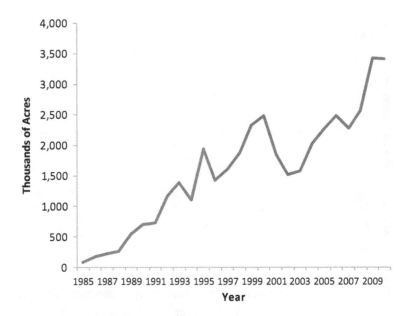

Figure 3.10 "Exploration effort"

Source: Own estimations

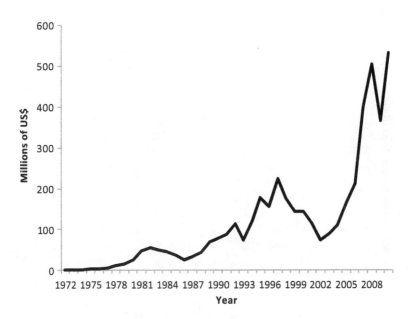

Figure 3.11 Spending in mining exploration in Chile

Source: Metals Economics Group

Notes

1 We thank Javier Tapia (Antofagasta Minerals), Medardo Lagos (Antofagasta Minerals), Carlos Gallardo (Antofagasta Minerals), Juan Carlos Guajardo (CESCO), Cochilco, and Alejandro Tejerina for helpful conversations on different topics regarding taxation and/or the functioning of the mining sector. Also, we thank Cochilco for helping us with data.
2 Pontificia Universidad Católica de Chile, rodrigo.fuentes@uc.cl
3 Inter-American Development Bank, pbernardita@iadb.org
4 Central Bank of Chile, mcalani@bcentral.cl
5 There are maybe two reasons for that, one internal and other external. After a coup d'état in 1973, the country was ruled by a military government until 1990, which passed (there was no Parliament in place during this period) all these laws related to FDI and mining concessions, explorations and exploitations. One hypothesis is that until democracy was reestablished in 1990, foreign capitals were not willing to flow into the country. Another hypothesis, which could be considered complementary to the first one, is that the external debt crisis experience by Chile (as in many other Latin American countries) prevented capital inflows of all types in the '80s. Some FDI did come to the economy, but that flow was small compared to the inflows in the 1990s.
6 Chumacero and Fuentes (2006) found a similar evidence for a sample of seven Latin American economies.
7 Borensztein et al. (2010b), using information of the Consejo Minero, gives support to Cochilco's information: between 2005 and 2009, labor and energy costs represented 35% and 25% out of the total operation costs, respectively.
8 Labor cost increase is explained by a rise of 53.7% of salaries in Chilean pesos, and a appreciation of 16.3% of the Chilean peso.
9 It is important to highlight that large-scale projects benefited strongly from the allowance under FDI status; especially, the accelerated depreciation of fixed assets, financial cost allowances and losses carried from one year to the next. All these exemptions had a large impact on tax collection from the sector.
10 It should be considered the annual sales of related firms.
11 Temporarily, during 2006 and 2007, mining companies could deduct 50% of the SMT payments from the income tax payments. The remaining 50% could be considered as a spending necessary to produce incomes.
12 Metric tons of fine copper.
13 That is, to have external audits for financial statements, and to send quarterly and annually financial statements plus an annual report to the Chilean Securities and Insurance Supervisor.
14 In 2006 and 2007, transitory investors who gave up the previous DL600 contract with the state could deduct from incomes accelerated depreciation spending for personnel income tax purposes.
15 From now on we refer to "copper revenues" as the sum of copper and molybdenum revenues.
16 The tax increased from 17% to 20% in 2011, and changed to 18.5% in 2012 in order to get resources to finance the reconstruction of the country after the earthquake that hit Chile at the beginning of 2010.
17 DL N° 2,398 of December 1978.
18 Law 20,026 of May 2005 and Law 20,469 of October 2010.
19 Known as "Ley Reservada del Cobre", it establishes that 10% of Codelco's copper and byproducts export revenues should be transferred to the military.
20 1.2% is explained by others' components.
21 The owners of Chilean copper mines are foreign investors or Chilean investors that have the controller firm registered abroad.
22 This section is based on Borensztein et al. (2010a).

23 There is a controversy between the members of the previous government and the actual government about what is the correct measure of the structural balance.
24 Before 2007, fiscal savings (fiscal withdraws) related to the cyclical component of fiscal revenues from copper and from the cycle were classified in different accounts under the line: copper savings in FEC and cycle savings in "other account".
25 In the case of the FEC, savings in or withdrawals from the FEC depended on a non-lineal function of the gap between spot and reference copper price. For more detail see Law – Ranking Decree 3,653 of March 1981.
26 Mining explorers have to pay a mining license related to the number of acres that she is exploring or developing: The amount is equivalent to one-fiftieth of UTM per acres of exploration and one-tenth UTM per acres of exploitation (UTM refers to Unidad Tributaria Mensual, an account unit used to pay taxes that is indexed to inflation. By the end of 2010 UTM had a value of US$79). For instance, Escondida Company paid in 2010 0.01% of its total income in mining licenses. Also, there is a real state tax that is applied to every person who owns a real state property in Chile.
27 We use only exploration spending since development spending was not available.
28 Historical data for years 1962, 1965 and 1972 from USGS show that in those years Chilean copper reserves represented on average 25% of world copper reserves.
29 Reserve data from USGS are updated every five years. In order to get a smoother series, we extrapolated data linearly for every five years.
30 *Servicio Nacional de Geología y Minería* (Sernageomin) published a homogeneous series of Chilean copper reserves from 2001 to 2008. Unfortunately, this series is too short for our estimation purposes.
31 The way to calibrate the cost function follows the appendix of Deacon (1993).
32 Fully allocated costs are total production costs, including operating costs (C1), depreciation and amortization charges, royalties, costs related to the head office and interest payments.
33 This price does not include the value of the byproducts contained in the reserves.
34 Financial statements report financial depreciation which is different from the depreciation allowed by the Internal Revenue Service (SII). In Chile, SII defines two types of depreciation: a normal one and an accelerated one. Based on information from the mining sector, we assume that normal depreciation is equal to the one reported in the financial statements.
35 In our analysis we do not consider the income tax to dividends and profits withdrawn (*Impuesto Adicional*). We assume that the decisions of production and financing are independent. That is, using profits or borrowing to finance investment do not affect the path of production.
36 A better way would have been to calculate normal and accelerated depreciation flows. Nonetheless, information of investment was not available.
37 In order to operationalize the new tax brackets we approximate the new SMT with a polynomial on operating income described by the following equation: τ^R=0.169–0.010 2OMB+0.0003OMB^2–4.17E-06OMB^3+2.92E-08OMB^4–8.17E-11 OMB^5, where OMB stands for operational margin and τ^R for effective SMT rate.
38 SMT revenues R^R are $R^R = (OMB - R^R)\tau^R$, where OMB is operating margin before SMT and τ^R is SMT rate. Solving the equation we have that $R^R = \dfrac{OMB}{1+\tau^R}\,\tau^R$.
39 According to the MEG definition, base metals are copper, nickel, and zinc.
40 Based on similar arguments, Deacon chose T=61 years for oil projects.

References

Braun, Juan, Matías Braun, Ignacio Briones and José Díaz. 2000. *Economía Chilena 1810–1995: Estadísticas Históricas*, Working Paper No. 187, Pontificia Universidad Católica, Santiago, Chile.

Borensztein, Eduardo, Bernardita Piedrabuena, Valerie Mercer–Blackman and Roberto Rigobon. 2010a. "El Manejo de los Ingresos del Cobre en Chile, segunda parte", document prepared by IADB to support the Comité Asesor para el Diseño de una Política Fiscal de Balance Estructural de Segunda Generación para Chile.

Borensztein, Eduardo, Bernardita Piedrabuena, Rolando Ossowski and S. Miller. 2010b. "El Manejo de los Ingresos del Cobre en Chile, primera parte", document prepared by IADB to support the Comité Asesor para el Diseño de una Política Fiscal de Balance Estructural de Segunda Generación para Chile.

Cariola, Carmen and Osvaldo Sunkel. 1982. *La historia económica de Chile: 1830–1930*, Instituto de Cooperación Iberoamericana, Madrid.

Chumacero, Romulo and Rodrigo Fuentes. 2006. "Economic Growth in Latin America: Structural Breaks or Fundamentals", *Estudios de Economía*, 33(2), 141–154.

Cesco. 2010. *Informe Financiero de la Minería, No. 10, 4to Trimestre 2010*, Centro de Estudios del Cobre y la Minería, Santiago Chile.

Cochilco. Various years. *Base de Datos*, www.cochilco.cl

Cochilco. 2006. *Impuesto Específico a la Actividad Minera: Características y Principales Implicancias*, Dirección de Estudios Cochilco, Santiago, Chile.

Cochilco. 2008. "Costos de la Minería: ¿Cuánto Impactan los Insumos en la Industria del Cobre?", Dirección de Estudios Cochilco, Santiago, Chile.

De Gregorio, Jose and Felipe Labbe. 2011. *Copper, the Real Exchange Rate and Macreoconomic Fluctuations in Chile*, Central Bank of Chile Working Paper 640, Santiago, Chile.

Deacon, R. 1993. "Taxation, Depletion, and Welfare: A Simulation Study of the U.S. Petroleum Resource", *Journal of Environmental Economics and Management*, 24, 159–187.

Díaz, Jose, Rolf Lüders and Gert Wagner. 2003. "La República en Cifras: 1810–2000", Mimeo, Pontificia Universidad Católica de Chile, Santiago, Chile.

Feenstra, Robert, Robert Lipsey, Haiyan Deng, Alyson Ma and Hengyong Mo. 2005. *World Trade Flows: 1962–2000*, NBER Working Paper 11040, NBER, Cambridge, Massachusetts.

Fuentes, Rodrigo. 2010. "Learning How to Manage Natural Resource Revenue: The Experience of Copper in Chile", in Collier, Paul and Antony Venables, eds., *Plundered Nations? Successes and Failures in Natural Resource Extraction*, Palgrave Macmillan, London, UK.

Fuentes, R. 2011. "A Unified Growth Model for Independent Chile", *Latin American Journal of Economics*, 48(2), 157–179.

Law – Ranking Decree 3,653, 1981.

Law 20,026, 2005.

Law 20,469, 2010.

Duke, J.M. (Murray). 2010. *Government Geoscience to Support Mineral Exploration: Public Policy Rationales and Impact*, Prospectors and Developers Association of Canada, Toronto, Ontario.

Radetzki, Marian. 2009. "Seven Thousand Years in the Service of Humanity: The History of Copper, the Red Metal", *Resources Policy*, 34, 176–184.

Sutulov, Alexander. 1976. *Minería Chilena 1545–1975*, Centro de Investigación Minera y Metalúrgica, Santiago, Chile.

4 Two sectors, two approaches

Resource taxation in Peru

Claudia Cooper and
*Eduardo Morón**

The performance of the mining and hydrocarbons sector has been one of the main drivers of continued economic growth in the last decade in Peru. According to Peruvian Central Bank (henceforth BCRP) data, the sector represented more than 50% of total exports during the period. In particular, gold and copper lead the list of main export products, with a participation in total mining exports value of 33% and 40% respectively in the last four years. Additionally, oil and derivatives exports accounted for 8% of the value of total exports between 2009 and 2010. Moreover, according to the Superintendence of Tax Administration (henceforth SUNAT), the mining and hydrocarbons sector represented during the last decade an average of 30% of total income tax revenues and 10% of central government tax revenues. Finally, the sector has had an important influence (mining companies account for approximately 75% of the Lima Stock Exchange Selective Index and 60% of the General Index) on the observed rise (30% annually during the same period) of the local stock market.

However, while the revenues generated by the sector in terms of total taxes are important and have been growing in the last decades, the social discontent with non-renewable companies' operations has not vanished. In Peru, the current mining income transfer system to affected regions is called the Mining Canon. It distributes the mining taxes among regional governments, local governments and public universities in the areas where the mineral is exploited (in percentages defined by law). Despite the large amounts involved (these transfers represent 50% of the income tax paid by mining companies), the system is not bringing the expected benefits to population in the areas of influence. This has already caused delays and suspensions of mining plants activities. Indeed, currently, mining activity rises as the main source of social conflict in Peru.

Therefore the large importance of the mining and hydrocarbons sector, the rising profits context for their companies (mostly induced by international boom in mineral prices) and their complex environmental/social influence have raised claims towards a redefinition of the social contract between the non-renewable companies, the government and the citizens. A critical point is the extent and scheme under which non-renewable resource companies pay taxes. This is a recurrent topic in the public policy agenda of a country such as Peru and, actually, the new government has recently introduced a modification on the royalty paid by the mining sector; it is currently renegotiating the contract with the main gas supplier; and has hinted a more direct involvement of the state in the oil sector.

In this context, the present paper assesses the efficiency of different tax regimes that are typically taken into consideration when looking for the best way to tax non-renewable resource activities. Based on Deacon (1993), we simulate a partial equilibrium model for a representative company operating in the non-renewable resource sector. In particular, we focus on three subsectors: mining (gold and copper), oil and gas. And observe the impact of different tax frameworks on the representative firm's decision about its output and exploration effort paths.

We refer to efficiency in the sense of unrestricted paths chosen by the firm being the least distorted by tax schemes. Then it is important to note that, since our approach does not necessarily incorporate all the externalities created by this kind of production, our analysis can be seen just as assessing a dimension of the whole problem. In particular, we assume it is desirable first not to move away from the unrestricted optimal path and, at last, not to reduce the total production along the project's lifespan.

Theoretical literature has demonstrated that taxes can cause high grading (the elimination or reduction of incentives to explore or produce) and can tilt the path of production towards the present or the future; see Krautkraemer (1990) for a survey of this literature. Deacon (1993) built on the general structure developed by Pindyck (1978) to quantify the two mentioned distortions for the US oil sector. We follow his simulation approach to examine the impact of different tax packages on the exploration and production paths of the non-renewable natural resources sectors in Peru.

Our results suggest that the presence of a royalty tax charged on gross income is highly distortionary, since it changes significantly the paths chosen by the firm in an untaxed scenario (which is our efficiency benchmark). Whereas the existence of (only) an income tax tends to leave production and investment decisions almost unaltered. Also, in our framework, including an income tax regime that allows for accelerated depreciation increases the drilling efforts and the production and reduces tax collection. These features are robust across the analyzed sectors.

The remaining of the paper is as follows: Section 1 describes the current institutional framework to which firms in these sectors are exposed. Section 2 explains the basic model in detail and introduces some particularities of each subsector. Section 3 discusses the limitations of available data and describes the empirical strategy implemented to deal with it. Section 4 presents the results and Section 5 introduces accelerated depreciation in Deacon's model as an important feature of the Peruvian framework. Finally, Section 6 points out some concluding remarks.

1 Institutional setting

In this section, we present a review of the institutional framework that each of the analyzed sectors faces. We begin by describing the tax and non-tax (e.g. compensations and contributions) obligations of each sector in subsection 1.1. Here, we emphasize the particularly relevant obligations of non-renewable natural resources sectors (e.g. royalties), which we later introduce in our model. In subsection 1.2, we move to the (rest of the) legal framework focusing in specific tax benefits for the analyzed sector, which had been placed to promote investment. We present a brief discussion and limit it to features we directly include in our model; for further details please see Appendix A. Finally, in subsection 1.3, we discuss the institutional framework of a particularly relevant gas project: Camisea.

1.1 Tax framework

In general, the taxes[1] and contributions that comprise the Peruvian tax system and that affect the mining and hydrocarbons sectors throughout the whole entire production chain[2] can be classified in four types: transaction taxes, wealth taxes, compensation for the exploitation of natural resources, income taxes (see Table 4.1).

Note that all taxes, with the exception of income taxes, royalties and contractual economic rights, are charged at pre-operating stages. This is especially relevant for natural resources sectors given that they are capital intensive and have an exploration phase (which determines if there will be production or not).

1.1.1 Mining

INCOME TAX

Income tax when applied to mining companies is applied on net profits generated; the current tax rate is 30%. Distributed dividends are also charged with a tax rate of 4.1% and employee profit sharing constitutes the 8% of firm net profit. All these rates add up to a total tax burden of 38.2% on income.

ROYALTIES[3]

The royalties' framework was recently changed (September 2011) from royalty rates applied on the value of gross sales to royalty rates applied on profits. Since

Table 4.1 Tax and non-tax obligations

Type of Tax	Tax or Contribution
Transactions taxes	IVA (value–added tax)
	Tariffs on imports
	Tax on financial transactions
	Capital gains
	Alcabala tax
	Selective Consumption Tax (ISC)
Wealth taxes	Property taxes
	Tax on equity: temporary tax on net assets
Consideration for the exploitation of natural resources	Royalties
	Contractual economic rights
Income taxes	Income tax
	Windfall profit tax
Others	Labor contributions
	Retentions
	Concession rights

Source: Zuzunaga (2011)

we analyze the performance of the sector under both frameworks, we discuss the principal features of each of them. Note that royalties are considered as a cost that is deductible for income tax calculation purposes under both regimes.

- *Old Royalties' Framework.* The reference basis on which the royalty rate is applied in this type of contract is the *gross value of sales minus costs and expenditures assumed by the exporter*.[4] For minerals that are traded at international prices, three rates apply depending on the range of annual sales: 1% (for sales under US$60 million), 2% (for sales between US$60 and US$120 million), and 3% (for sales over US$120 million).
- *New Royalties' Framework.* The new regime includes a law which modified the mining royalty regime. The law created the special tax on mining for firms not under juridical stability agreements (*Impuesto especial a la minería* [IEM]), and the law created the special tax on mining for firms under juridical stability agreements (*Gravamen especial a la minería* [GEM]). The law modifying the mining royalty regime establishes that the royalty is no longer based on sales, instead it will be determined according to a quarterly operational profits-to-sales ratio, with progressive marginal rates between 1% and 12%. The IEM and GEM are also calculated based on a quarterly operational profits-to-sales ratio with progressive marginal rates. The range of rates for the GEM (between 4% and 13.1%) is higher than the one set for the IEM (between 2% and 8.4%) because firms under juridical stability agreements continue to be exonerated from paying mining royalties.

1.1.2 Hydrocarbons

We focus on oil royalties[5] because we will consider them in the simulations in later sections. Royalties are a percentage of the production value of hydrocarbons extracted by the contractor, calculated on international prices. The four methodologies for the calculation are:[6]

- *The R factor*: It is defined as the ratio between cumulative income (X) and cumulative expenses (Y). It indicates the minimum royalty rate (or the base rate) from which negotiation between the company and the state can start. The bigger value of R, the bigger the minimum royalty rate applied. Final rates are defined in each contract.
- *Cumulative production*: The royalty rate is fixed in each contract and is adjusted according to the cumulative production and the average price per barrel of such production. As in the previous case, this method serves as a reference when negotiating the final rate on each contract.
- *Scale of production*: Minimum royalty rates are increasingly associated with production levels.
- *Economic outcome*: This method calculates the royalty rate with a fixed and a variable component. The fixed royalty is set at 5%. The variable royalty is applied once the R factor reaches 1.15, and the associated royalty rate is in the range of 0% to 20%.

The contractor has the possibility of choosing between these four alternative methodologies for the calculation of the basic royalty rate when making the Declaration of Commercial Discovery of Hydrocarbons. Once the methodology is chosen, there is no possibility of change. As well as mining royalties, hydrocarbons are also considered as expenses deductible for income tax calculation purposes.

1.2 Legal framework

1.2.1 Mining

Benefits[7] for mining companies can be summarized in five main groups: stability benefits, benefits for exporters, benefits in terms of value-added tax (VAT), benefits in terms of income tax and customs benefits. We focus on income tax revenues because they are directly included in the model; for further detail see Appendix A. First we describe the income tax benefits related to the pre-operation phase, and then, those related to the exploration and development phase.

Pre-operation phase. The most relevant features are the two special depreciation regimes that mining companies are allowed to use:

- The first regime applies to organization and pre-operation expenses. The taxpayer can either deduct all organization and pre-operation expenses in the first year of exploitation, or amortize them proportionally during a maximum period of ten years.[8]
- The second special regime applies to the exploitation expenses of the mining industry. The accelerated depreciation applies to fixed assets that are used by the taxpayers in their activities and that are subject to wear or exhaustion.

Investment, exploration and development. The exploration expenses incurred after the first production year can be deducted in the year incurrence or amortized proportionally during the probable life of the mine. The accelerated depreciation benefit applies to the mining activity holders that present investment projects for the initiation of a mining activity of US$20 million or more.

1.2.2 Hydrocarbons[9]

Incentives and benefits that seek to promote investment in the oil industry are quite similar to those of mining sector. Nevertheless, there are special regimes for the hydrocarbons sector. In this sense stability issues, imports of goods, as well as specific depreciation and amortization treatment of intangibles are regulated by the Organic Law of Hydrocarbons (OLE). In our modeling approach we do not include all these details, (although we do include accelerated depreciation with an approach similar to the one used in the mining sector), so we refer the reader to Appendix A for further discussion.

1.3 Gas: the case of Camisea Project

The case of gas will be analyzed through the study of the Camisea Project tax and production framework, due to its prevalence in the Peruvian gas market (Camisea comprises 92% of total cumulative gas production in 2010). In addition, the participation of the state in the final consumer price determination as well as in the guarantees scheme regarding supply (to the local market) and demand (minimum demand guaranteed to the consortium) require special attention. In this context, understanding the legal and tax framework that applies to gas exploitation in Peru implies necessarily understanding the conditions under which this project is being held. Next, we discuss the pricing and royalties' frameworks, which have direct consequences in our modeling. A detailed description of the project background can be found in Appendix B.

Pricing.[10] If the product is exported, the price is the result of a negotiation between private parties and depends on international market conditions. A protection against a collapse in international prices was established through the determination, in each export contract, of an inferior limit price of $0.60 for million BTU (British Thermal Units). On the other hand, the price faced by the transportation consortium for the gas (wellhead price) when the domestic market is the final destination is the final price faced by the local industry and is constructed adding to the wellhead price the transportation costs and other costs along the production line.

The wellhead price is determined in each contract between the exploitation consortium (Peru LNG) and the transportation consortium (TGP). However, despite the fact that these prices are a result of negotiations among private companies, they are subject to regulation depending on the final destination. That is, for gas destined to electricity generators customers, the maximum price set in each contract is $1 for a million BTU. And for gas destined to other users of local market, the maximum price is $1.80 for million BTU. These limits are adjusted yearly using an adjustment factor (which is a function of international oil prices[11]).[12]

1.3.1 Royalties' framework

Royalties paid by producers of the consortium depend on the type of hydrocarbon extracted. For the purposes of this study and for simplicity we will focus on the registered production of natural gas leaving aside oil and liquid hydrocarbons. The royalty rate is applied to the value of the registered production, valued at the price determined in each contract, and that depends on whether gas production is destined to local or foreign markets as specified in the previous section. The contract contemplates for the exploitation consortium a differentiated scheme of royalties to be applied to the three different products that are feasible to be exploited: oil, liquid gas and natural gas.

Oil: the royalty rate is 37.24% of the estimated value of the extracted resources, which is a result of multiplying the market price (obtained from an "oil basket" determined in the contract) by the volume of oil extracted. Liquid hydrocarbons: the same methodology applies, but a fixed $6.40 is subtracted from the market price (basket of liquids). This amount is detracted in order to recognize the additional costs of allocating the product (pipeline related costs, conversion of liquids into tradable products such as gasoline, liquefied petroleum gas.

Natural gas: royalties take the effective price paid by its users (product of nego-tiation between suppliers and consumers) as reference base. As in the two previ-ous cases, the royalty rate is 37.24% of the value of the gas sold in the market. The rate applied to the value of gas for local market is 37.24%, and the rate applied to the value of production destined to exports depends on the international price of gas (Henry Hub). That is, for prices equal to or less than $4 Henry Hub x MMBTU, a royalty rate of 30% is applied; and for prices equal to or greater than $5 Henry Hub x MMBTU, a rate of 38% is applied.

Finally, it is important to remark that in terms of taxes, tax stability, legal frame-work and other remaining aspects, the Camisea Project is under the regime of the Organic Law of Hydrocarbons; therefore, the assumptions that we will make in these regards for the oil sector will be the same for the gas sector.

2 The model

The dynamic partial equilibrium model presented in this section describes the behavior of a typical firm in a non-renewable resource sector. The model is based heavily on Deacon (1993) and, by extension, on pioneering studies by Hotelling (1931) and Pindyck (1978). The maximization problem faced by each sector's representative operator is simulated and solved computationally in Matlab using backward induction (i.e. starting from the last period of the project's life).

The per-period net cash flow of a firm arises from the difference between rev-enues and costs of operation. Besides, in non-renewable sectors, companies face costs associated with exploration efforts needed in order to incorporate new flows of the resource. Then, for year "*t*" the net cash flow of a firm in any of the assessed sectors is written as the following.

$$\prod_{jt} = p_{jt} y_{jt} - C\left(y_{jt}, R_{jt}\right) - D\left(w_{jt}\right) \tag{1}$$

Where p and y represents price and production amounts of the underlined good and R and w are reserves of the resource and physical exploration effort respec-tively. Upper case variables denote stocks measured at the beginning of year t and lowercase variables are flows during year t. Additionally, subindixes j and t refers to each sector and each year. In general, for any sector, we will assume that costs of production depend positively on current output and negatively on the remain-ing reserves at t. Where the latter condition relies on an increasing difficulty to extract the resource (so, an increasing production cost) as reserves run out. Also, exploratory costs will be represented by a concave monotone increasing func-tion $D(Wjt)$ just on exploratory effort. This first setting will represent hereafter the untaxed scenario for each sector and will be the benchmark reference against which we will compare each taxed scenario to assess the effects of their observed taxation scheme in terms of their efficiency paths of production and exploratory effort. Summarizing, the logic of the simulation exercise is as follows: we start from an explicit estimated relationship between paths of production and exploration effort and associated cash flows (functional forms and related parameters) to simulate the efficient paths that a representative firm will choose under the relevant scenario for each sector. Then, in an untaxed scenario, the relevant sector context will be set by preliminary particularities on price and output determination and differences on parameters. The setting of functional forms assumed by Deacon (1993) is usual in this literature. So, we will assign the same specification for functional forms for all sectors.

2.1 Oil and mining sectors

The setting is represented by three functions whose parameters have to be estimated: costs of production C(.), costs of exploration D(.) and a concave function F(.) (where F'>0, F''<0) of cumulative reserve additions (depending on cumulative exploration effort W), which combined with cumulative production (Y) determines the level of reserves for each period ($R_{ji} = F\ (W_{jt})\text{-}Y_{jt}$). Then, we have the following.

$$C\left(y_t, R_t\right) = \theta y_t^{\epsilon} R_t^{1-\epsilon} \tag{2}$$

With $C_y\left(.\right) > 0\ C_R\left(.\right) < 0$ (which requires $\epsilon > 1$)

$$F\left(W_t\right) = \Gamma\left(1 - exp\left(-\beta W_t\right)\right) \tag{3}$$

$$D\left(w_t\right) = \gamma w_t + \delta w_t^2 \tag{4}$$

For both oil and mining industries, the assumption of a competitive scenario on prices is quite acceptable. So the particular setting will be done just on estimated parameters. Therefore, the following represents the typical oil and mining firm's maximization problem in the untaxed scenario.

$$\left(y_t, w_t\right) \in argmax \sum_{t=0}^{T} \prod_{jt} \left(1+r\right)^{-t} \tag{5}$$

s.t.

$$W_{jt} + w_{jt} = W_{jt+1}$$

$$Y_{jt} + y_{jt} = Y_{jt+1}$$

Finally, given interest rate and price paths (exogenous to the extent that decisions of the industry do not alter the prices for their products), we simulate an oil and a mining firm that chooses extraction (Y) and exploration effort (W) paths to maximize the present value of its profits, subject to the transition equations of cumulative production (Y) and exploratory effort (W).

2.2 Gas sector

As we mentioned in Section 1, Camisea's project introduces particular features that make the general approach a poor approximation to reality for the Peruvian gas sector. To capture the relevant behavior of this sector, we consider the two markets (local and foreign, denoted by superscripts L and X respectively) where the firm can sell its product subject to the restrictions that apply given the existing regulation and contracts. Given that the firm has to ensure the supply for the domestic market, we assume that each year there is a minimum amount of production that has to be allocated to the domestic market; this amount grows annually according to the government projections ($\bar{y}_t^L$ will represent the local lower boundary that can change over time). Given the large investment committed in the LNG project, the existence of a contract where the firm commits to provide a minimum volume of gas to *Peru LNG* we also set an annual minimum volume of production to be directed to the foreign market ($\bar{y}^x$ will represent the foreign lower boundary that is assumed to remain unchanged by contract). This was a condition in the contract to make the project financially sustainable and it will play a role of a new constraint in the maximization process that we will simulate for the representative firm in the gas sector. Another particularity for this sector is that while both prices for domestic and foreign markets are taken as given (as in the general approach) only for the latter are they subject to international prices (such as in mining and oil). The domestic price was fixed in the concession contract. This involves only the specification of a constant price path for the domestic market in the simulation exercise. In addition, we will keep the same specification for the costs functions as in the oil sector. Then, the specification of net cash flow for the case of the Peruvian gas sector remains as follows.[13]

$$\prod_t = \bar{p}_t^L y_t^L + p_t^x y_t^x - C\left(y_t^L + y_t^x, R_t\right) - D\left(w_t\right) \tag{6}$$

And the new constraints in the maximization process:

$$y_t^L \geq y_t^{-L}, y_t^x \geq y_t^{-x} \tag{7}$$

2.2.1 Definition of the tax package for each sector

According to Table 4.1 there are a number of taxes that affect mining activity in the different stages of the production process. Nevertheless, taxes that constitute a higher burden on mining companies are income taxes and mining royalties. IPE (2011) revealed that nearly 90% of the amount of all taxes collected in the mining sector between 1999 and 2009 correspond to income taxes (including tax on dividends and employee profit sharing) and mining royalties. Due to the fact that exports are by far the main destination of mining production, where tax exemptions and benefits apply, only 10% of the mining taxes correspond to VAT. In this context, for gold and copper sectors, the tax package will be comprised by income taxes and mining royalties. Income taxes will be represented by a fixed rate of 38.2% applied on companies' benefits which summarizes the overall burden on income derived from income tax, dividends tax and employee profit sharing.

In the case of mining royalties, the package will comprise a scheme of legal royalties, where progressive rates apply depending on gross value of sales minus a series of expenses assumed by the exporter such as transport, storage and shipping (which was the effective scheme under which non-renewable sectors operated before recent changes introduced in the royalties' framework).[14] For simplicity, we will assume that the royalty rates are applied just on the gross value of sales.[15]

Another important component of tax packages are tax benefits. Due to the assumptions made so far, relevant tax benefits for the mining sector are stability benefits and income tax benefits. The stability framework will allow that the taxes and rates that comprise a standard mining tax package remain constant in the models. As mentioned in subsection 1.2, mining companies have the option to sign or not stability contracts. For those that do sign stability contracts, there is an increase of 2% of the income tax rate paid, which makes the income tax rate in the mining tax package increase from 38.2% to 40.2%. It is important to note that Yanacocha and Barrick's gold projects are subject to stability contracts; these companies are the current major producers of gold, accounting for more than 50% of total gold production in 2010.[16] For purposes of the estimation and due to availability of information, data from Barrick's gold projects will be used (more than 21% of total gold production in 2010).

The case of copper is quite different since two of the three more important projects, Antamina and Cerro Verde copper projects, are subject to stability contracts, while Southern copper project is not. These three companies account for 77.88% of total copper production in 2010 (26.02%, 25.04% and 26.82% respectively). Despite that, the assumption on stability of the tax regime along the life span of the project will be kept. And due to data availability, information from the major copper producer Southern will be used.

Finally, benefits in terms of income taxes will be also included in the mining tax package. It will be assumed for simplicity that all pre-operating expenditures are incurred before the stage of mandatory minimum production. Also, it will be assumed that companies take advantage of the benefit of smoothing pre-operating costs and they will do so along the first five years of operations. This assumption is made for simplicity since the law (General Mining Law) does not specify the exact rate and period; it only says that it will depend on the probable life span of the project and the amount of probable and proved reserves. Tax package for gold and copper sectors incorporated in the simulations are summarized in Table 4.2.

The study prepared by the Peruvian Economic Institute reveals that nearly 70% of the amount of all taxes collected in the hydrocarbons sector between 1999 and 2009 correspond to income taxes and mining royalties. It is worth noting that around 20% correspond to VAT and the remaining 10% to other taxes.

As well as in mining sector, income taxes in gas and oil sectors will be represented by a fixed rate of 38.2% applied on companies benefits. In terms of royalties, the tax package will differ between oil and gas sectors. Royalties in the oil sector can be calculated through four types of methodologies as described

Table 4.2 Gold and copper tax packages

	Gold	Copper
Income tax	τ_{Inc} = 38.2% on net benefits	τ_{Inc} = 38.2% on net benefits
Royalties	τ_{Roy} = 2% (< 30% of AMPP)	τ_{Roy} = 2% (< 30% of AMPP)
(two segments)	τ_{Roy} =3% (> 30% of AMPP)	τ_{Roy} = 3% (> 30% of AMPP)

Source: Energy and Mines Ministry

AMPP: Annual maximum amount of physical production. This bound is introduced for simulation purposes. All simulations will be done under stability contract assumption. Smoothing amortization of pre-operating costs (tax credit) in the correspondent five years forward. Minimum amount of reserves: 20% (for gold) and 20% (for copper) of probable reserves.

in subsection 1.1. However, for estimation purposes, we will assume as a representative case the case of Pluspetrol (offshore operations at the Peruvian north coast). This is the most important oil producer, which accounts for an average production of more than 50% of total oil production[17] in the last ten years. We take the case of a contract (for operations in lot 1-AB) which applies a basic rate on an average amount of production (determined in the contract) and another rate applied on incremental production. These rates depend on an average price per barrel of oil.

Royalties applied in the gas sector will follow the same structure presented in subsection 1.3. That is, for gas sold in local market, a rate of 37.24% is applied on the value of local production. And for gas exported, rates of 30% and 38% will be applied on the value of exports depending on relevant prices. It is important to remember that the price at which production is valued is determined in each contract and depends on whether production is sold in local or foreign markets (see subsection 1.3).

In terms of tax benefits, both oil and gas sectors behave in the same way. As established in the Organic Law of Hydrocarbons, stability of taxes will be granted by Perupetro during exploration and exploitation phases. That means that the tax rates that comprise oil and gas tax packages will remain constant along the life span of the projects.

Finally, for hydrocarbons, the amortization options for pre-operating expenditures, presented in subsection 1.2, are quite similar, but for estimation purposes, the second alternative will be assumed, since it implies no need of assumptions about the production units that investment in exploration and development – machinery and equipment – generates on each year of its life span, assumptions that may be very vague given the lack of information available in this regard. That means that oil and gas tax packages will include a linear amortization of exploration and development expenditures, deducted in equal portions over a period of not less than five fiscal years. Tax packages for oil and gas sectors incorporated in the simulations are summarized in Table 4.3.

We have to introduce these specifications in the model. Practically speaking, all sector's tax packages share a common structure: income tax, segmented royalties and amortization of costs of exploration in a period of no production. Sector particularities will be covered by differences in the tax rates and of royalties

Table 4.3 Oil and gas tax packages

	Oil	Gas
Income tax	τ_{Inc} = 38.2% on net benefits	τ_{Inc} = 38.2% on net benefits
Royalties	$\tau_{Roy=}$(pn* k1+K2)/100 (1) Basic production (contract): K1=0.8050, K 2=1,798 (2) Incremental production: K1=1.4,K 2=−0.5	(1) Local market: τ^{L}_{Roy} =37.24% on production value (2) Foreign market (exports): τ^{X}_{Roy} = 30% on production value

Source: Energy and Mines Ministry

All simulations will be done under stability contract assumption. Smoothing amortization of pre-operating costs (tax credit) in the correspondent five years forward. Minimum amount of reserves: 20% (for oil) and 0% (for gas) of probable reserves. Production value is adjusted deducting referential conversion costs of liquids into commerciable products.

segments. The specifications for net cash flows under taxed scenarios are similar for oil and mining sectors.

$$\sum_{t=0}^{T-1}(1+r)^{-t}\left(1-\tau_{Inc}\right)\left[p_{jt}y_{jt}\left(1-\tau^{j}_{Roy}\right)-C\left(y_{jt},R_{jt}\right)-D\left(w_{jt}\right)\right]$$

$$+\sum_{t=0}^{x-1}(1+r)^{-(t+x)}\tau_{Inc}\left[D\left(w_{jt}\right)\right] \tag{8}$$

The first sum represents the taxed firm's profit (by income and royalty taxes) and the second sum represents the amortization of pre-operation exploration costs as expenses deductible for income tax calculations. In particular, x denotes the first period of operation, τ_{inc} the income tax rate (which is greater than zero whenever the company generates profits) and τ_{Roy} the royalty tax rate of the correspondent segment "*i*" of production value (see Tables 2.2 and 2.3).

While for the gas sector, we have the following expression:

$$\sum_{t=0}^{T-1}(1+r)^{-t}\left(1-\tau_{Inc}\right)\left[\left(\bar{p}^{L}_{t}y^{L}_{t}\right)\left(1-\tau^{L}_{Roy}\right)+p^{x}_{t}y^{x}_{t}\left(1-\tau^{x}_{Roy}\right)\right.$$

$$\left.-C\left(y^{L}_{t}+y^{x}_{t},R_{t}\right)-D\left(w_{t}\right)\right]+\sum_{t=0}^{x-1}\left[\left(\bar{p}^{L}_{t}y^{L}_{t}\right)\left(1-\tau^{L}_{Roy}\right)\right.$$

$$\left.+p^{x}_{t}y^{x}_{t}\left(1-\tau^{x}_{Roy}\right)-C\left(y^{L}_{t}+y^{x}_{t},R_{t}\right)-D\left(w_{t}\right)\right] \tag{9}$$

3 Data

As has been mentioned before, the models that replicate the behavior of each of the four sectors require estimates for three functions: reserve additions, $F(.)$, drilling cost $D(.)$ and production cost $C(.)$ as in Deacon (1993). This estimation requires time series long enough to make feasible an econometric estimation on at least aggregated variables at the sector level in variables as production, reserves, a proxy variable for the exploratory efforts and costs of production and exploration. However, in the analyzed sectors, long enough time series are not available.

For the estimation of the reserve additions function $F(.)$ in the oil sector, there is enough aggregated data in terms of length – information of cumulative drilling[18] and cumulative reserve additions[19] for the period 1985–2010. However, the same number of observations is not available for the case of gas, due to interruptions in the Camisea exploration process and field development and an operation phase that has just begun in 2004.

Regarding firm-level information, there is no large series of public data for these sectors. Then, the empirical strategy will consist of collecting data from firms on which we want to draw conclusions in each sector (those companies representing the most important portion of each of the analyzed sectors' production). We got information on four series, primarily between 2004 and 2010. These series include production, reserves levels and operation and exploratory expenses. These data are enough to calibrate directly only one parameter of the cost function, namely ε in expression (2). This is calibrated as per Deacon (1993, pp. 184–185), namely based on a Cobb Douglas specification for the production function of each sector ($y=Ak^{\mu}R^{1-\mu}$) and determining as the inverse of the expenditure share of non-reserve inputs in total outlays (for K and R, i.e. non-reserve and reserve inputs respectively), that given the Cobb Douglas form equals μ. So, we define $\varepsilon = \dfrac{1}{\mu}$. The other cost function parameter, θ, has as its principal role to scale the cost level and the solution to the problem, so that it is calibrated indirectly. Particularly, it is defined at a value that gives a path where the representative firm chooses a non-trivial path of production. That is, a value that does not generate a zero-production level and where the firm distributes the extraction of its maximum level of probable reserves over its life horizon, just as it happens in Peruvian experience. The level of maximum reserves that a firm can hope to obtain as a result from its exploration effort is characterized by parameter " included in the function of reserve additions. This is calibrated on the base of probable reserves in each sector. Finally, the parameters β, γ and δ are calibrated, again, trying to get non-trivial paths of production and exploration effort for the Peruvian case. Table 4.4 reports the values calibrated for each sector. Our modeling approach allows us to analyze different tax packages by changing the policy parameters (τ_{Inc}, τ_{Roy}). We focus on the distortionary effects on the efficient paths of production and exploratory efforts induced by each alternative tax package. It is worth mentioning that we assume a stable path for prices for two reasons: the first is the volatility of analyzed markets (so trying to elucidate their evolution is outside the scope of this paper), and second, we did not want to induce the outcome by building a bias on the paths of interest (towards the end of the horizon when prices are rising or towards the beginning when prices are decreasing). Likewise, we assume the same life horizon for each simulated sector's project.

Table 4.4 Calibrated parameters

	Oil	*Gas*	*Gold*	*Copper*
P (Price)	$80	$5 (foreign market) $1.8 (local market)	$1600	$380
T (Life horizon)	30	30	30	30
r	0.05	0.05	0.05	0.05
θ	46	8	1020	285
ε	1.3922	1.9124	1.0122	1.0177
Γ	1500	8000	1700	2300
β	0.00288	0.005	0.004	0.004
γ	43	14.39	640	250
δ	0.205	0.35	0.65	0.3

Source: Own calculations

4 Results

The reference model adopted in this paper predicts a path of production and exploration effort, with consequences upon tax collection. The main result of the simulation exercise is that, as can be seen in Figure 4.1 and Figure 4.2, the presence of a royalty tax charged on gross income (royalties in Peru had this logic before the current administration) is very distortionary. Paths chosen by firms with respect to the untaxed scenario (which is our efficiency benchmark) depend significantly on the way royalties are applied. The existence of an income tax tends to leave production and investment decisions almost unaltered with respect to a scenario in which there are no taxes – a similar result is found in Deacon (1993). In other words, the case of an income tax with amortization of pre-operation costs fitted to the Peruvian case approaches a pure-profit tax.[20]

These simulations have been done assuming that the level (in present value terms) of tax collection remained the same as in the base scenario (in which we define policy parameters to replicate the current situation in Peru). Then, since both alternative packages are comparable and assuming that none of these options introduce unnecessary distortions, this result tells us that it is better to tax non-renewable industries charging profits instead of charging gross income.

These results appear to have been considered in the design of the recent framework of new royalties for the mining sector, which implied the transition from a gross income-based regime into a net income-based structure. This is an encouraging result on the Peruvian experience. Regarding this last point, in the lines 2–4 of Table 4.5, the existing royalty based on gross income is replaced by an extra levy on the income tax. This change could be understood as what has been approved recently for the mining sector. In these cases, the distortion is kept to a minimum while the tax collection could be higher. This result is highly relevant for policy decisions as the cost of imposing new royalties on gross income might have an impact on the amount of exploration effort (as a proxy

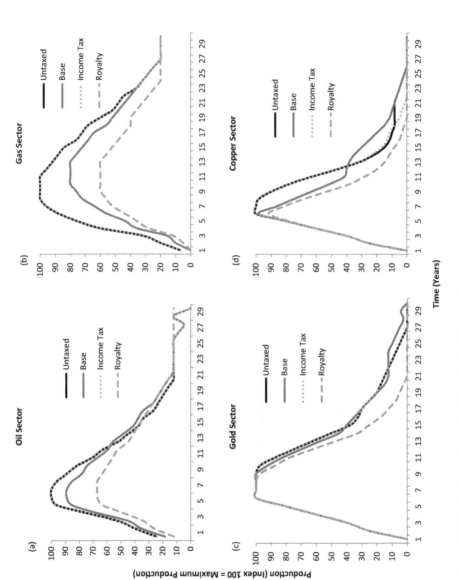

Figure 4.1 Production paths under alternative tax frameworks

Source: Own simulations

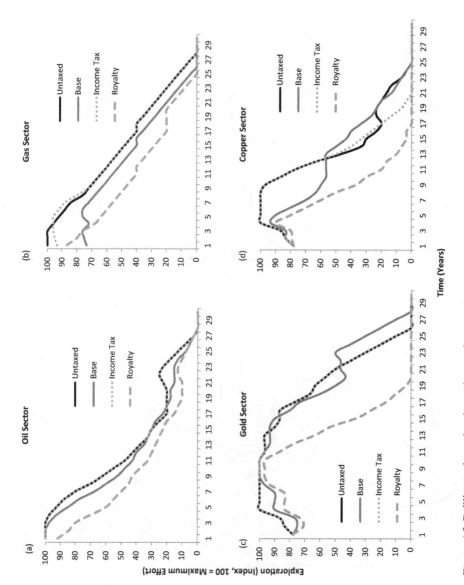

Figure 4.2 Drilling paths under alternative tax frameworks

Source: Own simulations

Table 4.5 Simulated tax packages summary

		Oil	Gas	Gold	Copper
		(Production deviation; exploration effort deviation; tax collection)			
τ_{Inc} = Base	τ_{Roy} = Base	10.57%, 9.80%, 10983	19.6%, 19.70%, 3508	5.38%, 10.88%, 166450	20.61%, 21.04%, 28426
τ_{Inc} = 45%	τ_{Roy} = 0%	0%, 0%, 10304	0%, 2.17%, 2693	0%, 0%, 200960	4.16%, 7.51%, 31338
τ_{Inc} = 55%	τ_{Roy} = 0%	0%, 0%, 12594	0%, 2.17%, 3292	0%, 0%, 237500	4.16%, 7.51%, 37036
τ_{Inc} = 65%	τ_{Roy} = 0%	0%, 0%, 14883	0%, 2.17%, 3890		
τ_{Inc} = 0%	τ_{Roy} = 10%			9.43%, 21.85%, 139880	31.65%, 46.39%, 31815
τ_{Inc} = 0%	τ_{Roy} = 15%	15.39%, 16.38%, 7931		17.82%, 35.82%, 195470	63.29%, 75.44%, 26548
τ_{Inc} = 0%	τ_{Roy} = 25%	26.04%, 29.52%, 11585			
τ_{Inc} = 0%	τ_{Roy} = 35%	39.37%, 47.93%, 13137			
τ_{Inc} = 0%	τ_{Roy} = 45%		29.83%, 27.72%, 2908		
τ_{Inc} = 0%	τ_{Roy} = 55%		38.99%, 34.61%, 3307		
τ_{Inc} = 0%	τ_{Roy} = 65%		50.36%, 41.71%, 3497		

Source: Own calculations

of investment) that companies might be willing to perform. Therefore, this low investment equilibrium will end up reducing the level of production and this might reduce the level of tax collection. These results are for those firms that already have signed a contract with the government. For the case of a new potential entrant, these changes in the tax package will reduce the willingness to invest in this country.

5 Introducing depreciation in Deacon's model

The Peruvian legislation includes the possibility to depreciate assets faster than the standard procedure. This was introduced as a tax incentive. In this section we attempt to demonstrate the importance of this accelerated depreciation regime in the income tax base determination, the tax incidence and consequently the drilling and production decisions of the firms. In particular we want to explore the distortionary effects of the real income tax regimes that include these depreciation accounting rules, in opposition of the neutral case very close to a pure-profit tax. Then the tax incidence analysis will require the comparison of four different tax scenarios: (1) untaxed (no taxes apply), (2) base case (income tax with depreciation and royalties apply), (3) income (income tax with depreciation applies solely) and (4) royalty (royalties apply solely). The new model specification will be the following (taking the mining and oil sector specifications as reference).[21]

$$
\sum_{t=0}^{T-1}(1+r)^{-t}\left(1-\tau_{Inc}\right)\left[\left(p_{jt}y_{jt}\right)\left(1-\tau_{Roy}^{j}\right)-C\left(y_{jt},R_{jt}\right)-D\left(w_{jt}\right)\right]
$$
$$
+\sum_{t=0}^{x-1}(1+r)^{-(t+x)}\tau_{Inc}\left[D\left(w_{jt}\right)\right]+\sum_{t=x}^{T-1}\tau_{Inc}*\delta_{t}*\kappa_{factor}\left[C\left(y_{it},R_{jt}\right)\right.
$$
$$
\left.+D\left(w_{jt}\right)\right] \qquad (10)
$$

The model framework under which the simulations have been implemented lacks an explicit measure for capital. Then, to account for depreciation (an inherent element of income tax regimes in most countries) in the setting of Deacon (1993) model, we use operation and exploration costs as proxies for capital stock. In particular, given the fact that natural resources exploitation is capital intensive, we assume the capital stock for each period to be proportional to the sum of operation and exploration costs. Then, the term K_{factor} is included only to scale this amount in such a way that the simulated paths are non-trivial. Then, given a proxy for capital stock, accelerated depreciation is introduced just through a decreasing depreciation rate. The results of this exercise over the production and drilling paths in each sector can be seen in Figure 4.3 and Figure 4.4.

The main conclusion provided by the simulation exercise is that an income tax regime that allows for accelerated depreciation will reduce the amount of taxes paid and therefore increase the drilling efforts and the production amounts in each of the sectors analyzed.

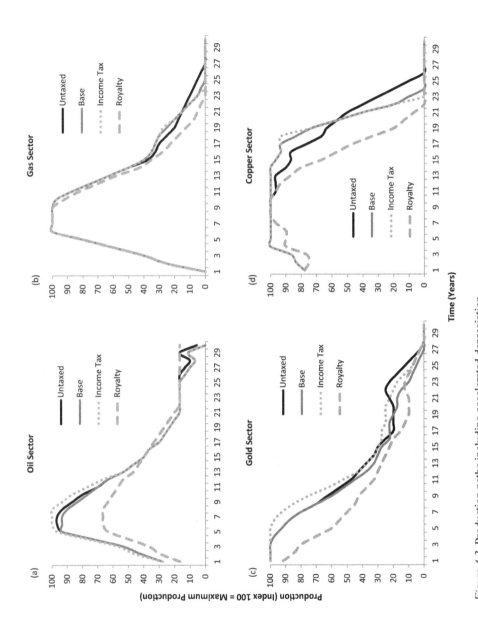

Figure 4.3 Production paths including accelerated depreciation

Source: Own simulations

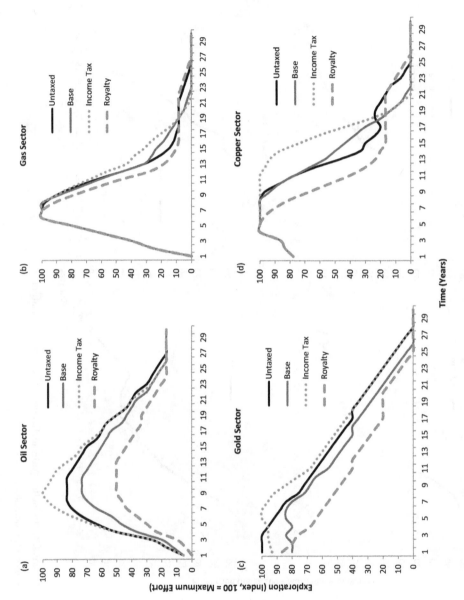

Figure 4.4 Drilling paths including accelerated depreciation

Source: Own simulations

6 Concluding remarks

The Peruvian tax and legal system in Peru can be summarized in three types of taxes: an income tax applied to net income, royalties applied to gross income and a value-added tax from which the natural resource sectors are mostly exempted through tax refund benefits. In addition, and given the high uncertainty of investing in these sectors, the government offers the possibility of signing a stability contract that will freeze the tax regime at the moment of signing this agreement and also the rest of the legal framework.

These features were introduced in the dynamic partial economic model developed by Deacon (1993). We did not include the possibility of the government ignoring the already signed stability contracts which would be an interesting extension for further research. The analysis of the several tax regimes was made under a calibrated model using available data for existing Peruvian firms, and the estimation results show that the fiscal regime applied to the natural resource sector in Peru is of significant importance in the firm's exploration, investment and exploitation decisions. The main conclusion for the three sectors considered refers to the fact that, in the case of a firm with a signed contract, taxes applied to profits (income tax) are less distortionary, or have positive distortionary effects on production and drilling, than the ones applied to gross income (royalties). Once we look at the different types of tax packages (taxes applied to profits versus taxes applied on gross income), the results are significant and clear: tax regimes applied to profit are more efficient, in the sense that investment and production paths are less or positively affected relative to the untaxed benchmark scenario.

It is important to note that we are using as a benchmark an untaxed scenario which does not necessarily reflect all the relevant externalities and consequently does not necessarily represent the social optimum. So the message could be restated. If a non-renewable industry ignores some externalities, it is important to identify and incorporate them. However, taxing based on gross income would not be a good instrument, unless your sole aim is to reduce production and therefore investment. So the simulation exercise ultimately states that if your aim is to collect taxes from a booming industry it is a better idea to tax profits than to tax gross income. And finally, once you identify and implement your social optimum of production (and investment), the more similar your tax scheme is (including tax benefits as accelerated depreciation) to the pure-profit tax case, the more efficient your economy will be.

Appendix A
Detailed legal framework

Mining

Stability benefits

These benefits arise as a result of the subscription of stability contracts by Mining Companies and provide the following advantages of the stability contract holders:

- Stability in terms of taxes, specifically, *stability of the rates applied on distributed profits* (this benefit applies on the investment company),[22] and *stability of the income tax rate and stability of the export regime*[23] (both benefits applied on the receptor company).
- *Stability of the exchange rate regime*, which guarantees the exporting company a flexible exchange rate regime (isolates it from the risk of the application of a fixed exchange rate if macroeconomic conditions deteriorate and massive devaluations occur). This advantage includes the stabilization of free availability of remittances. Both benefits are applied to investment and receptor companies.

Stability of the labor regime which applies only for the receptor company.

Benefits for exporters

These benefits establish that the export of goods, including minerals, is not affected by any tax.

Benefits in terms of IVA

IVA recovery regimes: The benefits for the mining sector include the refund of IVA paid in exploration operations such as imports or goods acquisition, construction and other services contracts, with no further obligation to refund them (for the non-exporting sector, the IVA refund in the pre-operating phase has to be repaid once productive operations begin).

Balance in favor of the exporter: Since the mining sector is almost entirely an exporting sector and exports in Peru are tax exempted, mining companies are unable to recover the tax paid in their purchases used in their production process because, in the general regime, a producer or retailer recovers the IVA assumed in its purchases through a "tax credit" against the tax to be paid when the final sales occur. But since exports are exempted of value-added tax, exporting companies are unable to recover the tax paid on the purchases made in the production process. Thus, mining companies, as exporters, are given the benefit of the *balance in favor of the exporter*, a regime that allows for a refunding request of the IVA paid in the acquisition of goods and services used in their production process.

Benefits in terms of income tax

ORGANIZATION AND PRE-OPERATION EXPENSES (GENERAL REGIME)

Article 6 of Chapter Six of the Income Tax Law, regarding corporate profit taxation, specifies two special depreciation regimes:

The first applies to organization and pre-operation expenses (including investment amount and interest payments of initial operations and expansion activities) where the taxpayer can choose between two alternatives. He can either totally deduct organization and pre-operation expenses in the first year of exploitation or production or amortize them proportionally during a maximum period of ten years.[24]

The second special regime applies to the exploitation expenses of the mining industry. The depreciation applies to fixed assets that are used by the corporate tax payers in their activities and that are subject to wear or exhaustion. Depreciation is calculated over the acquisition or production value of the asset, including permanent improvements.

INVESTMENT AND EXPLORATION AND DEVELOPMENT: MINING SECTOR

Title 9 of the Mining Law describes investment promotion measures implemented for the mining sector. In this context, Chapter 4 states that the Mining Rights (price of concession[25] and mining claims) and Exploration Expenses are amortized starting the year of production agreed by law, while the amortization term is determined depending on the probable life of the Mineral Deposit (taking into account proved and probable reserves as well as the minimum production mandate). SUNAT must be informed of the agreed term and amortization methodology before the year when amortization starts.

The exploration expenses incurred after the first production year can be deducted in the year incurrence or amortized proportionally during the probable life of the mine.

The accelerated depreciation benefit applies to the mining activity holders that present investment projects for the initiation of a mining activity, of US$ 20 million or more.

Custom benefits

There are a number of benefits in terms of tariffs that apply to the import of goods, whether raw materials, intermediate goods or capital goods. In the case of mining, the most important benefit lies in the ability to import certain capital goods (mostly machinery and equipment) at a 0% tariff rate.

Stability contracts

According to Peru's 1993 Constitution and 1984 Civil Code, companies can hold legal stability agreements with the Peruvian state.[26] Through these agreements, the state guarantees the stability of certain legal regimes. Currently, there are two types of agreements to which investments in the mining sector can qualify for. One is specifically applicable for mining companies, while the other applies to investors from any economic sector. There are two main differences between these types of agreements: (1) the minimum amount of investment required to qualify for the stability regime and (2) the advantages in terms of taxes. Since the stability contracts that are specific for mining sector imply larger benefits, this paper will focus on them. It is important to mention that (1) stability contracts for the mining sector are applied to each mining project and not to the company and that (2) they can be signed for a ten-year period in the case of projects with a minimum investment of $2,000,000 and for a 15-year period in the case of projects with a minimum investment of $20,000,000[27] or $50,000,000.[28]

Stability contracts protect the investors from unexpected changes in the regimes of relevant taxes and the exchange rate, as well as guaranteeing administrative stability.[29]

The Peruvian government charges the signing company for the stability benefits an additional 2% on actual tax rates.

Hydrocarbons[30]

Peruvian law promotes and protects private investment in Peru. At the beginning of the '90s, Congress delegated the executive branch to legislate in favor of private investment and two legislative decrees were enacted. DL No 757 (promotion of private investment) and DL No 662 (promotion of foreign investment) were put into effect. Since this legislation does not discriminate among sectors, incentives and benefits that seek to promote investment in the oil industry are quite similar to those of mining sector. Nevertheless, there are special regimes for the hydrocarbons sector. In this sense stability issues, imports of goods, as well as specific depreciation and amortization treatment of intangibles are regulated by the Organic Law of Hydrocarbons (OLH). Finally, benefits for exporters, IVA and custom benefits are applied to hydrocarbons in the same way as in the mining sector.

Stability contracts

Stability benefits do not arise as a result of a specific stability contract, as in the case of mining. These benefits are shaped in license contracts for exploration and exploitation of hydrocarbons. License contracts are signed under the OLH and ensure the free availability of oil and foreign currency as well as the stability of the tax and exchange rate regimes for a fixed term granted by Perupetro to explore or exploit hydrocarbons.

Benefits in terms of income tax

The general regime previously described applies also for the hydrocarbons sector.

INVESTMENT AND EXPLORATION AND DEVELOPMENT: HYDROCARBONS SECTOR

Article 53 of the fourth chapter of the OLH, referring to the amortization regime for tax purposes, states that exploration and development, as well as investment expenditures, made by contractors until the initiation of commercial extraction (including the costs of wells) have to be accumulated in an account, the amount of which can be amortized under two alternatives to be chosen by the taxpayer: (1) amortization based on production units,[31] (2) linear amortization, where equal deductions apply during a period not shorter than five years.

Once commercial extraction is initiated, all the expenditures lacking recovery value must be deducted in the year of incurrence.

The depreciation of the main pipeline can be fixed by the Ministry of Energy and Mining and cannot be less than five years. Each contract must include the amortization regime used by the contractor, which cannot be changed. If the linear method is chosen, the period must also be specified in the contract.

Regarding the particular case of Camisea, which will be detailed in Appendix B, the contract specifies that each of the enterprises that are part of the contractor are to adopt the linear amortization method during a five-year period, starting at the commercial extraction year. This methodology applies for exploration and development as well as for all other investment expenses incurred by the contractor before the initiation of the commercial extraction. The amortization term can be extended, without exceeding the contract term, if because of price reasons or other reasons agreed by the parties, the financial statements show a negative result that cannot be compensated for by taxing effects.

Imports of goods

Imports of goods and services required in the entire exploration phase of each hydrocarbons contract are exempt from all taxes.

Appendix B
Camisea Project background

In 1981, the Peruvian government signed a contract with Shell Company for the exploration of oil in the south area of the Ucayali Basin. In 1987, after a long exploration period, two gas reservoirs were found in the Camisea area, located in the Cuzco region. This discovery led in early 1988 to the signing of a preliminary exploitation agreement between Petroperu and Shell. By August of that year, the Peruvian government decided not to go on with the project, although at the time, the sole gas purchaser of natural gas and liquids was the state implying a high political risk (the Peruvian energy and hydrocarbons sectors were vastly in public ownership), Shell's position was to go on with the project. Thus, negotiations ended in August of that year without reaching an agreement. In March 1994, an agreement for the evaluation and development of the Camisea deposits between Shell and Petroperu was signed. A consortium of Shell and Mobil started to develop the fields but, due to political concerns, they cancelled all projects in Peru in July 1998. In May 1999, the Commission for the Promotion of Private Investment agreed to conduct a promotional process to develop the Camisea Project through a scheme involving three independent businesses, exploitation, transportation and distribution.

Law No. 27133 was enacted establishing that reserves of block 88 can only be assigned to cover the domestic market almost permanently (20-year horizon), while reserves from block 56 were allowed to be exported. Finally, in 1999, two international public tenders for awarding the contract for the exploitation, transportation and distribution of liquids and gas were initiated and by December 2000 contracts were signed between the Peruvian State and an international consortium, which after a number of changes, now includes Pluspetrol (27.2%), Hunt Oil Company (25.2%), SK Corporation (17.6%), Repsol YPF (10%), Tecpetrol (10%), and Sonatrach (10%). The whole process ended in May 2002, when the transportation concession contract between the Peruvian government and Transportadora de Gas del Peru (TGP) was signed.

Nevertheless, discussions regarding the more convenient use of the Camisea gas reserves continue now. The development of an ambitious and expensive export project ($2,000 million) between the Peruvian state and a foreign consortium (Peru LNG) lead by Hunt Oil, required some guarantees of the availability of gas reserves to allow for the feasibility of the project, and therefore amendments to Law No. 27133 were made in order to reduce export constraints of gas from block **88**. The amendments started a debate regarding the allocation of the Camisea reserves (between local and foreign markets), a discussion that lead to the current re-negotiation of the contract between the Peru LNG Consortium and the Peruvian State.

Notes

* Corresponding author: emoron@up.edu.pe. We want to acknowledge the excellent research work of Maria Alejandra Amado, Fernando Mendo and Cristhian Seminario. We are also grateful for the comments and suggestions from the participants at the IADB research project. The views presented in this paper do not necessarily represent the views of Universidad del Pacífico. As usual, any errors are ours.
1 This section includes the analysis not just of taxes, but also of compensations and contributions such as royalties and concession rights.
2 This implies the exploration, evaluation, construction, production, transport, commercialization and closure stages of any project.
3 Royalties paid by mining companies are not a tax per se; they are a compensation that companies pay to the government for having the right to exploit their natural resources.
4 These costs are those not related to the production process, including all rates, indirect taxes, insurance, transportation costs, storage, shipping and stevedoring, and other expenses assumed by the exporter and agreed upon according to the international commerce terms. For those companies that transform their own products (integrated companies), these costs are not relevant and the royalties are applied just on the value of sales of the final product. Besides, adjustments such as discounts, sales returns and other concepts of a similar nature are also discounted from the reference basis on which the royalty is applied.
5 Oil royalties are defined as the "consideration of the license contracts, which are the mechanism through which the individual is enabled to explore and exploit hydrocarbon resources becoming the owner of the resource extracted" (see Zuzunaga 2011, page 3). In other words, license contracts give the company the permission to explore and exploit hydrocarbons in the area of contract while transferring the contractor the ownership of the hydrocarbons extracted in exchange of a royalty payment.
6 For further detail see Ernst & Young (2011).
7 For simplicity, benefits such as exoneration of municipal taxes in rural areas, or the deduction of investment in public infrastructure from taxable income, are not going to be detailed in this section.
8 Once the amortization regime is chosen, it can only be changed with a SUNAT authorization.
9 Based on the Organic Law of Hydrocarbons, Peru (2002).
10 Based on the Law of Promotion of the Development of the Natural Gas Industry, Peru (1999).
11 Two price reference indexes are considered: (1) the arithmetic average of the Oil Field and Gas Field Machinery (WPS1191) index, and (2) the arithmetic averages of the Fuel and Related Products and Power (WPU05) index. The Department of Labor of USA publishes both indexes.
12 The idea behind this adjustment factor is to protect the final consumer from the volatility of the price of oil at international market. It is important to note that when the Camisea Project contracts were signed, international prices were considerably high, and therefore, at that time, the price paid by local consumers was less than the price paid by foreign customers. However, international price of gas have been decreasing considerably, reversing the local consumer price advantage and leading to a lower price for the gas appointed to foreign markets, generating social unrest domestically, and consequently increasing the political pressure to increase export constraints. In front of these social pressures stand those opinion leaders who consider that limiting

106   *Claudia Cooper and Eduardo Morón*

the export potential would reduce incentives for investment in the gas industry and therefore reduce the possibility of new discoveries.

13 It is important to note that these two additional constraints can force the firm to operate under negative results. An implicit assumption of our model is that firms cannot choose to exit the market (set zero output). Indeed, this is an important feature of the regulated Peruvian gas sector.

14 We simulate higher royalty rates as production value rises. This is implemented by segments, as in the Peruvian taxation framework. See subsection 1.1.

15 In fact, allowed deductible transport, storage and shipping expenses are in general negligible.

16 Each of the remaining companies accounts for less than 9% of total production (Ministry of Energy and Mines, 2010). The majority of firms developing large projects sign stability contracts.

17 We are referring specifically to the oil projects of Pluspetrol in the north area of Peruvian territory, leaving aside oil production as result of exploitation of block 56, which belongs to the Camisea Project. For purposes of this study, oil production will not consider production that arises from block 56 or 88 of Camisea Area, for simplicity and since they do not account for a significant share of total oil Peruvian production.

18 Cumulative drilling footage is computed from series on cumulative numbers of wells drilled for oil and depth per well. Numbers of wells drilled each year since 1985, and depth per well drilled in each oil project are obtained from the Annual Statistical Oil Report by Perupetro, the National Agency of Hydrocarbons.

19 Cumulative reserve additions for 1985 will be computed as cumulative oil production through that year plus the 1985 level of reserves. Data on reserves additions for subsequent years is obtained from the annual Report on Reserves, prepared by the Energy and Mines Ministry.

20 In the next section we present the extension of the model that considers accelerated depreciation.

21 For the gas sector, the extension is done in similar fashion.

22 It is very common in the mining sector to distinguish between the company that provides the funds and invests in the project and the company that executes the investment or the receptor of the funds. For example, Minera Mexico and Buenaventura are both investment companies while Southern and Yanacocha are both companies that receive the funds and execute the investment, respectively.

23 As will be seen later, there are some benefits in terms of taxes applied to exporters. The stability of the export regime means that these benefits will be maintained through the years.

24 Once the amortization regime is chosen, it can only be changed with a previous SUNAT authorization.

25 Includes the price paid, the mining rights requests as well as the drilling and exploration investments.

26 Represented by the Mining and Energy Ministry of Peru.

27 If the company has not started mining activities.

28 If the company is already doing mining activities.

29 This means stability of Concession Rights, applied on the concessions involved on the execution of the project and stability of mining royalties, applied on minerals extracted from concessions that form part of the project. Other types of taxes that are subject to the stability benefit are the ones that affect assets or property (ITAN and predial), financial transactions (ITF) and consumption.

30 Information on this section is based on Organic Law of Hydrocarbons Law No. 26221.

31 The value of the asset is divided by the number of units that it can produce during its life span. The resulting depreciation cost by unit of production is multiplied by the number of units produced in the year.

References

Deacon, Robert. 1993. "Taxation, Depletion, and Welfare: A Simulation Study of the U.S. Petroleum Resource", *Journal of Environmental Economics and Management*, 24, 159–187.

Hogan, L. 2010. "International Minerals Taxation: Experience and Issues", in Daniel Philip, Michael Keen and Charles McPherson, eds., *The Taxation of Petroleum and Minerals: Principles, Problems and Practice*. Routledge Explorations in Environmental Economics.

Hotelling, Harold. 1931. "The Economics of Exhaustible Resources", *Journal of Political Economy*, 39, 137–175.

IPE. 2011. *La Tributación Minera en el Perú: Contribución, Carga Tributaria y Fundamentos Conceptuales*, Peruvian Institute of Economics, Lima, Peru.

Krautkraemer, Jeffrey. 1990. "Taxation, Ore Quality Selection, and the Depletion of a Heterogeneous Deposit of a Nonrenewable Resource", *Journal of Environmental Economics and Management*, 18(2), 120–135.

Otto, James. 2011. *Analysis of Peruvian Mineral Sector Fiscal Reform Options*, Ministry of Economy and Finance, Lima, Peru.

Pindyck, R. 1978. "The Optimal Exploration and Production of Nonrenewable Resources", *Journal of Political Economy*, 86(5), 841–861.

Zuzunaga, Fernando. 2011. "La Tributación Minera en el Perú", *III Encuentro Regional Latinoamericano IFA*, Bogotá, Colombia.

Legislation and government reports

Ernst & Young. 2011. *Second National Reconciliation Study of the Extractive Industries Transparency Initiative (EITI) in Peru (2008–2010)*, Consultancy for the EITI Peru Multi-Sector Working Committee.

Ministry of Energy and Mines. 2010. *Mining Yearbook*, Lima, Peru.

Peru. 1999. *Law of Promotion of the Development of the Natural Gas Industry*. Law No. 27133, November 18, 1999.

Peru. 2002. *Organic Law of Hydrocarbons*. Law No. 26221, September 24, 2002.

5 Not all fields are created equal

The challenge of oil taxation in Venezuela

Osmel E. Manzano M

One of the singular characteristics of the Venezuelan oil sector is its diverse resource base. Current reserves in Venezuela range from extra-heavy oil and what is called bitumen,[1] to light crudes, comparable to the West Texas Intermediate (WTI) or Brent crude. Consequently, the major concern in Venezuela is whether the current tax system allows for the development of this resource base, rather than whether each field is being developed efficiently.[2]

As a consequence, important changes have been made in recent years to the tax system in Venezuela. The economics and political economy of oil production in Venezuela is, of course, well-documented;[3] basically, the regulation framework was the same since 1944, except for changes in tax rates until the reforms on the '90s. Petróleos de Venezuela S. A.[4] (hereinafter PDVSA) paid a one sixth of revenue in royalty and income tax at a rate of 67% (the royalty is tax deductible). In 1991, operating agreements (*convenios operativos*) were introduced, and marginal fields that, under normal circumstances, were not going to be exploited by PDVSA, were instead given to private operators – companies that would produce the oil for a certain fee per barrel. Next, in 1993, associations for heavy and extra-heavy oil production were introduced (*asociaciones estratégicas*). One could describe these crudes in two ways: either as low-commercial-value crudes or as those requiring a special "pre-refining" that would make them suitable for any refinery and, consequently, characterize them as high-production-cost crudes. Around 60% of the reserves discovered in Venezuela represent one or the other of these crudes; thus it was argued that, thanks to the existing tax structure, they would not be exploited, leading to a new regulation being approved both for their extraction and the production of offshore gas.[5] In 1996, new areas were given over to private investors for exploration and exploitation. This was termed the "opening-up" of the oil sector (and I am going to refer to them as "exploration at risk"); however, although these areas were supposed to possess light and medium crudes, little or no exploration was actually carried out. Once again, it was argued that – thanks to the current tax system – there were few incentives to do so; once again, a new tax system was introduced in an attempt to remedy this.

However, all these reforms were pushed back after 1998. In November 2001, the Organic Law of Hydrocarbons (OLH) was reformed and, since 2002, a new tax system has taken effect, indicating that any field must pay 30% royalties, excepting non-viable both "mature" or extra-heavy oil fields of the Orinoco Oil Belt (OOB) which could vary between 20%–30% or non-viable projects of a mixture of bitumen from the OOB which could vary between 16.7%–30%. At the same time, the income tax rate was set at 50%, setting a rate of 34% only for gas-related projects and for companies exclusively dedicated to refining hydrocarbons or to upgrade heavy and extra-heavy oil. In 2006, a new reform started a "migration" process to extinguish the operating agreements and the associations giving full structure to the so-called mixed enterprises (*empresas mixtas*) – i.e. companies where PDVSA have more than 50% shareholding. This reform also leaves aside the bitumen reference to resources extracted from OOB, formalizes an extraction tax and an export registration tax, and increases the income tax rate from 34% to 50% to all OOB's associations – retaining the right to receive a 12% tax credit for new investment. More recently, a new windfall profit tax called Special Contribution on Extraordinary Prices was added to the fiscal regime but the royalty and the income tax remained the same.

This chapter uses a panel of 821 Venezuelan oil fields to estimate a model of the economics of the sector and measure those effects. The primary conclusion is that tax reforms based solely upon the effects of the tax code on marginal fields overlook the distortions that the tax system creates in non-marginal fields, which can be even greater.[6]

The chapter is organized as follows: Section 1 presents a quick review of the theory on the effects of taxes upon oil production. Then a discussion of the singular characteristics of the Venezuelan case is done in Section 2, followed by the estimation of the tax effects in Section 3. Section 4 briefly reviews what has happened in the oil sector in Venezuela since the reforms. Finally, Section 5 presents some concluding remarks.

1 The theory on oil production and taxes

The theory on the effects of taxes on oil production have been documented in the introduction of this book and in Manzano (2004) and Corbacho et al. (2013), among others. Therefore, we will just summarize the relevant implications of this literature for this chapter. Subsection 1.1 reviews the Hotelling model. Next, the effects of the two main tax instruments used in Venezuela –income tax and the royalty – upon the amount of reserves developed and the entry conditions are analyzed, in subsections 1.2 and 1.3, respectively.

1.1 The producers problem

As in other chapters of this book, we use the problem of the producer of a natural resource developed by Hotelling (1931) in its seminal work.[7] Basically, the producer maximizes:

$$\max_{\bar{R},q,T} V = \int_0^T \pi(q)\, e^{-rt}\, dt - C(\bar{R}) \tag{1}$$

subject to

$$\dot{R} = -q$$
$$R(0) = \bar{R}$$
$$R(T) = 0$$

where π represents profits, q the extraction rate, r the discount rate, C the development and exploration cost and $\bar{R}$ reserves.

In this paper, I am going to assume that:

$$\pi(q) = pq - c(q)$$

which implies that:

1   There are two different types of costs involved in producing oil: (1) $C(\bar{R})$ or the cost, in money, of period 0 of the reserves. This is basically made up of exploration expenses, and may include such costs as connecting to the distribution infrastructure, etc.[8] And (2) $C(q)$, which represents the costs of oil extraction, and includes labor costs, gas injection, etc.[9]

2   This problem assumes that oil companies are price-takers, an assumption that is not so very removed from reality, at least not from the point of view of PDVSA or any operator in Venezuela.

The producer will choose the extraction path (q and T) and the amount of reserves that maximizes the profit function subject to the constraint, which implies that the total amount extracted should be equal to the reserves at the beginning of the exploitation.

The problem of the government will be to try to capture V. As explained in the literature, since the optimal mechanism – a competitive auction – is usually not feasible to implement, it will introduce special taxes to capture V. The most common are royalties and income taxes.

This model does not consider the market power of resource producers and how to induce efficiency in domestic resource markets.[10] In countries like Venezuela the government is more concerned with the development of the oil sector and the collection of revenue coming from the sector. Domestic markets are usually subsidized and only represent a relatively small fraction of the total production of oil.

1.2 Tax effects on reserves developed

A first alternative with which to check whether the current tax system affects, negatively, the development of certain kinds of fields is to check the effects of the tax system, by field, on the amount of reserves developed. We will do this in this subsection.

Royalties: The royalty is similar to a revenue tax; however, it is called a royalty because the government is the owner of the oil field and thus collects its royalty from the business. The effect of royalties is well-documented in Heaps and Helliwell (1985) and later extended in Manzano (2004).

Most of the literature on the topic has thus far focused on the tax burden.[11] I am going to refer to this tax burden as the Net Present Tax Rate (NPTR). The tax rate is going to be higher for those crudes with lower value (p), higher production costs ($c(q)$) and higher development costs ($C(\bar{R})$).

However, this analysis does not take into account the fact that producers will adjust when they face a tax; consequently, we cannot draw conclusions regarding just which fields are going to be more affected based solely upon the analysis of the NPTR. For this reason, Manzano (2004) derives the change in the amount of reserves developed from the change in the royalty rate. From here it calculates how that derivative changes with respect to the parameters that we are interested in: reserves in fields where costs increase at the fastest rate – either in production or development – are going to be less affected by the royalty. These results are similar to well-known results from the standard literature in public finance concerning inelastic agents. In fact, the development costs result is already mentioned in Heaps and Helliwell (1985).

Another result is that reserves developed in high value fields are going to be more affected by the royalty than reserves in low value fields. The reason for this is that high-value fields are going to lose more value relative to the costs of developing those crudes than are low-value fields. Consequently, there will be a larger reduction in reserves.

Income tax: It is clear that if we have a tax system that allows us to deduct all expenses, the optimal solution will not be affected by that system.[12] However, most of the tax codes do not recognize, or allow for, the amortization of these $C(\bar{R})$. Instead, they offer a tax credit for them. Looking at the net present tax rates, the fields that will pay a higher rate are those that have a lower value, higher development costs and higher operating costs.

However, we have – once again – the same problem we had with royalties: this analysis does not consider that producers will adjust when they face a tax. Consequently, we cannot draw conclusions regarding which fields are going to more affected solely as a result of analysis of the NPTR.

If we look at elasticities, we see that the results are like those in the royalty case. The main difference here is that the marginal cost has a more direct effect. This is because the royalty is based only on the price, while the profit tax takes into account the cost of producing oil. Fields with lower marginal costs will reduce their level of reserves, because of the introduction of an income tax, more than do those with higher costs. The reason is that, in fields with lower costs, the government take with respect to development costs is going to be greater than is the case in fields with higher costs.

1.3 Tax effects on entry conditions

The next step is then to explore the effects of the tax system on the entry of oil firms into different kinds of fields. The first step is to divide the space into dimensions representing the differences between the projects that we are interested in. Manzano (2004) chose three properties relevant to the Venezuelan situation: namely, the quality of crude, the degree of difficulty in extracting and the degree in difficulty in finding the crude in the area.

As a consequence, our problem in (1) becomes:

$$
\max_{\bar{R},q,T} V = \int_0^T \pi(q,\Theta,\mu_1)e^{-rt}dt - C(\bar{R},\mu_2)
$$

$$
= \int_0^T (\Theta pq - c(q,\mu_1))e^{-rt}dt - (F + f(\bar{R},\mu_2)) \tag{2}
$$

subject to

$$\dot{R} = -q$$
$$R(0) = \bar{R}$$
$$R(T) = 0$$

where the new variable Θ will represent the oil quality, and μ_1 and μ_2 will represent the ease of extracting oil and the ease of finding it respectively. The objective is then – with the optimal paths – to find the combinations of Θ, μ_1 and μ_2 that produce zero profit, assuming that there are fixed costs of development.

This is illustrated in Figure 5.1. For the sake of simplicity, I will focus only on Θ and μ_1. In this figure, the Y axis measures the easiness of extracting oil space, and the X axis measures the quality. As shown in equation (2) there is a negative relationship between Θ and μ_1: if we lower oil quality, we need to increase the easiness of extracting oil to maintain zero profits. This is shown by the thick line, which represents the level curve for 2. In the figure, the projects to the right of, and above, the curve will operate. They have either higher quality or easier-to-extract reserves than do projects that make zero profits and will thus produce positive profits. On the other hand, projects to the left of, or below, the curve will not produce. They have either lower quality or harder-to-extract reserves than do projects that make zero profits, and would thus make negative profits if they were to operate.

With this framework, Manzano (2004) introduces taxes and checks to see how the Zero-Profit Condition (hereinafter, ZPC) shifts. The ideal tax will avoid these shifts. This can be done with a "pure" profits tax and any other tax will shift the curve. In Manzano (2004) the shifts of the ZPC are compared to a lump-sum tax to include the "income effect" of the tax.

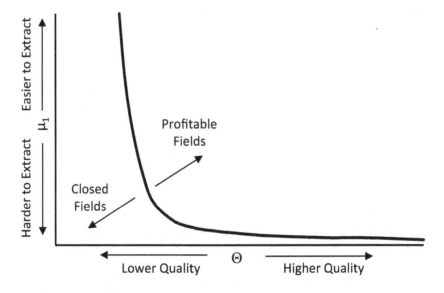

Figure 5.1 Zero-Profit Condition for field development

Royalty: Manzano (2004) shows that the ZPC rotates counterclockwise. Consequently, compared to a lump-sum tax, in this case a royalty leaves out fields of high quality but where oil is harder to extract, and allows the operation of fields of low value but where oil is easier to extract. The reason is that this is a tax that does not take into account the costs of producing the oil, favoring fields that are low cost and easier to extract.

This result has important welfare implications. The total surplus V represents a producer's surplus, and therefore welfare surplus. The original ZPC represents an "iso-surplus" line, in other words combinations of Θ and μ_1 that have the same amount of welfare. Any point above it has a higher welfare. The line that represents the lump-sum tax is also another iso-surplus. In the ZPC without tax the welfare level was zero, in the ZPC for the lump-sum tax the welfare level is the amount of the tax.

The fact that ZPC with royalty crosses the ZPC for the lump-sum tax will imply that the tax system is shifting the composition of producing fields towards fields where less welfare is generated. In other words, the fields that, with the introduction of a royalty (substituting a lump-sum tax), produce will generate less welfare than the fields that close.

Repeating this analysis on the plane defined by Θ and μ_2 yields similar conclusions (Manzano, 2004). The royalty shifts the ZPC, rotating. The rotation favors fields of lower value against fields that are harder to find. On the other hand, the royalty has no effects on the plane defined by μ_1 and μ_2.

Income tax: On the Θ and μ_1 plane, the income tax will not have an effect. However, as with the royalty, Manzano (2004) shows the income tax discriminates against fields where oil is harder to find. Finally on μ_1 and μ_2 plane, the slope will shift biased towards fields that are harder to extract. This is due to the fact that extraction expenses are fully deductible from the income tax. Actually, if there is full deductibility of investment on field development the slope will be the same as that without taxes.

2 The Venezuelan case

The previous section developed the basic framework on oil exploitation and taxation. In this section the particulars of the Venezuelan tax system and its effects are described and discussed. First, I am going to describe the common rules that the tax system possesses and the ways in which it departs from the theoretical model in section 1. Next, I will describe the particular rules pertaining to different kinds of oil activity.

2.1 Common rules

In this subsection, I will analyze the effects of the common rules – in particular, those referring to development costs.

1   First, there is a tax credit on the investment in field development. This credit works in the following way: each year, firms are allowed to deduct 12% of their investment as an expense for income tax purpose.

2   Second, there is another allowance for development costs. In the case of Venezuela, they are recognized in a particular way as, each year, you are allowed to deduct a portion of them from your taxes – a portion equal to the proportion of the reserves of the field used that year. It is important to mention that this deduction is called *depreciation allowance* according to the tax code, but that, as I will show, it will have effects upon oil production, even if the project exhibits no depreciation at all.[13] Consequently, Manzano (2004) refers to it as *development cost allowance* and thus avoids introducing depreciation considerations that will simply complicate things. There, it is shown that this kind of allowance is not equivalent to expensing and distortions will arise. However, it could reduce the distortions of the income tax.

Finally, one should mention a couple of distortions that, though not mentioned before, are nonetheless important. The reason for not mentioning them in the theoretical framework is that the way they are written in Venezuelan law does not allow us to analyze them in the simple Hotelling model:

1   The deduction of 12% of investment in field development cannot be greater than 2% of the before-tax net income of the year in which the investment is made. When firms hit this last limit – i.e. 12% of investment is greater than 2% of the before-tax net income – they are allowed to carry forward the remaining portion of the 12% of investment for up to three years. This method of deduction can only be used by operating firms (since the carry forward is limited); consequently, it generates a new form of discrimination between newer and older firms. Also, if we allow for field development after the field is in operation (as Pindyck, 1978, does), it will further distort the timing of the development. However, this is a different model, and one we will not consider here.
2   The same can be said about losses. The analysis in Manzano (2004) was carried out under the assumption that the rules apply everywhere, even if the firm makes losses. However, the tax system does not allow for losses. Rather, you can carry them forward for up to three years for deduction against taxable income in future periods. This will be important for two reasons: (1) Firms tend to have losses in the first years, and not all of them would be deducted and (2) If Venezuela continues to experience the high inflation of recent years, then, even if firms can deduct losses in the future, the deductions will represent less than the real value of the losses.

2.2 Particular rules

PDVSA traditional areas (until 2001): As mentioned in the introduction, PDVSA paid one-sixth royalty and 66.7% income tax.

   Heavy oil associations: The changes in the tax code pertaining to these kinds of projects were that the income tax rate was set at 34%, and the royalty was changed into a variable royalty ranging from 1%–16.67%, depending on the profitability of the project. As mentioned earlier, the reason for the changes to the tax rules for these projects was that these were low-value fields.

Operating agreements: Here, as said in the introduction, a firm operates a "mature" field on behalf of PDVSA and receives a fee per barrel. In this case, the company producing for PDVSA pays the tax rate that applies to all non-oil companies (30%). PDVSA pays its standard tax rate and the royalty for production of the field; however, the way these agreements are designed completely changes the tax effects on the firm's objective function.

As explained in Manzano (2004), the optimal design of this agreement is such that firms bid for a schedule of fees per barrel that in the optimum will imply that the income tax distortion is removed. The situation in Venezuela is different to that presented here. The firms do not bid for the schedule of fees. The schedule is preset before the bidding, and what the agents bid is a bond payable at the beginning of operations. Clearly, if the preset schedule differs from that which the contractors would themselves have chosen, distortions will arise. Therefore, the system would imply that PDVSA will maximize a function where the distortion of the income tax rate is not completely eliminated.

Exploration at risk: Here, as described before, a firm carries out the complete operation – right from the initial exploration of the field – but these areas are supposed to be areas of high quality crude. The tax system pertaining to these areas is more complex: (1) there is a variable royalty, (2) the tax rate is still 67% and (3) an auction was called in which companies bid upon the government participation rate in the post-tax "economic" profits – i.e. including developmental costs. This was called the PEG rate.[14] However, the PEG was set to a maximum of 50%. Therefore, if two or more companies bid 50%, a second auction was made but firms bid upon an up-front payment. In such a case, the winning firm would pay the 50% PEG and the up-front payment.

As discussed in Manzano (2004), the optimal design of these contracts will imply that the PEG rate and the upfront payment will not affect decisions on reserve development and production. The upfront payment may affect entry decisions. However, the actual setting is different, because the amount of $C(\bar{R})$ that is allowed to be deducted changes with the profitability of the project, and it does so in brackets. Therefore, the income tax distortions are not fully removed. Another important factor is that it exhibits variable royalty levels, too. It is clear that the reduction of the royalty will have the effects presented in section 1.2.

2.3 New common rules

The 2000s reforms revert the changes made in the '90s on tax rates on particular areas and, with that, the current tax system reduces the tax "discrimination".

1   The applicability of the 12% investment credit is back to all areas.
2   A fixed royalty of 30% was established on any profitable PDVSA traditional areas, including the mixed enterprises created in the OOB for heavy and extra-heavy oil production – i.e. formerly known as strategic associations. These associations should pay an additional special advantages royalty of 3.33%, a 1% tax to develop endogenous projects, a superficial tax of idle

Table 5.1 Summary of the main tax changes

Area	Tax system		
	1990	*1990s*	*Current*
PDVSA Heavy oils		No change Income tax = 34% Royalty = 1%–1/6	
Operating agreements	Income tax = 66.7%	Investment credit = 100%	Income tax = 50%
	Royalty = 1/6	Income tax = 66.7% PDVSA	Royalty = 30%
	Investment credit = 12%	Income tax = 30% contractor	Investment credit = 12% Windfall tax
Exploration at risk	Depreciation = $q.C(\bar{R})/\bar{R}$	Royalty = 1%–1/6 "After–tax" tax by bidding: PEG%.π, if PEGB < 50% a,b,c 50%.π–BOND,d if PEGB > 50%	

[a]PEG=government participation in after-tax profits; [b]π=after tax profits; [c]PEG[B]=PEG bided; [d]BOND=up-front bond payment bid

fields and a "shadow" tax guaranteeing that the sum of royalty, additional royalty and income tax reach a minimum of 50% of their income.

3   A general income tax was set at 50% to companies dedicated to oil exploitation and related activities. Previously, the income of companies exclusively dedicated to refining or to upgrading heavy and extra-heavy oil were taxed at 34%. Nevertheless, this "special" treatment has no current practical application. The heavy and extra-heavy areas are vertically integrated so that a mixed enterprise which refines and upgrades also explores and explodes, thus being taxed at 50%.

4   A "windfall tax". This is a tax that levies the revenues generated by an increase of oil prices in two brackets. If the oil price rises above US$70 (later modified to US$80) a tax of 50% will be applied to the difference between the price and the threshold. If the price rises above US$100, it will be 60% of the difference between that price and the second threshold.[15]

We can summarize the tax system in place in Venezuela in Table 5.1.

3 Estimating the effects upon oil exploitation of the tax rules

As mentioned earlier, the changes to the tax code were introduced because the fields were different to PDVSA's fields. In Manzano (2004) there is a discussion of the expected theoretical effects. In this work we focus on measuring them. This is carried out in this section.

There are two different approaches to estimate those values. The first approach would use data from the situation before the taxes were introduced and data from the situation after and compare both cases. Alternatively, knowledge of the oil sector can be used to estimate the situations before and after a tax reform. In the Venezuelan case, the reforms are relatively recent given the characteristics of the oil industry.[16] Therefore the latter approach would be used.

This approach has already been used in the past to study the effects of taxes on oil field development.[17] However, in the previous literature producers are not allowed to adjust the amount of reserves developed and/or the production path over time in reaction to the taxes introduced. In this chapter, I will estimate the parameters needed to calibrate a model of the oil sector for a panel of 821 fields, and predict with that model the effects of the reforms. This approach allows for the agents to adjust to the presence and the changes of the tax code.

In subsection 3.1 an estimation of the theoretical model of oil exploitation is done. Section 3.2 presents the estimation of the tax effects on the oil sector, given the parameters estimated in section 3.1.

3.1 Calibrating the model

I use Manzano's (2000) panel of 821 fields, including their expected production over the next 20 years and their operational costs. The next two Tables 5.2 and 5.3 show some summary statistics for the data on the panel.

With these fields, I can construct parameters for a cost function and carry out a calibration of the model developed in the previous section. With this calibration I can evaluate the different tax structures. In the following subsections I will use the panel to construct the parameters needed to evaluate the tax reform.

3.1.1 Determining cost functions

The main drawback of the panel is that it does not include information about the amount of reserves developed in each field and the costs of doing so. Therefore,

Table 5.2 Variables: summary statistics

Variables	N	Mean	Std. dev.	Min.	Median	Max.
Production	14001	1.9480	4.8359	0.0037	0.6315	132.6045
Costs	14001	8.5072	15.6457	0.0044	3.2951	237.6725
Total prod.	821	33.2206	73.5820	0.2446	12.3042	965.9616
Degrees API	821	28.3079	9.1515	8.5000	30.4000	54.2000

Table 5.3 Correlations

	Production	Total prod.
Costs	0.7367	
Degrees API		−0.0524

I use an estimation arrived at by Medina (1997). He used aggregate data to estimate the optimal time path of oil production in Venezuela, and then checked the effects of different taxes on that path. He estimates the following functions:

$$R_t = \Gamma\left(1 - e^{-\beta W_t}\right) \tag{3}$$

and

$$C(w_t) = \varepsilon + \gamma w_t + \delta w_t^2 \tag{4}$$

where Γ represents the total amount of reserves discovered at time t, W_t represents the total number of wells drilled *up* to time t and w_t represents the total amount of wells drilled at time t (i.e. $W_T = \sum_{t=0}^{T} w_t$). These functions are based on a model developed previously by Deacon (1993).

In the appendix we explain in detail the estimation. Table 5.4 summarizes the parameters used:

Table 5.4 Parameters used

Reserves	$\Gamma =$	$167.6578 * 10^6$
	$\beta =$	0.0210
Costs	$\varepsilon =$	$5.57 * 10^6$
	$\gamma =$	$2.2551 * 10^6$
	$\delta =$	0

For the cost function in, I will use the following specification:

$$c(q) = a + bq + cq^2 \tag{5}$$

I need to define where I am going to introduce the cost effect per field. In the Appendix I show how I determine to use individual effects on the value of c. In other words, a and b are common to all fields.

3.1.2 Results

The estimations done will imply that 2 will be simplified to:

$$\max_{\overline{R}, q, T} V = \int_0^T \pi(q, \Theta, \mu) e^{-rt} dt - C(\overline{R}) \tag{6}$$

subject to

$$\dot{R} = -q$$
$$R(0) = \overline{R}$$
$$R(T) = 0$$

where Θ still represents the oil quality, and μ will represent the ease of extracting the oil. In our estimation, $\mu = \dfrac{1}{b}$.

After repeating all the steps we follow in section 1.3, we will have a graph like Figure 5.2.[18] Again, ZPC plots the level curve for those projects that are going to result in zero profits. Projects above the line will produce, while projects below it will not.

With the parameters, we can check the distribution of fields in the space depicted in Figure 5.2. For that purpose, Table 5.5 shows some statistics, Figure 5.3 shows us the fields and Figure 5.4 their histogram.

One of the striking characteristics of this graph is the concentration of points around the value of 1.5653. Therefore, I checked my sample composition. In Table 5.6 I show the expected reserves of oil, calculated by PDVSA, in my sample, compared to the expected reserves in the whole country, divided by oil

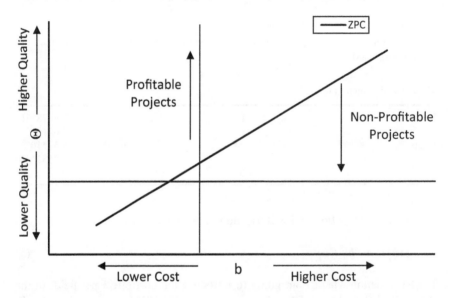

Figure 5.2 Zero-Profit Condition, level curve

Table 5.5 Summary of the parameters estimated. Distribution of fields' dimensions

	Θ	$1/\mu_l = b$
Mean	1.0426	1.5653
Std. dev.	0.1305	1.9039
Min	0.7601	−14.2714
10th percent.	0.8386	−0.0949
25th percent.	0.9652	1.0510
Median	1.0725	1.8319
75th percent.	1.1238	2.3020
90th percent.	1.2237	2.6179
Max	1.4119	9.7710
Correlation Θ, $1/\mu_l$	−0.0949	

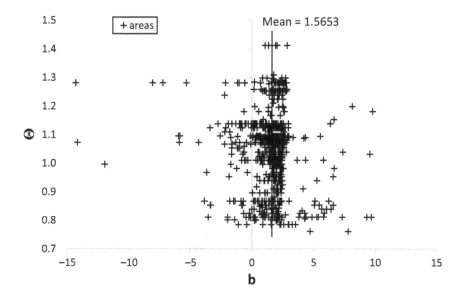

Figure 5.3 Distribution of fields

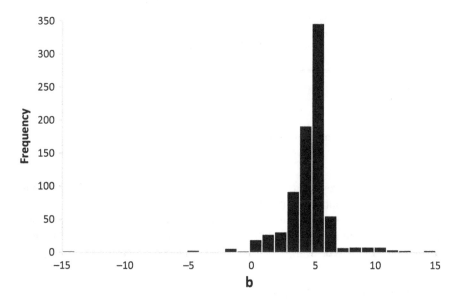

Figure 5.4 Histogram on individual effects

quality. It clearly shows that my sample is not a representative sample of the total fields in the country. Therefore, sample bias may explain the concentration of fields around a type of cost.

With these results, I can calculate the Zero Profit Conditions level curves. This is represented in Figure 5.5. There, I show four different curves: one without taxes

Table 5.6 Sample selection

	Expected reserves	
Crude		Sample/country
Light/condensated		78.0%
Medium		57.4%
Heavy		38.8%
Extra–heavy		0.3%

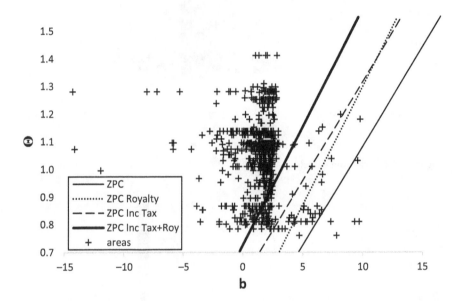

Figure 5.5 Fields and entry conditions ('90s)

("ZPC"), one with royalty ("ZPC royalty"), one with income taxes ("ZPC inc tax") and one with both taxes ("ZPC inc tax+roy").

Thus we see that five (5) fields will not produce, even without the taxes.[19] Once the taxes that were in place in 1990 in Venezuela were introduced, 99 additional fields would be closed.[20]

3.2 Evaluating the tax changes

3.2.1 Assigning areas to tax codes

One of the problems I have with the panel is that it does not match the areas to the new tax regimes. For that reason, I use the motives given to change the tax code for each area in order to assign each to its corresponding tax regime.

Heavy oils: As I mentioned in Section 2.1, these areas are of low value. Conse-quently, of the areas that are not produced, I will consider heavy oils those whose Θ is less than 0.9418 (i.e. areas with crudes of 20 or less degrees API). These represent 87 of the closed areas.

Operational agreements: Here I put all the other areas that are not produced under the current tax system. This means that there are 12 areas.

Exploration at risk: As I mentioned, these areas may be interpreted in dif-ferent ways. I have chosen to assume that they have a higher fixed cost of devel-opment than do the other areas. This implies that their ZPC is different too. To determine the areas assigned to this group I did the following:

1 Calculated a new ZPC with an additional fixed cost of development of US$92 million,[21] with income tax and royalty.
2 Calculated a new ZPC with the same fix cost, but without royalty (reform proposed).
3 Took those areas that were not produced under (1) and are produced under (2). Total: 38 areas. It is important to recall that these areas were not previ-ously counted as closed ones under the current tax system. The inclusion of these areas means that 137 areas are closed thanks to the current tax system.

3.2.2 Results

The next tables show the results of the calibration. The first step is to evaluate the reform according to the arguments given for it. For that purpose, Table 5.7 shows the amount of reserves developed in each area as a fraction of the total resource base available in those areas, for different scenarios.

The table first shows the situation as it would be with no taxes. We see that the total amount of areas that are available for production would produce under this scenario. Next, under the tax arrangement of 1990, we see that only PDVSA areas produce. Then we see the improvements brought about by the new changes, as a result of which 112 of the 137 areas are recovered.

However, we see that once the new tax agreements introduced in the 2000s are in place, there is a loss in number of areas and reserves. Seventy-seven areas that would be producing with the tax schedules introduced in the 1990s will close. In particular, all the operational agreements areas will close and most of the areas of heavy oils, and only three explorations at risk will open. Since there is a reduction in income tax, PDVSA areas will develop more reserves.

A final scenario is made with applying the different tax schedules of the '90s to PDVSA areas. The argument behind this scenario is to see the welfare impact of changing the tax treatment of PDVSA. Clearly, if the reform is applied to PDVSA areas, no improvement will be made in terms of the number of areas producing. However, more reserves will be developed. The total fraction of reserves produced in PDVSA areas if these areas were operating under the vari-ous new tax systems would be greater than would be the case in the non-PDVSA areas. Nevertheless, the marginal recovery of reserves in PDVSA areas, thanks to the tax change, is lower than the marginal recovery in the non-PDVSA areas.

Table 5.7 Evaluating the tax reform: target variables

Variables	Areas			
	PDVSA	Heavy oil	Op. agr.	Expl. at risk
With no tax				
Reserves used $\left(\dfrac{\sum \bar{R}}{\sum \Gamma}\right)$	0.8494	0.6872	0.6902	0.9027
Areas producing	679	87	12	38
Under the tax agreement of 1990				
Reserves used $\left(\dfrac{\sum \bar{R}}{\sum \Gamma}\right)$	0.5018	0	0	0
Areas producing	679	0	0	0
Under 1990s tax reforms				
Reserves used $\left(\dfrac{\sum \bar{R}}{\sum \Gamma}\right)$	0.5018	0.5567	0.4729	0.6877
Reserves used $\left(\dfrac{\sum \bar{R}_{new\,tax}}{\sum \bar{R}_{no\,tax}}\right)$	0.5908	0.6891	0.4568	0.6015
Areas producing	679	74	8	30
Under the current tax agreement				
Reserves used $\left(\dfrac{\sum \bar{R}}{\sum \Gamma}\right)$	0.5216	0.3399	0	0.7051
Reserves used $\left(\dfrac{\sum \bar{R}_{new\,tax}}{\sum \bar{R}_{no\,tax}}\right)$	0.6140	0.0284	0	0.6783
Areas producing	679	5	0	33
Value for PDVSA areas under the current/previous tax agreement				
Reserves used $\left(\dfrac{\sum \bar{R}}{\sum \Gamma}\right)$	0.5216	0.7467	0.7188	0.5591
Change		0.2251	0.1972	0.0375
Areas producing	679	679	679	679
change		0	0	0

In terms of the framework developed in Section 1, this is due to the functional form chosen. Development cost curve becomes more inelastic as the amount of reserves developed increases. Since PDVSA areas have already developed reserves, they development cost are more inelastic than those of the non-PDVSA areas, compensating for the fact that these areas have other disadvantages – higher extraction costs, lower prices, etc. Therefore, in terms of the arguments given for the reform, the reform was successful.

Table 5.8 focuses upon welfare variables. In it, I present the total surplus generated by each area, the total tax collected and the social surplus of the marginal barrel, for each area under each different scenario.

On the first set of results, I show the total surplus in each area that would be produced if there were no taxes. Obviously, under this assumption, the marginal surplus would be zero in all fields (social λ =private $\lambda = C'\left(\overline{R}\right)$). We cannot compare absolute magnitudes here, because of the overwhelming difference in the number of areas between the different types. For that reason, I will focus my discussion in the marginal surplus.

In the next set of results, I calculate the same variables again, this time under the 1990s tax system. Because, under this assumption, there is no production in areas other than PDVSA areas, those areas have no surplus. Consequently, the surplus of the marginal barrel is the surplus of the first barrel produced.

Note that, even though we do have production in PDVSA areas, the surplus of the marginal barrel there is higher than in almost all other areas. This is because

Table 5.8 Evaluating the tax reform: welfare variables

Variables	*Areas*			
	PDVSA	*Heavy oil*	*Op. agr.*	*Expl. at risk*
With no tax				
Surplus (.10⁹)	485.05	23.79	3.21	43.40
Marg. surplus	0	0	0	0
Under the tax agreement of 1990				
Surplus (.10⁹)	378.01	0	0	0
Tax (.10⁹)	322.37	0	0	0
Marg. surplus	4.1367	3.8050	3.3317	11.2813
Under 1990s tax reforms				
Surplus (.10⁹)	378.01	21.34	2.26	29.52
Tax (.10⁹)	322.37	12.67	1.51	23.48
Marg. surplus	4.1367	1.2694	1.8541	5.0506
Under the current tax agreement				
Surplus (.10⁹)	384.05	1.28	0	33.95
Tax (.10⁹)	316.47	1.13	0	26.11
Marg. surplus	3.7067	3.0766	1.8613	4.5920
Value for PDVSA areas under the 1990 tax agreement for . . .				
Surplus (.10⁹)	384.05	470.66	461.86	405.48
Change (.10⁹)		86.61	77.81	21.43
Tax (.10⁹)	316.47	244.16	241.53	331.44
Change (.10⁹)		−72.31	−74.94	14.97
Marg. surplus	3.7067	1.9589	2.1488	3.8286

these areas have lower value, higher costs, etc. As a consequence, the best strategy is to increase production in PDVSA areas rather than in the other areas.

The next step is to introduce the recent reforms. Because the PDVSA areas have not experienced a change in their tax structure, we see nothing change for them. I find that an extra-surplus is generated in all the "new" areas; nevertheless, the social value of the barrels produced is much higher in PDVSA areas than in the case of other areas – except for exploration at risk. Therefore, it would be welfare improving to switch production to PDVSA areas from other areas.

The third exercise is to apply the 2000s reforms to the different areas. Since many closed, the total surplus is reduced. In addition the marginal surplus increases in those new areas. However, in PDVSA areas the total surplus increases. This is because more reserves are developed. This result implies that the marginal surplus in PDVSA areas falls, though it is still higher that in most areas.

Then, as in the previous table, I calculate what would happen if the PDVSA tax regime was modified so as to match those of the different special agreements. It can be seen that the extra-surplus generated in PDVSA areas is generally greater, except in the case of the exploration-at-risk areas. The main reason for this is that the barrels produced in PDVSA areas, as a consequence of the tax changes, are of higher value than those resulting from the special agreements.

Finally, I have calculated the level of government revenue created under all these scenarios. It is clear that, as a result of all the changes, the government gains more revenue if it applies the exploration-at-risk tax treatment to PDVSA areas. This is another way of measuring tax distortions. The fact that more tax revenue can be generated under the "easing" of the tax rules means that the sector is in a point where the marginal change in the tax rate would be more than offset by the marginal change in production.[22]

4 A brief review of the performance sector

As mentioned before, given the time frames of oil exploitation, we cannot do a full comparison between ex-ante and ex-post. In addition, there have been events not described here that complicate the analysis.

First, there was a strike in 2002 that practically paralyzed production and that resulted in the firing of more than 18,000 workers. This has an impact on operations. In addition PDVSA has been tasked with functions beyond the oil business: to distribute food, to build houses, etc. This has impacts on profits.

However, in this section we will look at a couple of variables to see if in the aggregate some of the conclusions apply. The first issue is the change in the composition of production, shown in Figure 5.6. As expected, PDVSA shares in production fell. This is in line with the expected results where the changes in the tax system were biased against PDVSA areas. After 2006, there was an increase in PDVSA's share as it took part of the share of the new areas. However, even after that, the incentive for PDVSA was to produce in *empresas mixtas* rather than in its own fields.

In addition, there were changes in the composition of revenue. As Figure 5.7 shows, there is a shift towards royalty revenues in PDVSA. In other areas, once

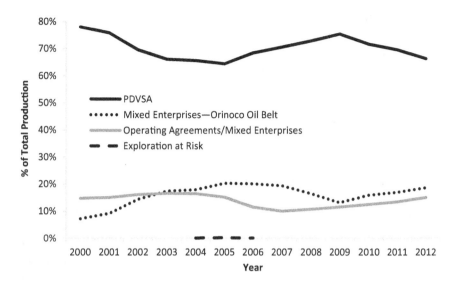

Figure 5.6 Composition of total production of oil

Source: Ministry of Petroleum and Mining of Venezuela (2010 and 2012)

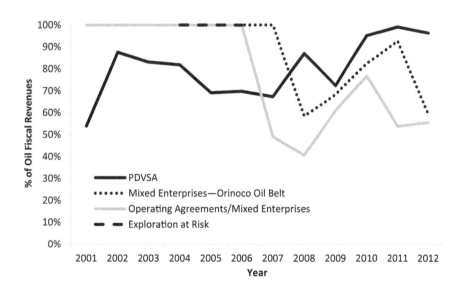

Figure 5.7 Share of royalty revenues on taxes collected

Source: Ministry of Petroleum and Mining of Venezuela (2010 and 2012)

they started to turn in profits – through higher production, income tax increased its share. However even there, the share of royalties increased even as prices were going up. Because of that, the elasticity of tax revenue to operational income is low. This explains why the government changed again the rules in 2006, though the change was in levels and the fundamental issue was not changed.

5 Concluding remarks

This paper has shown that a comprehensive tax reform of the oil sector should consider not simply whether projects are being developed under the current tax system but, rather, the effects of the tax structure on the whole oil sector and the distortions it creates.

The recent reforms in the Venezuelan oil tax system have pointed towards the development of marginal areas. The argument behind these reforms was that these areas either had the highest burden or were not being developed at all. However, it may be the case that these areas are also the ones that the tax system distorts the least. Therefore, there would be areas where the tax system generates more distortions and thus a tax reform should also include and focus on those areas. Estimating a model of the Venezuelan oil sector, I found that this is what happened in Venezuela.

In the margin, those reforms could have had a positive impact if the areas that were the most tax system distorted were tackled by them. In other chapters, we have seen that in other countries more "integral" reforms were adopted. However, it is also fair to point out that the case of oil, Venezuela presents a very heterogenous resources base which highlights the need of a more complex tax structure, which could be a challenge for policymakers.

Appendix

Estimating development costs

Using the totals from the Venezuelan oil sector since 1960, the results of Medina's (1997) estimation were (*t-statistics* in parentheses):

$$R_t = \underset{(not\ estimated)}{\underset{\Gamma^M}{420*10^9}} \left(1 - e^{\underset{(-72.7539)}{-8.4369*10^{-6}}\, w_t} \right) \underset{\beta^M}{} \tag{A.1}$$

and[23]

$$C(w_t)*10^{-6} = \underset{\varepsilon^M}{(4.8746)} + \underset{845.13}{\underset{(4.0514)}{}} w_t + \underset{\gamma^M}{\underset{0.7574}{(2.6268)}} w_t D + \underset{\delta^M}{\underset{0.0039}{(1.3100)} w_t^2} \tag{A.2}$$

for $D=1$, after 1983.

In equation A.1, the results imply that Medina chose not to estimate Γ^M, but, rather, to use the estimates given by the geology department of PDVSA and estimate from there. In equation A.2 the results imply, first, that the quadratic term is not significant and, second, that there is a time break in the cost function. The reason for this time break is that, originally, Deacon (1993) uses the total amount of feet drilled. However, as this information was not available for a long period for Venezuela, Medina uses the number of wells. Nevertheless, it is known that the average depth of the wells drilled increased significantly after 1983, when a major exploration campaign commenced. Therefore, Medina introduces the change of the slope in the estimation of A.2.

I used his parameters scaled to the fact that Medina's model is designed for the aggregate and here is used for for individual areas. For the scaling, I used the fact that these areas represent 39 billion barrels out of the total of 119 billion barrels of reserves that Venezuela possesses. I assumed that the fields were of equal size. This then implies that, if 821 fields represent 39 billion barrels, there will be a total of 2,505 fields. Consequently, if we divide the total resource base by 2,505, each field will have a resource base of 168 million barrels.

In addition, for the scaling of Γ, I assumed that the marginal cost of the first barrel of oil in the aggregate is equal to the marginal cost of the first barrel of oil in each area. Finally, the fixed cost of 3.4 was divided by the number of fields, and a net present value of it for 40 years (the average life of a field) was used as a fix cost for the purposes of our estimation in Table 5.4.

Estimating development costs

There is a problem, however, with carrying out a simple least square regression for this purpose. In Figure 5.8, I show the different costs and production levels of the different fields. It is clear from the graph that fields with lower costs will also be the fields in which production is higher. This is part of the result of a maximizing process, and will cause the estimation of c on 5 to be negative.[24] A solution would be to estimate the equation 5 individually for each field, but the problem is that for some fields we may have few observations.[25]

For that reason, I use the Hotelling model in 2. I know from our original problem that:

$$q_t = \frac{p - b - \lambda e^{rt}}{2c} \tag{A.3}$$

The problem is that I do not have λ. Nevertheless, I do have the total production for each field for the years in the sample, and integrating 3.6:

$$\int_0^T q_t dt = T \frac{(p-b)}{2c} - \frac{\lambda}{2c} \frac{\left(e^{rT} - 1\right)}{r} \tag{A.4}$$

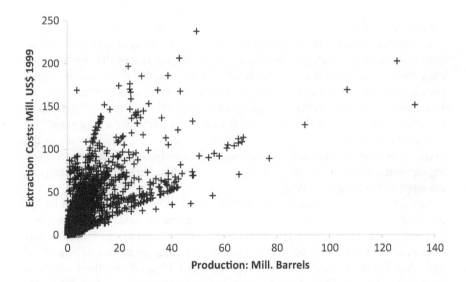

Figure 5.8 Production and extraction costs

Table 5.9 Results from the non-linear estimation. Dependent variable: extraction costs

	No individual effects	Individual effects		
		on constant	on q_t	on q_t^2
	(1)	(2)	(3)	(4)
constant	4.9888		8.4824	4.1401
	[19.1025]		[42.5589]	[37.2828]
q_t	1.1989	1.0164		0.7705
	[43.7885]	[52.6138]		[28.6826]
q_t^2	0.1993	0.2033	0.3776	
	[130.0402]	[152.951]	[90.043]	
N	14001	14001	14001	14001
SSE	11,773,896.6	5,140,730.6	4,886,777.8	1,631,859.0
F–test for I.E.		20.71	22.62	99.76

t-statistics in brackets

Consequently, I substitute (A.4) on (A.3), that value on 5, and then use non-linear least Squares to estimate the resulting expression.[26]

Table 5.9 shows the results of the estimation. Column (1) shows the estimation assuming no individual effects. The coefficients are of the expected sign and significant.

The next three columns show the results with different individual effects. All specifications in the table reject the restricted model in (1). I am going to choose column (3) for three reasons:

1   In Figure 5.3 it seems that the difference is on the slope of the cost functions and not on the intercept.
2   Theoretically, it is also more plausible to have different marginal costs than different fixed costs, because the differences are going to be caused by differences in the characteristics of the field that are going to affect the extraction pattern (pressure, viscosity, etc.).
3   Finally, if we do a Haussman Test on the value of c, the test rejects (2).[27]

Notes

1   Heavy oil associated with other elements.
2   The latter is probably the major concern in most other countries and, therefore, in most of the literature. See, for example, Lund (1987), Kemp (1989) and Kemp and Rose (1984). In these texts the main concern is that fields involving high developmental costs are not going to be exploited.
3   A good view of the different aspects and the different views that exists about these topics can be gotten with three papers: Espinasa (1997), Mommer (1998) and Rodríguez and Sachs (1999).
4   The oil company was created in 1975, following the nationalization of the oil sector.
5   Actually, the project for off-shore gas was the first approved by Congress.
6   It is important to clarify that in this research those fields that were not active under the past tax structure will be called marginal and will produce under the new tax code.

7   I am using Heaps and Helliweel's (1985) formulation here.

8   C($\bar{R}$) will be the present value of all the expenditures in exploration and development of the field.

9   There is an important branch of literature on the nature of C(q). In particular, Pindyck (1978), who assumes it depends on the amount of reserves present at the time of extraction, also introduces the possibility of adding reserves through the lifetime of the field. However, one can safely say that the simple framework used in this research will be sufficient to ascertain the effects of the tax system on the development of different kind of fields.

   Models like Pindyck (1978) will help us to understand the effects of the tax system on the timing of extraction and the timing of field development, which, though non-trivial, are not the focus of this research.

10 See Karp and Livernois (1992) and Rowse (1997).

11 Kemp (1989) and Kemp and Rose (1984), for example. This is not a bad approach if you consider that most of that literature was written to consider the tax effects on oil field development in places like the North Sea, where adjusting is costly. A detailed explanation of the characteristics of oil exploitation in the North Sea can be found in Lund (1987).

12 In this case 1.1 will be multiplied by (1-τ) and it will disappear once we set the first order conditions.

13 Formally, this provision in the law allows not only for expenses in C($\bar{R}$) but also for the investments made to produce oil. It is easy to see that the investment carried out in C($\bar{R}$) is different to investment in the production infrastructure. Once you have discovered the reserves, you enter in the producing phase of the project. And given the property of the field in Venezuela, the expenses incurred in exploration cannot be recovered by means of selling the field after the firm discovers the reserves. These expenses do not have any depreciation or cost attached to them throughout the exploitation of the field.

   On the other hand, investment in production will exhibit the standard depreciation costs. Clearly, in the latter case, the way depreciation is being allowed to be deducted will have important consequences regarding the allocation of capital in the production of oil. Since the focus of this research is the amount of reserves developed, Manzano (2004) assumes that there is no depreciation in the capital invested in oil production.

14 PEG are the Spanish initials of Government Take on Profits.

15 In our estimations, we will not consider this tax, since we use a long-run price that is below the threshold. However, this will be relevant for an extension of the analysis considering the impacts of oil price volatility on firms' decisions.

16 The first reforms were introduced at the beginning of the 1990s and the latest in the early 2000s.

17 See for example Kemp (1987) and (1989), Kemp and Rose (1984) and Lund (1987). For the Venezuelan case see Office of the Chief Economist (1998) and Smith (1995).

18 Note that, for visual reasons, I have changed the position of the axes.

19 It is important to remember that what I had from PDVSA were geologically optimal paths that did not consider whether exploration costs, in particular fixed costs, were covered.

20 This relatively low number also seems to add to the evidence that the panel represented here is a biased panel of fields. The reader can see that in Figure 5.5 there is almost a "gap" between the fields that actually produce with the taxes and the fields that do not produce at all.

   This seems to suggest that the panel represented here is only or mainly of PDVSA fields (i.e. few heavy oils, operational agreements and exploration-at-risk areas). As we will discuss later, this will actually make our results more relevant.

21 This magnitude comes from the following numbers: The expected initial exploration effort for the eight areas was expected to be US$485 million and the total "lump-sum" posted in the eight areas was US$250 million. I added up these numbers and divided by eight.

22 This is just an example of the "Laffer Curve". The results imply that the oil sector is in a point beyond the maximum revenue.
23 All monetary values are in US$, 1999.
24 The OLS result for c is -0.01363.
25 It is true that we have the projected production for the next 20 years, but that does not mean that each field is actually producing in each of the next 20 years. The average time is 17, but the minimum time is nine.
26 By the time the panel was done, the expected price of the Venezuelan basket was US$13.96. Given that crudes usually are priced in absolute spreads over a reference value, this will imply that I can price other crudes based on the following formula: P=8.9192+0.1991*Degrees API.
27 In addition, looking at the distribution of possible effects, for (2) and (3) the average effect will be negative. This will imply non-convex costs.

References

Corbacho, Ana, Vicente Fretes and Eduardo Lora, ed. 2013. *More Than Revenue: Taxation as a Development Tool*, Inter-American Development Bank and Palgrave Macmillan, Washington DC.

Deacon, Robert. 1993. "Taxation, Depletion, and Welfare: A Simulation Study of the U.S. Petroleum Resource", *Journal of Environmental Economics and Management*, 24(2), 159–187.

Espinasa, Ramon. 1997. *Política Petrolera y Desarrollo Económico [Oil Policy and Economic Development]*, Petróleos de Venezuela S.A, Mimeo, Caracas, Venezuela.

Heaps, Terry and John Helliwell. 1985. "The Taxation of Natural Resources", in Auerbach, Allan and Martin Feldstein, eds., *Handbook of Public Economics Volume I*, North-Holland, Amsterdam.

Hotelling, Harold. 1931. "The Economics of Exhaustible Resources", *Journal of Political Economy*, 39, 137–175.

Karp, Larry and Jjohn Livernois. 1992. "On Efficiency-Inducing Taxation for a Non-Renewable Resource Monopolist", *Journal of Public Economics*, 49, 219–239.

Kemp, Alexander. 1987. *Petroleum Rent Collection Around the World*, The Institute for Research on Public Policy, South Halifax.

Kemp, Alexander. 1989. "Development Risks and Petroleum Fiscal Systems: A Comparative Study of the UK, Norway, Denmark and the Netherlands", *The Energy Journal*, 13, 17–39.

Kemp, Alexander and David Rose. 1984. "Investment in Oil Exploration and Production: The Comparative Influence of Taxation", in Pearce, David, Horst Siebert and Ingo Walter, eds., *Risk and the Political Economy of Resource Development*, pp. 169–195. St. Martin Press, New York.

Lund, Diderik. 1987. *Investment, Taxes and Uncertainty, With Applications to the Norwegian Petroleum Sector*, Dissertation submitted to the department of Economics in Partial Fulfillment of the Requirements for the Degree of Ph.D., MIT Press.

Manzano, Osmel. 2000. *Tax Effects Upon Oil Field Development in Venezuela*, Center for Energy and Environmental Policy Research Working Papers Series Number 2000–006, Center for Energy and Environmental Policy Research, MIT.

Manzano, Osmel. 2004. "Efectos teóricos de los impuestos en el desarrollo de los campos petroleros en Venezuela", *Revista BCV*, 18(2), 119–154.

Medina, Humberto. 1997. *Evaluación de los efectos de diferentes esquemas impositivos sobre la senda de exploración y producción de una empresa petrolera en el tiempo (un análisis para el caso venezolano) [An Evaluation of Different Tax Schemes on the Path of Exploration and Production of an Oil Firm (an Analysis for the Venezuelan Case)]*, Petróleos de Venezuela S.A., Mimeo.

Ministry of Petroleum and Mining of Venezuela. 2010. *Petróleo y Otros Datos Estadísticos 2009–2010*, Ministry of Petroleum and Mining, Caracas, Venezuela.

Ministry of Petroleum and Mining of Venezuela. 2012. *Petróleo y Otros Datos Estadísticos 2012*. Ministry of Petroleum and Mining, Caracas, Venezuela.

Mommer, Bernard. 1998. *The New Governance of Venezuelan Oil*, Oxford Institute for Energy Studies, WPM 23, Oxford Institute for Energy Studies, Oxford, UK.

Office of the Chief Economist of Petróleos de Venezuela. 1998. "El Marco Fiscal Petrolero Venezolano: Evolución y Propuestas [The Legal Framework for the Venezuelan Oil Sector: Evolution and Perspectives]", Presentation at the Central Bank in Venezuela.

Pindyck, Robert. 1978. "The Optimal Exploration and Production of Nonrenewable Resources", *Journal of Political Economy*, 86(5), 841–861.

Rodríguez, Francisco and Jeffrey Sachs. 1999. "Why Do Resource-Abundant Economies Grow More Slowly?", *Journal of Economic Growth*, 4, 277–303

Rowse, John. 1997. "On Ad Valorem Taxation of Nonrenewable Resource Production", *Resource and Energy Economics*, 19, 221–239.

Smith, James. 1995. "Calculating Investment Potential in South America", *World Oil,* June.

6 Regulation and state intervention in non-renewable natural resources

The cases of the oil and gas sectors in Argentina[*]

Enrique Kawamura

1 Introduction

Argentina is an interesting example of a country traditionally specialized in the production of agricultural commodities that also developed relatively important energy-related, non-renewable resources, mainly, oil and gas[1]. That development became stronger in the 1990s, becoming the third largest oil producer in South America (after Venezuela and Brazil) during part of that decade and the first years of the new century. To provide a quantitative reference, in 1990 Argentina's natural gas production was 23.02 m^3 billions, while in 2004 the production was 52.38 m^3 billions. That production growth allowed Argentina to become a net exporter of crude-oil and natural gas.

Yet, production and exports of both resources started to sharply drop by the mid-2000s on[2], implying also a reverse of the trade balance from surplus to a deficit already in 2006. From a conceptual perspective, part of the potential explanation for such decline might be found in traditional rent-extraction problems common in such sectors in different oil and gas abundant countries. Indeed, both at the policy as well as at the academic level, a common concern in those countries is the "temptation" that governments in such countries may want to extract rents from the firms in those sectors. (Below is a brief account of the academic literature related to that discussion). Yet, in the case of Argentina the type of government intervention seemed much more different and much more complex to understand.

This paper has then a double goal. It first documents a list of major stylized facts about both production and exploration investment in the oil and gas sectors in Argentina, and especially a description of the new regulation regimes introduced by the Argentine government during the period 2002–2012. In brief, those facts can be summarized as follows: oil production decreased about 25%, gas production decreased 15% between 2004 and 2012 and exploration activity steadily decreased at least until 2010. The government started to almost completely control the resources (oil and gas) prices as well as energy prices. Both were kept way below their corresponding international prices. At the same time, natural gas consumption heavily increased (about 48%). This combination of decline in production, increase in domestic energy demand and domestic low prices implied an explosion in the trade deficit, especially in natural gas, whose physical volume reached values even higher than the maximum trade surplus reached in 2004. As Navajas (2006) and other authors state, such regulation can hardly be reconciled with standard theories regarding dynamic regulations or taxation in non-renewable resources.

Given those facts, the paper then presents a stochastic, partial-equilibrium, inter-temporal model of a non-exhaustible resource and energy production with price regulations and implicit quantity restrictions imposed by the state, whose values arise endogenously in equilibrium, whose technical details appear in a companion paper[3] . The major goal of the model is to rationalize the facts presented in the first part of the chapter. Embedded in a well-known model of non-renewable-resource taxation, such as Deacon (1993), the framework considers explicit (incumbent) politicians (and not benevolent planners) who have the capacity to set the values of such policies, but that could be removed from office by elections. The model introduces a *self-enforcing equilibrium* concept as an adaptation of the sustainable equilibrium developed in the macro-political economy papers by Yared (2010) and Acemoglu et al. (2010 and 2011), among others. This concept internalizes self-enforcement constraints, requiring that for a policy to be part of an equilibrium the government must have no incentive to deviate from that policy in any period. Thus, the sequence of policy variables arising in such equilibrium is time consistent by construction.

In the model, upstream firms produce a non-renewable resource that is used as the only input to produce a final consumption good called energy, produced by a downstream firm. Those firms face two types of regulations: the prohibition to export as long as domestic demand is not fully satisfied (a constraint that binds within the equilibrium analyzed in this paper) and prices completely controlled by the government. Energy is one of the three goods consumed by consumers, the other two being a numeraire of good and leisure. Consumers receive a stochastic endowment of an international energy-unrelated commodity. The government is run by one of many possible (identical) bureaucrats. These consume a fraction of fiscal revenues coming from the taxes on the energy-unrelated commodity. On the other hand, when the government sets the price of energy received by the downstream firm, it may potentially have to compensate the downstream firm to cover losses through subsidy payments. Also, in the latter case, there is a potential need for resource imports (also paid by the government in equilibrium) given the domestic shortage of the resource production relative to energy consumption.

The model considers a repeated game that represents a political interaction process between consumers and bureaucrats. The main assumption is the existence of elections at the beginning of each period, where consumers may choose to re-elect the incumbent government or else to replace it with another bureaucrat. The model assumes that consumers enjoy some intrinsic utility coming from the replacement of the incumbent (preference for turnover). Also, any incumbent bureaucrat faces an intrinsic utility cost of being expelled from power. Thus, these two preference parameters shape the bureaucrat's incentives to set low prices for energy to allow for re-election to occur in a self-enforcing equilibrium.

The main results of the theoretical model are as follows. First, domestic energy prices are way below the international price of the resource as long as both the incumbent government's utility cost of being expelled from power and the voters' preference for political turnover are high enough (subject also to high enough values of the endowment of the energy-unrelated commodity). The intuition for this result is simple. Under the last condition tax revenues are high to get enough consumption for the incumbent in case that his or her re-election takes place. High utility costs for the incumbent after losing the election imply lower benefits from setting high energy prices (and low subsidies) rather than low. The high value of preference for turnover makes the incentives to reduce the energy price even stronger, to ensure that voters have enough incentives to re-elect the incumbent. Note that such conditions also ensure strictly positive subsidies paid to the energy producer (downstream firm), a fact that characterizes the natural gas sector in Argentina especially after 2008.

Other results from the theoretical model include conditions under which resource imports occur in equilibrium. Such conditions are those that imply a very low price-to-marginal-cost relation in the upstream sector. On the other hand, the model also predicts that, by the time the domestic reserves of the resource are exhausted, the domestic price is a constant fraction of the international price, where this fraction reflects the share of variable inputs in the resource-extraction technology. For periods before reserves exhaustion, domestic prices of the resource follows a dynamic that is consistent with declining expected domestic prices.

It is important to stress that, at this stage, the model in this chapter is the first in endogenizing regulations in the non-renewable resource sector and the energy sector through a dynamic repeated game between non-benevolent governments and voters (consumers). Indeed, the now very extensive[4] literature on taxation and regulation of non-renewable resources do not include such an endogenous taxation analysis.[5] In particular, such papers do not take into account the endogeneity of the risk of expropriation. However, for Latin American countries such as Argentina this type of risk is clearly of a first-order importance, provided the regular instability of governments and, especially, public policies in the region. The relevance of this risk has already been pointed out by Garnaut and Clunies Ross (1975).

However, only much more recently there has been an increase in the analysis of formal models with expropriation risk within the natural resource sector. An early example is the model by Gaudet, Laserre and Long (1995). The basic version of this model assumes two periods and no commitment on behalf of the government, and so the second-period royalty rate is (re)set after the first period's tax rate has been set. To my knowledge, this constitutes one of the few models assuming an explicit problem of time inconsistency. Clearly, their model does not capture the problem of expropriation and other types of risks associated with a not-fully-benevolent government. The model fills this gap by assuming a politician's objective function that combines a rent-seeking behavior with a political-power-keeping behavior, the second of which is more consistent with a benevolent uninformed government than the first type of behavior.

Another related study is Bohn and Deacon (2000). These authors develop and estimate a theoretical model of asset expropriation. When estimated with an international panel data they find that ownership instability indeed reduces the speed of oil exploitation.[6] This type of expropriation risk is also a major subject in several chapters of the book by Hogan and Sturzenegger (2010).[7] In the end, this expropriation risk reflects a time-inconsistency problem by a government that may want to extract more rents by increasing tax rates over the original arrangement after the international price of the resource increases. This time inconsistency issue is discussed in more detail when presenting the formal model presented in this paper.

The rest of the paper is organized as follows. Section 2 presents some key facts about the oil and gas sectors in Argentina after the abandonment of the currency board system in 2002. Section 3 presents the model with the analysis. Section 4 presents the main results concerning the equilibrium characterization of the model. Section 5 presents several policy implications coming from the equilibrium analysis of the model. Finally Section 6 presents the conclusions with several suggestions for future research.

2 Some facts about the oil and gas sectors in Argentina after the 2001–2002 crisis

This section presents a brief summary of major empirical facts characterizing the gas and oil sectors in Argentina for the years following the abandonment of the currency board in January 2002. A steady increase in regulations on producer prices, energy tariffs and trade restrictions characterize that period, with a consequent impressive drop (followed by a minor recovery) in both production and investment in exploration, in the latter case, at least until 2010. Thus, it is apparent that those stronger regulations seemed to have affected the incentives to invest and to produce oil and especially natural gas. These and other facts are presented as follows.

1   **Fall in production**. In the period considered here, the decrease in domestic production of both oil and natural gas (in this last case, since 2004) has been an increasing public concern. Figures 6.1 and 6.2 below document such fall for each of these two energy resources.

   Indeed, the cumulative decrease in oil production between 2002 and 2012 is above 25%. The decrease in gas production between the 2004 peak and 2012 is more than 15%. As Navajas (2006) and other authors state, such a decrease (together with a sharp increase in domestic gas use, see Figure 6.5 below) explains a big portion of the energy problems faced in Argentina, especially after 2007.

2   **Fall (and mild recovery?) in exploration investment**. Those drops in production shown in fact 1 can also be linked to a decrease in exploration activity. Figures 6.3 and 6.4 below illustrate this fact.

   These figures clearly emphasize that, between 2005 and 2010 (with some exceptions) the number of wells dedicated to exploration of new reserves in oil and gas fairly decreased. This seems to show a short run reversion in 2011

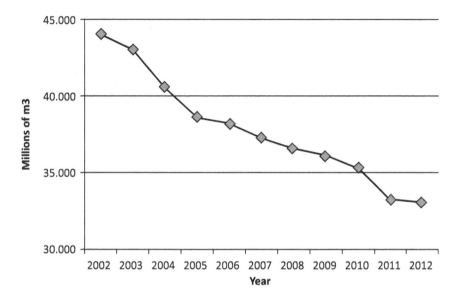

Figure 6.1 Oil production in Argentina, 2002–2012

Source: IAPG

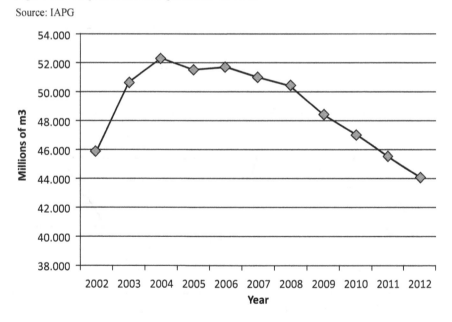

Figure 6.2 Natural gas production in Argentina, 2002–2012

Source: IAPG

and 2012, possibly as an effect of the restatization of the major oil and gas company in Argentina, *Yacimientos Petrolíferos Fiscales* (YPF). Yet, during all this period, the quantity of wells are significantly below the technical level

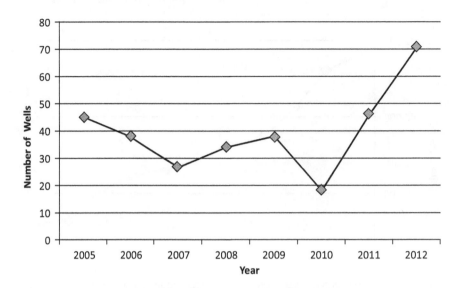

Figure 6.3 Number of exploratory oil wells in Argentina, 2005–2012
Source: IAPG

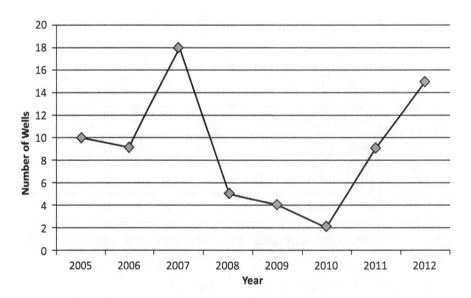

Figure 6.4 Number of exploratory natural gas wells in Argentina, 2005–2012
Source: IAPG

to increase production significantly. Overall, beyond these short-term fluctuations, the general level of this variable suggests a strong lack of incentives to invest in the sector.

3   **Reversion of international trade balance in gas: from surplus to deficit**. Both the decrease in domestic production and the increase in the domestic demand for natural gas led to the reversion of the trade surplus that existed by the early 2000s, turning it soon into a deficit.

Figure 6.5 shows indeed a steady increase (only interrupted by the international financial crisis in 2008–2009) in natural gas consumption. The increase between 2002 and 2012 is in the order of 48%. As stated above, these figures suggest that the immediate consequence would be the reversion of the trade surplus in gas into a deficit, confirmed in Figure 6.6 below.

The dynamics of the trade deficit in the last figure is a key aspect of the domestic natural gas sector in Argentina after the 2002 crisis. Especially after 2006, exports decreased to almost zero in 2011 and 2012 (they are not exactly zero just because of the pre-committed sales to Chile). Imports, on the other hand, have steadily increased since 2008 until 2012. The trade deficit in physical volumes is 43% higher than the peak of the trade surplus in 2004.

4   **Government intervention on producer prices (lower than international prices)**. As early as February 2002 President Duhalde's administration set export taxes on oil and gas by decree[8] (see fact 6 below). Several other policy decisions also introduced tight restrictions regarding the capability of selling oil and gas abroad. In a sense, several of these policy decisions implied a

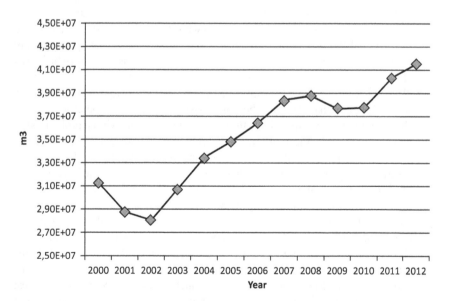

Figure 6.5 Natural gas domestic consumption in Argentina, 2000–2012

Source: Secretary of Energy

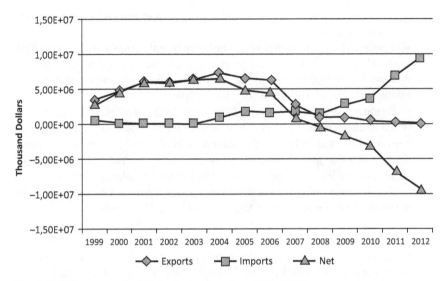

Figure 6.6 Natural gas trade balance in Argentina, 1999–2012

Source: IAPG

complete departure from the policy implemented by the Menem administration in the '90s, which included market deregulation and privatization of
YPF.[9] These interventions have implied a departure of domestic prices for oil
and gas from international prices, at least until the 2008 crisis and later.

Figure 6.7 shows that, after two years with domestic prices higher than the
international WTI spot price reference, since 2004 the latter was systematically
above the domestic one, except for the international crisis years (which was
clearly a transitory event). In the natural gas case the difference is even more
clear; at least since 2007, the estimated import price from Bolivia[10] is at least 2.5
(typically, more than 3) times the volume-weighted average domestic price, as
shown in Figure 6.8. This price difference, combined with a virtual prohibition to
export gas (given by the domestic-market priority rule introduced in 2004) seems
to partially explain the decrease in domestic production and the low level of
investment exploration within the period in which YPF was still private (mainly,
until 2010, as seen above). Given that economic costs include some measure of
opportunity costs, in this case by import prices, then such a regulation strongly
would lead to very high costs and low profits, as Navajas (2006) and Scheimberg
(2007 and 2011) state, and unlike what other papers such as Kozulj (2005) state.[11]
If one accepts that profitability is key to understand incentives to invest then this
may help explain the lack of investment in recent years. A recent paper by Barril
and Navajas (2015) reinforces this view through a model-based econometric test
to study the determinants of the decline in production, using a panel-data set at
the area level from 2004 through 2009. That paper explains the rate of growth in
natural gas production as a function of different variables, including the ratio of
cumulative production to resource size, exploration investment effort and some

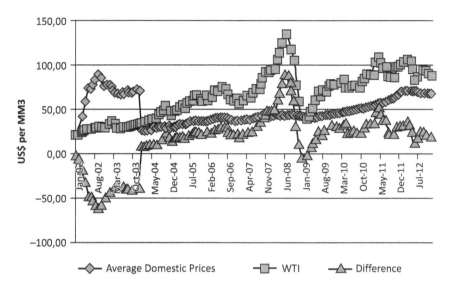

Figure 6.7 WTI monthly spot prices and volume-weighted average oil domestic prices for Argentina, 2002–2012

Sources: EIA and Secretary of Energy

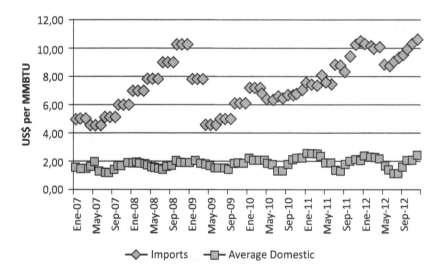

Figure 6.8 Natural gas prices: imports from Bolivia and average domestic producer prices

Sources: Hidrocarburos Bolivia and Secretary of Energy

concession-renegotiation dummies. One of their main results is that an increase of 1% in the ratio of cumulative production to resource size implies a 20% decrease in the rate of growth of natural gas. The extension of the concession given to the company Pan American Energy in 2007 by the government of the Chubut province also explains a significant increase in the rate of growth of gas for that specific company. *Ceteris paribus* this concession implies a 39% increase in the growth rate. These and other results induce the authors to suggest that such a decline can be attributed mostly to "depressed economic incentives" on intra-marginal reserves and depressing also incentives to invest.

5   **Natural gas tariffs (for final demand) much below the import prices (implying high levels of subsidies).** Since the 2002 crisis, the government kept tariffs for final use in the natural gas markets clearly below different measures of opportunity costs, mainly, those based on import prices. Hancevic et al. (2016) estimated such differences, which are illustrated in the next figure.

In Figure 6.9 the diamond-dotted line shows the upward evolution of the import price of natural gas from Bolivia. The square-dotted and triangle-dotted lines show the evolution of tariffs for final users in the city of Buenos Aires and the metropolitan area (the Greater Buenos Aires area). For the 2008–2010 tariffs the observation corresponds to the upper scale of use (more than 1,800 cubic meters per year). Even for such intensive users of gas (some which correspond to the upper decile of the income distribution in this area) the price paid is way below the cost of importing it. This is the origin of the increasing value in the subsidies that the government had to pay to gas distributors as a compensation for such price disparity.[12]

6   **No major changes in taxation on the upstream of oil and gas.** Regarding taxation on this sector, upstream companies face two separate types of fiscal costs. The first corresponds to the regular taxes applied to all businesses. The

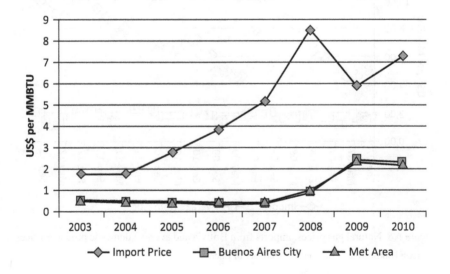

Figure 6.9 Natural gas prices: imports from Bolivia and tariffs for final use in the city of Buenos Aires and its metropolitan area

Source: Hancevic et al. (2016)

main ones are corporate income taxes (with a flat tax rate of 35%), value-added taxes (a flat rate of 21%) and a tax on major shareholder assets. The first two are the most important regarding impact on fiscal revenues. However, until 2006 there has been no differentiated treatment towards oil and gas companies regarding the application of those taxes. In that year the government released Act 26154 with the intention of providing investment and production incentives to the sector. Such incentives included a faster accounting-based capital depreciation for computing the corporate income tax base and also faster reimbursement of VAT retentions, among others. However, according to tax law experts, this act never was effectively applied.[13] The evidence above (especially in Figures 6.1–6.4) confirms this absence of any relevant reaction towards this particular tax policy measure. The second source of fiscal cost for companies comes from royalties. In the 1990s the Menem's Administration released Act 24145 (1992). According to the latter, the ownership of oil, gas and minerals passed from its original national domain to the provinces. The constitutional reform in 1994 confirmed this reform. This implied that the provinces were now the state levels receiving royalty revenues, not the national one. However, the same legislation confirmed the royalty rate that was in the old regime (12% over output value at domestic prices) and, since then, such rate has not been not modified.[14] Thus, there has been no relevant reform regarding the fiscal cost imposed on upstream oil and gas companies coming from royalty rate changes. As stated in fact 4, during the crisis following the abandonment of the pegged or fixed exchange rate in January 2002, the government in that year implemented tax reforms to increase its revenues. One of them was the introduction of a tax on oil exports. Initially the tax rate was a flat 20% independent of the value of exports. However, in 2004 the government changed this tax introducing a stepwise tax rate regime, up to a maximum of 45%, as a function of the international price of a barrel. The increase in the rate was three percentage points per each $2 increase in the price. In 2007 the government set a completely contingent tax rate that implied a price cap of the barrel of $60.9. However, such export tax is currently (at least, since 2010) not very relevant, given the low volume of oil exports (corresponding to oil types not used for the distilling process to get gasoline and other type of fuels). In sum: this brief summary shows that taxation legislation changes in oil and gas has not shown to have an important impact on investment and extraction decisions. This was mainly due to government decisions implying almost null changes in the fiscal costs for those companies. Royalty rates did not change. Corporate income tax and VAT rates remained also unchanged. Export taxes became important but also for a limited period of years. In summary, as stated below and especially since 2010, other regulations were more relevant to understand the production, investment and trade balance negative performances in the sector.

These six facts characterize key variables (regulated prices and tariffs, production, energy consumption and investment) of the oil and gas sectors in Argentina after the abandonment of the convertibility regime. For several authors who studied them in more detail some of those facts constitute a clear unsustainability problem regarding the long-run performance of this sector. Also, for critics of the administration who decided such policies these facts show some form of "irrationality", based on those sustainability issues. The question is whether it is possible to at least qualitatively interpret or explain part of those facts. The model presented in the next section is an attempt to do so.

3 Making sense of regulations: a dynamic political-economy agency model of state intervention in the gas market

While several pieces of work in the related literature focused on the link between regulations and performance in these sectors, it seems harder to explain a possible rationale for the implementation of such regulations. Indeed, in the context of the first decade of the 21st century, the part of the popular press that showed criticisms against such regulations qualified them as "energy populism". Would it be possible to explain such "populism" from a political-economy perspective? This section introduces a first answer through an intertemporal theoretical model from Kawamura (2016) to understand the potential driving forces behind the type of the state intervention observed in the gas sector and, less strongly, in the oil sector. The model's assumptions mainly reflect institutionally relevant features of those two markets partially collected in the last section.

3.1 The set-up

Consider an economy lasting for an infinite number of periods dated as $t=0, 1, \ldots$. In each period there exists several types of decision-makers, described as follows:

3.1.1 Domestic households

Consumers care for leisure and two goods: energy and an internationally tradable *numeraire* good denominated in dollars, called the *consumption* good from here on. There is a third good not consumed by agents, an internationally tradable commodity whose units are also denominated in dollars, called the *exported commodity*. Each consumer receives two endowments in each period t: one unit of labor time and a random amount ξ_t of the exported commodity. The endowment of the commodity follows some exogenous (stochastic) process where its minimum realization $\underline{\xi}$ is assumed to be strictly positive. For simplicity, suppose that the consumer can work as much as she wants and produce the consumption good using a linear production with a stochastic productivity (equal to the market wage) given by ω_t. Assume that the minimum value of this wage $\underline{\omega}$ is also strictly positive. The price of energy in dollars is denoted as π_t. The model assumes that the consumer's preference is represented by the following expected utility function:

$$E_0 \left\{ \sum_{t=0}^{\infty} \beta^t \left[\frac{(Z_t)^{1-\frac{1}{\varepsilon}}}{1-\frac{1}{\varepsilon}} + \frac{c_t^\alpha l_t^{1-\alpha}}{\alpha^\alpha (1-\alpha)^{1-\alpha}} \right] \right\} \tag{1}$$

where z_t is the consumption of energy, l_t is the consumption of leisure and c_t is the quantity of the consumption good. Here the assumption is that $0 < \beta < 1$, $\varepsilon > 1$ and $0 < \alpha < 1$. Consumers pay a tax on the endowment of the exported commodity, whose rate is τ_t. Consumers cannot save nor borrow. Thus, the problem of each consumer in each period t is to choose (z_t, l_t, c_t) to maximize each term in (1) subject to the following budget constraint:

$$\pi_t z_t + c_t = (1-\tau_t)\xi_t + \omega_t(1-l_t) \tag{2}$$

The solution for the energy demand function is

$$z^d(\pi_t, \omega_t) = \frac{\omega_t^{\varepsilon(1-\alpha)}}{\pi_t^{\varepsilon}} \tag{3}$$

Consumers have an active role in the political process[15] that implicitly determines the regulations. At the beginning of each period consumers decide (through an implicit voting mechanism) which politician (bureaucrat) in power or replaces her for a different one (although with the same characteristics). The binary choice reduces to either re-elect the incumbent or to choose another one out of the outside pool. Consumers derive an intrinsic periodic utility $\chi^e > 0$ from replacing a bureaucrat with a new one. This assumption comes directly from Yared (2010) and captures aversion to political persistence.

3.1.2 Downstream energy producer

Energy is supplied by a regulated monopoly.[16] The unique downstream firm faces a production function for z_t given by:

$$z_t(y_t^L; y_t^m) = \begin{cases} y_t^L & \text{if } z_t \le y_t^L \\ y_t^L + y_t^m & \text{if } z_t > y_t^L \end{cases} \tag{4}$$

In expression (4) the variable y_t^L denotes the quantity of a non-renewable resource bought to the upstream firm (both of them are described below) while y_t^m is the quantity of the same resource imported from abroad. Thus, production function (4) states first that there is a one-to-one relationship between the resource and the final quantity of energy produced by the downstream. Second, such produced energy is obtained with domestic resource extraction only when total energy production (and consumption) is less than or equal to the quantity of the domestic resource. On the contrary, when total energy to be produced exceeds domestic resource extraction then imports are needed to cover the difference. International price for the resource is equal to p_t. This price is the relevant reference for the upstream firms, and it is also the price of resource imports when needed. Thus the minimum cost function for the downstream company is obviously piecewise linear in z_t:

$$C^D(z_t; p_t) = \begin{cases} \bar{p}_t z_t & \text{if } z_t \le y_t^L \\ \bar{p}_t y_t^L + p_t[z_t - y_t^L] & \text{if } z_t > y_t^L \end{cases} \tag{5}$$

This minimum cost function states that the marginal cost of production is exactly the regulated domestic price of the resource domestically extracted if and only if the amount of energy to be served is below the quantity of that domestic resource. Otherwise, the marginal cost is the international price of the resource. This technology suggests that the government's upstream-market regulations may affect the downstream regulated energy monopoly.[17] The latter produces energy with the technology (4) to satisfy the consumers demand of energy given by (3).

3.1.3 The upstream firms

In each period there is a large number of a unique type of (upstream) firms. Risk-neutral shareholders are the owners of upstream firms. The latter produce an international-tradable *natural*, possibly *exhaustible*, *resource*, whose main use is the production of energy (either within the country or abroad). The specific technology of the upstream firm comes is taken directly from Deacon (1993)[18] chosen for the quantitative exercise performed in that paper. Let x_t be the quantity of the variable input and R_t the stock of available reserves at the beginning of period t. Then the following production function represents the upstream firm technology:

$$\zeta F(x_t, R_t) \tag{6}$$

with

$$F(x, R) = x^\mu R^{1-\mu} \tag{7}$$

where the parameter μ, the share of the variable input in total output, is positive and less than one. That is, the resource production function within the economy is constant-return-to-scale Cobb-Douglas with respect to reserves and the input. The latter represents all possible material inputs and labor used in the extraction of the resource. The term ζ denotes the total factor productivity in the production function. In this basic version it is assumed to be constant. On the other hand, available reserves in period t is an increasing function of the cumulative drilling up to that date and decreasing in cumulative production. Reserves in period t equals the cumulative reserve additions up to that date less cumulative production. Using Deacon's notation, let W_t be the cumulative drilling and Y_t be the cumulative output (extracted resources). Thus the remaining reserves follows the equation:

$$R_t = \Phi(W_t) - Y_t \tag{8}$$

where

$$\Phi(W) = \Gamma.(1 - \exp(-\gamma W)) \tag{9}$$

where Γ and γ are strictly positive constants. The cumulative investment is in fact the addition of all exploration investment decisions made up to any period t.

Denote w_t as the exploration investment decision made at date t. Associated to this investment there is a drilling cost $D(w_t)$ expressed in dollars.

The latter is assumed to be equal to:

$$D(w_t) = w_t \tag{10}$$

This means that w_t not only expresses a physical quantity of investment effort but also a monetary amount, given the linearity of the cost function D. Given this investment effort, the evolution of W_t and Y_t through time are respectively:

$$W_{t+1} = W_t + w_t \tag{11}$$

$$Y_{t+1} = Y_t + \zeta x_t^\mu R_t^{1-\mu} \tag{12}$$

The upstream firm sells total production in potentially two markets. The first market corresponds to where the downstream firm demands the resource to produce *energy*. Thus, the variable y_t^L introduced in subsection 3.1.2 denotes the upstream firm production for domestic use. On these domestic sales, the upstream firm receives a price equal to $\bar{p}_t$. The latter is directly set by the government, as it is described below. Thus, the firm chooses y_t^L given the regulated price $\bar{p}_t$. If allowed, the upstream firm would also sell part of the output abroad, at the international price p_t. However, this possibility depends on the regulation that the government imposes regarding a priority rule for domestic sales. In each period the upstream firm decides the input quantity x_t and the investment amount w_t that maximizes the expected discounted profits, taking the foreign price of the resource good p_t, the regulated local price $\bar{p}_t$, the domestic sale restriction $\bar{y}_t$ and the price of the q_t input good as given. The model assumes that the prices (p_t, q_t) are also exogenous and stochastic, although both are always strictly positive.

The upstream-firm owner assumed to be risk neutral has a discount factor equal to β, the same one as that of consumers. Thus, the upstream firm chooses a plan $\{x_t, w_t\}_{t=0}^\infty$ $\{xt, wt\}CXJ$ that maximizes the expected discounted value of dollar profits until depletion of the reserves. The exact expression of such profits is presented below after introducing the government policy decisions (since these decisions affect the explicit form of the upstream firm's profit function). Also, as a consequence of the interaction between the upstream firm's decisions and the government's decisions, as well as the exogenous variables, there may exist an endogenous random date T (where at least one of the realizations may be infinite) in which resource reserves are completely exhausted. Thus, whenever T is finite then in periods $\{T + j\}_{j=1}^\infty$ reserves are equal to 0, i.e. $R_{T+j} = 0$, and so the upstream firm is shut down after reserves are exhausted.

3.1.4 Government decisions and upstream firm profits

This model assumes the existence of a (national-level) government run by one of many ex-ante identical politicians or bureaucrats, whose preferences depend on their own consumption of the numeraire good, denoted as g_t. The following expected utility function represents their preference:

$$E_0\left\{\sum_{t=0}^{\infty}\beta^t g_t\right\} \tag{13}$$

where the discount factor β is the same as that of the upstream firm owners and consumers. The government decides the final price of energy π_t and the price paid to the upstream producers of the input good for domestic sales, $\bar{p}_t$. Potentially the government could also set a tax rate on potential foreign sales (which becomes effective only when exports are positive). The model assumes that the government takes as given a rule that restricts that upstream firm's domestic sales which must satisfy first the whole domestic demand from the downstream energy producer. There is of course an implicit assumption that the government has the power to close down any upstream firm that intends to violate such rule. Thus, upstream firms can only export the remains of production after servicing the local demand. If production is below the local demand, then all domestic resource production goes to the downstream regulated monopoly. On the other hand, given that the government directly sets the price of energy, it must compensate the energy producer when the latter incurs losses. Let S_t denote the dollar amount of compensation (subsidies) paid by the government to the energy producer. The latter satisfies:

$$s_t = \max\{(p_t - \pi_t)z_t^d(\pi_t,\omega_t)-(p_t - \bar{p}_t)y_t^L; 0\} \tag{14}$$

where $z_t^d(\pi_t,\omega_t)$ satisfies equation (3). Subsidies are defined as total costs of producing the total quantity of energy demanded, $z_t^d(\pi_t,\omega_t)$, minus revenues. Subsidies become potentially positive when charging a low value π_t of the energy price to consumers compared to the value of importing the quantity of the resource (the excess of resource use over the local production y_t^L) at a higher (international) price, p_t. Thus, there is an implicit rule stating that subsidies are active as long as the downstream firm incurs losses.[19] Finally, the government taxes a fraction $T_t \in$ (0, 1) of each consumer's commodity endowment.

Thus, the period-t budget constraint relevant for the national government's incumbent in period t is

$$g_t = \tau_t \xi_t - S_t \tag{15}$$

If the incumbent is finally kicked out of power in a given period t, the former sets the policy variables so as to obtain a maximum consumption in period t. These decisions include the confiscation of positive profits that the downstream firm may get given the price π_t^{out} set by the exiting incumbent. In that period the latter gets a utility loss of $\dfrac{x^N(1-\beta)}{\beta} > 0$ in addition to the loss of future rents (consumption).

On the other hand, the expelled incumbent gets a total utility loss of $\frac{\chi^g}{1-\beta}$.

The government decisions, together with assumptions on the exogenous variables and parameters introduced below, imply that, in equilibrium, y_t^L is strictly less than z_t in every period t. In other words, upstream firms will just produce in equilibrium only to satisfy the local demand. Therefore, in such an equilibrium

$$y_t^L = \zeta x_t^\mu R_t^{1-\mu} \tag{16}$$

Thus, export taxes become non-existent here. All these conditions allow writing the (equilibrium) period-t profit for the upstream firm as

$$\Pi_t \equiv \bar{p}_t \zeta x_t^\mu R_t^{1-\mu} - q_t x_t - w_t \tag{17}$$

Given the objective of the upstream firm, as long as exports are zero in the analyzed equilibrium, then the government may affect production and investment decisions by the upstream firm only through the regulated domestic prices $\{\bar{p}_t\}_{t=0}^\infty$. Thus, the optimality problem set-up can be written as follows. Let

$$s_t \equiv (\xi_t, \omega_t, p_t, q_t) \tag{18}$$

be the state vector of exogenous shocks. Whenever T becomes the last period with positive reserves then the firm solves a static profit-maximization problem

$$V_T^u(s_T, R_T, \bar{p}_T) = \max_{x_T \in \mathbb{R}_+} \left\{ \bar{p}_T \zeta_T x_T^\mu R_T^{1-\mu} - q_T x_T \right\} \tag{19}$$

whose solution is equal to

$$V_T^u(s_T, R_T, \bar{p}_T) = \left[\left(\frac{\mu}{q_T} \right)^\mu \zeta_T \bar{p}_T \right]^{\frac{1}{1-\mu}} (1-\mu) R_T \tag{20}$$

The right-hand side of (20) is the textbook-standard maximum profit function out of a Cobb-Douglas technology with a fixed factor, reserves R_T. For the other dates $t < T$ the upstream firm's problem can be written recursively[20] as:

$$V_t^u(s_t, R_t, \bar{p}_t) \tag{21}$$

$$= \max_{(x_t, w_t) \in \mathbb{R}_+^2} \left\{ \bar{p}_t \zeta_t x_t^\mu R_t^{1-\mu} - q_t x_t - w_t + \beta \mathrm{E}_t [v_{t+1}^u(s_{t+1}, R_{t+1}, \bar{p}_{t+1})|t+1 < T] \right.$$

$$\left. + \beta \mathrm{E}_t [V_T^u(s_T, R_T, \bar{p}_T)|t+1 = T] \right\}$$

The first line of the right hand side in (21) represents the period-t profits or cash-flows, constructed as total domestic sales minus variable costs (associated with the use of the variable input, x_t) and the investment in new drilling, w_t. The following term of the right-hand side in (21) denotes the expected discounted values of cash-flows provided that reserves are not exhausted in the following period. The last term on the right-hand side in (21) denotes the expected discounted values of cash-flows provided that reserves are exhausted in the following period. This Bellman's equation is one of the key basis to characterize the upstream-firm equilibrium decisions in an equilibrium.

3.2 The political game

The interaction between consumers, producers and the government is summarized in a (repeated) game whose main features come from the sustainable taxation literature in macroeconomics.[21] The particular elements of this model correspond to the dynamic extension of the well-known agency models à la Ferejohn (1986), including the recent work by Yared (2010) and Acemoglu et al. (2010 and 2011). The particular timing chosen here is taken directly from Yared (2010). The sequence of actions within any period t is as follows:

- At the beginning of the period, and after observing the realizations of exogenous variables and the history of all endogenous variables, domestic consumers choose to re-elect the incumbent government or else a different one.
- After the election stage, the incumbent politician in power chooses regulation variables and tax rates.
- Given regulatory and tax policies, markets open and consumers and upstream firm owners make their respective decisions.
- Whenever is applicable, government replacement takes place at the end of the period.

Under this within-period timing, the government faces the decision of investing in political reputation for period $t + 1$ on or just decide to extract as much surplus as possible provided that at the end of the period she will be removed from power. Hence, this timing implies that in every period t the bureaucrat in power wishing to stay sets values for the policy variables that provide incentives to consumers to vote again for her at the beginning of period $t + 1$. At the same time, for this re-election to be rational for the bureaucrat such policy must give her more utility value of remaining in power than of being expelled from office. These constraints can be formalized as follows. Suppose that the incumbent does not follow what will be the equilibrium choices of policy variables, implying she will not be re-elected. In this last case, consumers perceive that any new incoming bureaucrat would also deviate from the equilibrium policy, thus obtaining

$$v^{out}(p,\omega) = \frac{\frac{1}{(\varepsilon-1)}\left(\frac{\omega(1-\alpha)}{p}\left(\frac{\varepsilon-1}{\varepsilon}\right)\right)^{\varepsilon-1} + \omega^{\alpha}}{1-\beta} \qquad (22)$$

Therefore, the function v^{out} denotes the utility that consumers get when all possible bureaucrats deviate from the choices that allow their own re-election. Consumers, then, choose re-electing the incumbent as long as the total expected utility from re-electing the incumbent (denoted as v) in next period is at c least as high as v^{out}

plus the total intrinsic utility of bureaucrats' turnover, $\dfrac{x^c}{1-\beta}$. The last condition can be recursively written as:

$$v(s') \geq v^{out}(p',\omega') + \frac{x^c}{1-\beta} \qquad (23)$$

for every possible s', and where the prime used on states is equivalent to the next-period. On the other hand, the incumbent government's value of deviating from the choices that ensure re-election must satisfy

$$v^{g,out}(p,\xi,\omega) = \max_{\tau} \; \tau\xi = \xi \qquad (24)$$

In this setting, incumbents "betraying" their voters collect as much revenue as possible. Of course, this implies zero subsidies paid to the downstream monopoly as a necessary condition. Yet, it also implies full tax on commodity endowments. Thus, to ensure that the incumbent wants to be re-elected the next-period value of the latter, $V^g(s', v'(s'))$, must be at least as high as the value of deviating from that choice, $V^{g,out}$, subtracting the cost of being removed from the government from the next period on, $\dfrac{x^g}{1-\beta}$ The last condition can be written as:

$$v^g(s',v'(s')) \geq v^{g,out}(p',\xi',\omega') - \frac{x^g}{1-\beta} \qquad (25)$$

for every future state s'. The incumbent's problem can be recursively written as:

$$v^g(s,v(s)) = \max_{\tau,\Pi,\bar{p},(v(s'))_{s'}} \left\{ \tau_t\xi_t - s_t + \beta\sum_{s'\in s} v^g(s',v(s'))Q(s,s') \right\} \qquad (26)$$

with S_t given by (14) and where the maximization is subject to the constraint that total utility for consumers (voters) must satisfy:

$$v(s) = \frac{1}{(\varepsilon-1)}\left(\frac{\omega^{(1-\alpha)}}{\Pi}\right)^{\varepsilon-1} + \omega^\alpha + \frac{\xi(1-\tau)}{\omega^{1-\alpha}} + \beta\sum_{s'\in s} v(s')Q(s,s') \qquad (27)$$

and the inequalities (23) and (25). The optimization problem in (26) states that the maximum utility value for the bureaucrat depends on policies that determine the utility value delivered to consumers. Constraint (27) states that the total present and future value for consumers is equal to the contemporaneous consumer's welfare (the first three terms on the right-hand side) plus the discounted expected values from the next-period on, which is summarized in the last term on the right-hand side of (27).

3.3 The equilibrium notion

Given the within-period timing presented in the subsection above, and the absence of asymmetries of information in the model, then the basic equilibrium notion follows very closely that in Yared (2010), which is a variant of that in papers like Acemoglu et al. (2010b). Provided that the interaction between policymakers (politicians), consumers and producers is repeated through time, then such an equilibrium considers not only the realization of all stochastic variables up to period t but also the history of decisions made by policymakers, consumers and producers from period 0 up to that date t. That history of decisions is usually referred as the history of play, using basic repeated game terminology. The equilibrium concept then specifies plans of decisions for each relevant agent (present and future) such that for every possible history of play the continuation plans are individually optimal. More specifically, the following definition provides details on such equilibrium concept.

Definition 1 *A self-enforcing equilibrium is a plan of governments* $\{\tau^{x^*}, \tau^*, \bar{p}^*, \Pi^*\}$, *a plan of output, investment and input use by upstream firms* $\{y^*, w^*, x^*\}$, *a plan far consumers* $\{z^*, c^*, l^*\}$ *and random period* T^* *such that:*

(1)   after every history of decisions onpolicies and private decisions, each plan maximizes each agent's utility value from that stage onwards, subject to incentive constraints in the case of politicians and consumers;
(2)   at the random date T^*, reserves are equal to 0 from that period onwards.

The expression *self-enforcing* in the equilibrium concept refers to the incentive constraints (23) and (25) that plans must satisfy. Relative to the literature, this definition adds to the equilibrium concept in the above-mentioned papers by Yared (2010) and Acemoglu et al. (2010b) the random period T^* when reserves are exhausted. The incentive constraints ensure that the plans in the equilibrium are free of "time inconsistency" issues. In other words, this equilibrium notion in this model captures some dimensions of well-known (complex) political processes that characterize several emerging markets countries such as Argentina, considered relevant for the analysis of state intervention in the exhaustible-resources sector. It is a concept that allows rationalizing the values of regulation policies as the result of the political interaction presented in this paper.

4   Self-enforcing equilibrium characterization with no exports, positive imports and positive subsidies

This section characterizes the self-enforcing equilibrium when the upstream firm does not export in any given period t. As stated in the introduction, this type of equilibrium in fact reflects mainly the features of the natural gas and a possible future oil market in Argentina. Of course, the 0-export condition is part of a self-enforcing equilibrium when several conditions over exogenous variables hold. Those conditions are provided also in this section.

4.1 Upstream firm's optimal choice under no exports

The equilibrium begins by the characterization of the optimal plan decided by each upstream firm. The following proposition characterizes the solution to this problem (all proofs are in Kawamura 2016).

Proposition 1 *Suppose a self-enforcing equilibrium with 0 – exports. Thus the optimal policies by each representative firm are given by the following equations: for period T*[22]

$$x_T = R_T \left[\frac{\mu \xi_T \bar{p}_T}{q_T} \right]^{\frac{1}{1-\mu}} \tag{28}$$

and for periods t < T

$$x_t = R_t \left[\frac{\xi [\mu \bar{p}_t - \wedge_t]}{q_t} \right]^{\frac{1}{1-\mu}} \tag{29}$$

where

$$\wedge_t \equiv \beta \left\{ E_t \left[\frac{q_{t+1} x_{t+1}}{R_{t+1}} | t+1<T \right] + E_t \left[\frac{q_T x_T}{R_T} | t+1 = T \right] t + 1^R T \right\} \tag{30}$$

The optimal level of investment w_t in any self-enforcing equilibrium is given in the following expression.

$$wt = -w_t + \frac{1}{\Upsilon} \ln \frac{\beta(1-\mu)\Gamma\Upsilon}{(1-\beta)\mu} + \frac{1}{\Upsilon} \ln \wedge_t \tag{31}$$

Finally, in period T the following condition must hold:

$$\left[y_T - \Gamma \left[1 - \frac{\Gamma\Upsilon\beta E_{T-1} \left[\frac{q_T x_T}{R_T} \right]}{1-\beta} \right] \right] \left[1 - \xi^{\frac{1}{1-\mu}} \left[\frac{\mu \bar{p}_T}{q_T} \right]^{\frac{u}{1-\mu}} \right] \geq 0. \tag{32}$$

Several comments are worth making regarding the upstream firm equilibrium decision. Period *T* corresponds to that in which reserves are exhausted. The exhaustion condition in inequality (32) states that the accumulated production exceeds the accumulated investments. These are sufficient conditions to provide no incentives to invest in this last period. By that date, the equilibrium use of the variable input becomes a textbook-standard demand function from a Cobb-Douglas technology – equation (28) – coming from the standard equality between the value of its marginal product and the input price.

For periods before the exhaustion of the resource (*t < T*) the demand for the input not only depends on the current values of the TFP shock and prices (including the price of the resource set by the government) but also on the variable $\wedge_t$, whose value depends on expectations of *future* values of those same prices and TFP shocks (but not on present ones). Variable $\wedge_t$ is equal to the discounted expected per-unit-of-reserve variable cost in the following period. Equation (29) is obtained from a first-order condition that is a variant of the well-known Hotelling rule.[23] It relates the price-marginal-cost difference of two consecutive periods. However, it explicitly takes into account the fact that reserves could be exhausted in the next period – which is given by the second expression within brackets in equation (30). Given the presence of randomness in the model, such possibility cannot be ruled out (and it should even have positive probability, at least for t not too small).

On the other hand, given the particular assumptions on technology used here, the optimal investment decision depends on the accumulated investment spending W_p, as well as on the variable Λ_t described above. On the one hand this feature is consistent with the view about the dependence of the investment in natural resources to future "perceived macroeconomic risk" and future "perceived political risk", as discussed in, e.g., Navajas et al. (2005). Also, this dependence combined with a constant-return-to-scale technology, a lack of commitment by the incumbent and the lack of access to public debt makes the decision on export taxes independent on the investment behavior. The domestic price set in a given period t could have only affected the investment decision in $t-1$, but the incumbent takes such investment already as given. If the incumbent government had partial commitment for, say, one period ahead, then the decision in period t would also include one-period ahead tax rates, affecting the investment decision in the current period.

4.2 Self-enforcing-equilibrium tax and regulation policies

The next step is to present a characterization of the self-enforcing equilibrium policies, summarized in the following proposition:

Proposition 2 *In any self-enforcing equilibrium with no exports and both positive imports and subsidies the following statements characterize the major policy variables.*

(1) *For any period t:*

    (a) *the self-enforcing equilibrium price of energy* Π_t^* *follows the following law of motion:*

$$\Pi_t^* = \begin{cases} \overline{\pi}_t \equiv \left(\dfrac{\varepsilon}{\varepsilon - 1 - v_\nu^g \left(s, \dfrac{v^{out}(p,\omega) + x}{1-\beta} \right) \omega^{-(1-\alpha)}} \right) & ptif\ \pi_{t-1}^* > \pi_{Lt} \\[3em] \left[\dfrac{\varepsilon}{\left[\left(\dfrac{pt-1}{\pi t-1} - 1 \right)\varepsilon + 1 \right] \left(\dfrac{\omega_{t-1}}{\omega_t} \right)^{(1-\alpha)} + \varepsilon - 1} \right] & ptif\ \pi_{t-1}^* \in [\pi_{Lt}, \pi_{Ht}] \quad (33) \\[3em] \pi_t \equiv \left(\dfrac{\varepsilon}{\varepsilon - 1 - v_\nu^g (s, \overline{v}(s))\omega^{-(1-\alpha)}} \right) & ptif\ \pi_{t-1}^* < \pi_{Ht} \end{cases}$$

Where

$$\pi_{Lt} \equiv \frac{\varepsilon p_{t-1}}{\left[\varepsilon\left(\frac{pt}{\pi t}-1\right)+1\right]\left(\frac{\omega_t}{\omega_{t-1}}\right)^{(1-\alpha)}+\varepsilon-1}$$

$$\pi_{Ht} \equiv \frac{\varepsilon p_{t-1}}{\left[\varepsilon\left(\frac{pt}{\pi t}-1\right)+1\right]\left(\frac{\omega_t}{\omega_{t-1}}\right)^{(1-\alpha)}+\varepsilon-1} \quad and \; where \; -v_v^g\left(s,\frac{v^{out}(p,\omega)+x}{1-\beta}\right)$$

represents the government's marginal value of decreasing the consumer's total expected discounted welfare at the outside option value (i.e. when consumers are indifferent between reelecting the incumbent and not doing so), and also where $-V_v^g(s,\overline{v}(s))$ is the same marginal shadow value of when the incumbent is indifferent between continuing in power and not doing so.

(b) Let p_{max} be the maximum value that the resource international price p_t can take, and q be the minimum value that the variable input price q_t can take; furthermore assume that $0 < \delta < 1$, where δ is defined as:

$$\delta \equiv \beta\left[(1-\mu)\mu\left[\frac{\xi p \max}{q^\mu}\right]^{\frac{1}{1-\mu}}+1\right] \tag{34}$$

and assume that ω, χ^g and χ^c are sufficiently high; then the energy producer receives strictly positive subsidies with probability 1.

(c) For sufficiently high values of ω, the tax rate on the endowment τ_t^* is equal to 1.

(2) For histories s^t with $t = T^*$, then the self-enforcing-equilibrium domestic price $\overline{p}_T^*$ paid to the upstream firms equals μp_T

(3) For any period $t < T^*$, then the self-enforcing-equilibrium domestic price $\overline{p}_T^*$ paid to the upstream firms satisfies:

$$\overline{\overline{p}}-\mu\tilde{p}_t = \left\{\left[\left[(1-\mu)\xi^{\frac{\mu}{1-\mu}}\left(\frac{\overline{\overline{p}}_{t+1}}{q_{t+1}}\right)^{\frac{\mu}{1-\mu}}-1\right]\mu\tilde{p}_{t+1}+\overline{\overline{p}}_{t+1}\right.\right.$$

$$\left.-2(1-\mu)\mu\left[\frac{\xi\overline{\overline{p}}_{t+1}}{q_{t+1}^\mu}\right]^{\frac{1}{1-\mu}}\right|t+1<T^*\right\}$$

$$-\beta\xi(1-\mu)\mu^{\frac{2}{1-\mu}}E_t\left\{\left[\frac{p_T}{q_T^\mu}\right]^{\frac{1}{1-\mu}}\right|t+1=T^*\right\} \tag{35}$$

Where

$$\tilde{p}_t \equiv \mu p_t - \wedge_t$$

$$\tilde{\bar{p}} \equiv \mu \bar{p}_t^* - \wedge_t$$

and where Λ ,follows (30).

(4) *Imports are strictly positive in every period t where the values of ω_t and q_t and histories of endogenous variables up to t induce the inequality:*

$$y_t^L(qt,s^t) < z_t^d(\pi_t,\omega_t)$$

where s^t denotes the history embedded in available reserves in period t, $z_t^d(\pi_t,\omega_t)$ is as in (3), πt follows (33), and x_t satisfies (29).

(5) *The self-enforcing-equilibrium exhaustion period T^* is characterized by the minimum T such that*

$$\left[\sum_{j=1}^{T}(-1)^{j-1}\left(1-\frac{\beta(1-\mu)\Gamma\Upsilon}{(1-\beta)\mu}\wedge_{T-j}\right)\left[\Pi_{l=1}^{j}\left[\varsigma_{T-l}\left[\frac{\tilde{\bar{p}}_{T-l}}{q_{T-l}}\right]^{\mu}\right]^{\frac{1}{1-\mu}}\right]\right.$$

$$\left. + \frac{\Gamma\Upsilon\mu^2\varsigma\beta E_{T-1}\left[\left[\frac{p_T}{q_T^{\mu}}\right]^{\frac{1}{1-\mu}}\right]}{1-\beta} - 1\right]\left[1-\varsigma^{\frac{1}{1-\mu}}\left[\frac{\mu^2 P_T}{q_T}\right]^{\frac{\mu}{1-\mu}}\right] \geq 0 \quad (36)$$

In this equilibrium, the incumbent at the national government level never leaves office.

The last proposition presents the main characteristics of regulated prices in a self-enforcing equilibrium. A first salient feature is that a condition for positive subsidies includes sufficiently high values of the vector (χ^g,χ^c). The interpretation of this property is not too difficult to see. High values of such parameters induce the incumbent to maintain energy prices *low* enough in any given period to ensure re-election. Of course, sufficiently cheap energy ensures that consumers want to re-elect the incumbent for the next period. The higher are both χ^c and χ^g, the stronger is the effect on depressing energy prices to provide that re-election incentive.

Regarding the evolution of the self-enforcing-equilibrium energy prices π_t, a remarkable feature is the existence of (state-contingent) lower and upper bounds π and $\bar{\pi}$.[24] Clearly, such bounds come from the incentive constraints, one for the consumers formalized by inequality (23) and the other for the incumbent government, in inequality (25). Each threshold energy price π and $\bar{\pi}$ corresponds to values of exogenous variables such that either (23) or (25) binds. Interestingly, the middle expression in (33) states that, as long as the last period energy price is within the two current-period bounds, then the current-period price is increasing in the last-period price. This shows some (weak) tendency towards an increase in the price of energy, although this is subject to the condition of past prices within the bounds. This feature may be read as partially consistent with the evidence observed in Argentina after 2011.

The result of the tax rate on the exportable endowment being equal to 1 comes from both consumers' preferences and also the fact that consumers do not value the exportable commodity. Preferences determine that a marginal increase in the tax rate decreases the consumers' utility by an amount which, being proportional to the commodity endowment ξ, its absolute value is decreasing in the realized wage ω. On the other hand, given the linearity of bureaucrats' preferences, the period-t utility is obviously increasingly linear in the tax rate. In this case, a marginal increase in the tax rate is also proportional to that endowment. Thus, for the bureaucrat, a marginal increase in the tax rate on the one hand increases both his utility but on the other hand makes the incentive constraint for the consumers tighter (since it represents a decrease in their utility). However, with the assumption of the wage being high enough, then the first effect dominates the second. This implies that the net effect of increasing τ is always positive, thus providing the final result of full taxation of the exportable commodity (given that energy prices are low enough, and so compensating for this full taxation outcome).

A drawback from this equilibrium is that the domestic price of the natural resource is marginally independent of the price of the energy good. There are two aspects behind this independence result. On the one hand, bureaucrats are risk-neutral, and, on the other hand, the technology of energy production is also linear in the resource. The model introduced those two assumptions since they ensure a relatively simple characterization of the equilibrium law of motion of these prices. Admittedly, the prediction of an independence between those two prices may be at odds with the empirical evidence in Argentina.

5 Rationalizing facts on Argentina's oil and gas in the 2000s with the model results; some policy implications

Results of Proposition 2 are helpful to rationalize some of the facts presented in Section 2. Statement (1.b) presents a sufficient condition to understand what it may be behind the fifth fact, namely, that domestic energy price was much lower than the import price. Note that these sufficient conditions include a adequately high value of the endowment of the minimum realization of the commodity shock. The rationale for this result is as follows. High enough values of both χ^g and χ^c induce the bureaucrat to set very low energy prices to keep incentives for re-election, implying subsidies. For this to be a self-enforcing equilibrium the bureaucrat should get enough revenue from other sources. That revenue undoubtedly comes from commodity taxes. Thus, one way of rationalizing fact 5 is that regulations would keep energy prices low enough following electoral incentives, being that "sustained" by tax revenues from other commodities (i.e. tax on cereals exports such as soybean).

Statement 2 of Proposition 2 states that, at the exhaustion equilibrium date T^*, the price paid to domestic producers of the resource is strictly less than the international price given that $\mu < 1$, mimicking what is documented in fact 4. For earlier periods, equation (35) characterizes such domestic price. At first glance, this does not provide a straightforward condition to undoubtedly state whether the price for the domestic producer of the resource p-* is below the international price p_t. Nevertheless, the same equation suggests that a sufficient condition for it to hold before T^* is that the expectation of the net-of-expected-variable-cost future domestic price, p^*, is strictly greater than half of net international price, p^{t+1}, and less than or equal to that net international price multiplied by parameter μ. There are clearly less demanding conditions for p-* $< p_t$ to hold, but the last discussion at least gives a clear idea that such conditions between those two prices depends heavily on expectations about future domestic prices themselves.[25]

Statement 4 of Proposition 3 characterizes the conditions leading to positive resource imports in equilibrium, imports that have arisen in Argentina according to fact 3. Given the characterization of energy prices, a sufficient condition for such inequality to hold is a domestic resource price much lower than the input price q_t, i.e. a very low domestic-price-to-marginal-cost ratio. Part of this is consistent with fact 4, but given lack of reliable data on unit production cost, the precise inequality in statement 4 cannot be put under test properly. Yet, fact 4 emphasizes that part of the explanation of energy imports in Argentina is indeed the low incentive to produce, given the low domestic producer resource price.

What kind of policy (or institutional) implications do these results suggest? From a normative perspective, the answer would require the full characterization of the Pareto-efficient allocation, which is out of the scope of this chapter.[26] However, a broader intuition emerges directly from the model itself. The latter assumes that policymakers are selfish agents who consume units of the numeraire goods. In making decisions, the bureaucrat only takes into account political incentives coming from the interaction with consumers, who are responsible for electing the bureaucrat in charge of the government in every period. Bureaucrats have no explicit interest in the "long-run sustainability" of upstream production (extraction) of the non-renewable resource. The intuition then is that a more benevolent government may weigh the benefits of a possibly low domestic price paid to the upstream firms for the resources (and low expected future prices embedded in the variable Λ_t) in the short run with the cost of such policy to the upstream firm in the long run, especially concerning the features of the equilibrium exhaustion period T^*.

Paradoxically, the main proposition states that, if the goal were to reduce the amount of subsidies paid by the government, the parameter χ^g (or χ^c, or both) should not be "high enough". Thus, any "reform" inducing a lower value of such parameter may relax the government's incentives to keep the price of energy very low. However, as long as equilibrium subsidies paid by the government are still positive, then the latter policy may not affect the domestic price of the resource paid to upstream firms, at least when the "decrease" in the parameter value is marginal. This is because that domestic price only depends on exogenous variables and other parameters, not on χ^g. This also applies clearly to the exhaustion time T^*. Thus, in such equilibrium, no marginal change in policy can change the dynamics of the domestic price of the resource.

Therefore, the only possible relevant reform to analyze is a *discrete* change of the values of χ^g (and/or χ^c), so that in equilibrium subsidies may become null.[27] But then, the question would be about the type of such reform that meant that all potential bureaucrats in power have a lower intrinsic cost of not being re-elected. One possible guess on these concrete reforms may be a policy that guarantees to politicians in power that must leave the government a certain type of "compensation" to reduce that cost. Yet, this seems a very artificial interpretation since the parameter is independent on an amount of consumption that such policy implies. A more natural possible reform may include restrictions on the process to become elective candidates for government positions. Such restrictions should induce a change in the politicians selection process, a change that should point towards candidates that "signal" an intrinsic lower cost of leaving power. It is far from obvious what those signals would be. In fact this is part of a broader debate on political reforms that ensure a better "selection of politicians" that leads to better public policies in general (not only for the energy and non-renewable-resource sectors).

6 Concluding remarks

This chapter has presented the main facts about the dynamics of about production, investment and, especially, government regulations in the Argentine oil and gas sector between 2002 and 2011. It has also developed a theoretical intertemporal model to rationalize such regulations. The assumptions of the model partially reflect some of the distinctive features of those two sectors. Although very stylized in several dimensions, in terms of its results, the theoretical model, can qualitatively replicate several features of those regulations observed in Argentina. The model also predicts energy downstream prices below the import resource prices (consistent with the facts) as long as the threat of exclusion from power for the regulator is strong enough. Another prediction is that, with low enough resource-regulated prices relative to the variable input price then the economy imports resources from abroad. This prediction is consistent with the actual behavior of natural gas imports observed in Argentina after 2008. The model also predicts a forward-looking behavior for the domestic-producer price of the resource. This behavior is at least consistent with a decrease in investment coming from a perception of lower future (expected) prices of the resource. That is, this model would associate the decline in exploration investment seen in the data with an expected future decline in the resource domestic-market regulated prices.

Regarding policy and institutional implications, this model suggests that the major issue is to change government's incentives regarding price and quantities regulations in energy-related, non-renewable sectors. This goal demands several political reforms regarding how the political system selects candidates for elected government positions. In particular, how the electoral system favors either political turnover or political stability is not neutral relative to government incentives to keep prices too low. As discussed in Section 5, changes in the intrinsic cost of not being re-elected for the incumbent government may affect such incentives in subtle ways. It is important to keep producing further research to get a more precise answer about which type of electoral reforms may improve government regulations to induce a reversion in the decline of both investment and production.

As discussed in several parts of this paper, there is a lot of room for other extensions and improvements of this basic model. First, although the model can qualitatively predict the equilibrium behavior of different policy variables, it does not provide precise quantitative results to compare them with the quantitative aspects of the facts in Section 2. In particular, knowing how the equilibrium dynamics of resource and energy prices, as well as its effect on production, investment and the average duration of reserves, vary with the values of the incumbent's intrinsic cost of leaving power or the consumer's intrinsic benefit of political turnover parameters, may help energy-regulation designers to understand not only the qualitative types of changes in political constraints to implement but also more quantitative answers regarding such reforms.

Also, as stated in subsection 3.1.4, the subsidies considered on this model are compensations for the losses in which the energy monopoly incurs given the regulations on the energy price. Subsidies paid by the Argentine government in the gas sector after 2004 are somehow different. The targeted population (usually the poorest quantiles) receives a direct discount on the price of energy that they pay. Thus, it may be of interest to consider the same model as in this chapter but introducing his specific form of subsidies as a policy tool to analyze whether the behavior of such subsidies resembles that of the regulated energy prices of the current version of the model, or else there are important differences.

One major assumption in this model is the long-lived politician who in equilibrium never leaves power and that affects the way that government sets taxes and regulations. However, as different authors (such as Spiller and Tommasi 2003) stress, the political dynamics in Latin America is perceived as much more complex. That complexity may have different implications regarding the stability of different political actors. Spiller and Tommasi (2003) emphasize how bad incentives coming from the design of political systems may imply that politicians act as if they only care about the short run. Indeed, Manzano and Monaldi (2008) also stress this point applied specifically to the oil sector. Thus, different assumptions on preferences or different political types can be added to the benchmark model to deal with more complex political dynamics. However, such change in those assumptions is hardly free. More complex political dynamics may threaten the possibility of getting readable and policy-oriented results out of the modified model.

Another aspect is the exogeneity of the type of concession contracts assumed in this model. In reality, concession contracts are endogenous outcomes of auctions. A possible extension to the benchmark model then is to introduce an analysis of an auction mechanism, in the spirit of the analysis by Engel and Fisher (2010).[28] This modification may lead to regulations and taxes different from those in the current model, where the precise shape of those regulations may depend on the type of contract arising from that mechanism. Particularly important is the paper by Stroebel and van Benthem (2013). The latter develops a dynamic contracting problem taken from Thomas and Worrall (1994) and applied to non-renewable resources. The theoretical results regarding the contract design is tested using a Wood-Mackenzie dataset of hydrocarbon contracts, showing that the theoretical predictions are consistent with this evidence. Such an exercise may be embedded in the model here to get simultaneous results concerning regulations and contract features.[29]

Other relevant issues have been left out of the analysis. One of them is the relationship between corporate governance, regulation design and political incentives. This issue is basically motivated by the Argentine government's decision to re-nationalize YPF in 2012. This fact induces one to think that governance problems may start interacting in subtle ways with the policy and regulation decisions. In the benchmark model the owners of the upstream firms are risk neutral and unique for each firm. An extension would entail multiplier owners for the upstream firms, even with risk averse preferences instead of risk neutral. But then a possible problem[30] is the lack of a well-defined objective function for the upstream firm. With multiple risk-averse owners and incomplete financial markets there is usually disagreement about the relevant discount factor. The static general equilibrium with incomplete markets (GEI) literature solves this problem introducing voting mechanisms inside the firm. A dynamic model then demands an adaptation of such voting mechanism. A possible idea is to use an extension of the self-enforcing voting model in Maggi and Morelli (2006). In the latter the voting decision in each stage must be part of a perfect-equilibrium notion. This will clearly complicate the equilibrium characterization, but it could be useful to analyze such an interaction.[31]

Another venue for future research is the consideration of asymmetric information between the government and the voters. A first way of asymmetric information may come from the well-known model by Osmundsen (1998). The latter, assuming full commitment,[32] considers the optimal contract under asymmetric information, as well as the tax systems that implement such contract. The extension of the model in this paper would consider also an extension of Osmundsen's analysis from a two-period model to the infinite horizon case. A second and different way of considering asymmetric information comes from Ales et al. (2014). The latter adapts Yared (2010) to an asymmetric information environment, where there are multiple types of bureaucrats but the specific type is private information. This extension, unlike the original Yared's framework, explains political turnover. Thus, this extension seems very useful to adapt it to a non-renewable resource endogenous regulation (and taxation) problem to analyze the interaction between political turnover and regulation instability in this sector.[33]

Finally, a more recent issue opened in the Argentine gas and oil sector with the recent discovery of shale gas and shale oil reserves in the Vaca Muerta area, in the province of Neuquen. This new and unconventional source of gas seems to play a key role in the future regarding regulations in the gas sector. It is then a natural next step to extend the model to include this type of discoveries of new technologies. How the availability of these new technologies affect the incentives by the incumbent national-government politician to regulate the gas market in certain ways is an almost mandatory exercise to provide precise policy recommendations for the future gas sector.

Notes

* This chapter has been developed with the financial support of the Research Department of the Inter- American Development Bank. I deeply thank Fernando Navajas for the comments he gave me on the proposal of this paper. They helped a lot in terms of the modelling strategy. I also thank the coordinators, Andy Powell and Osmel Manzano, for their comments. The usual disclaimer applies.

1 For a historical perspective on these sectors, see Favaro (1992) and Gadano (2006 and 2010).

2 For example, by 1996 Argentina's oil production represented 16.4% of total oil production of South American countries (and 27.2% when excluding Venezuela from the sample), while ten years later Argentina's oil production represented only 10.4% of total South American oil production, according to the site of BP, www.bp.com.

3 See Kawamura (2016).

4 For comprehensive surveys on this literature, see the classic works by Heaps and Helliweel (1985) and the more recent by Lund (2010).

5 The classical treatment based on Hotelling's (1931) model is surveyed by Section 5 in Heaps and Helliweel (1985). Within this tradition we find Manzano's (2000) extension considering a "quality" dimension in the profit function applied to the analysis of the Venezuelan market. For the case of Argentina, Vera (2000) presents a Hotelling model to analyze two types of royalties: a sales-based tax and a long-run sustainable revenue tax system. The extension to stochastic environments includes Leland (1978), Campbell and Lindner (1985), Ball and Bowers (1983), Lund (1992) and Zhang (1997). Postali (2007) applies an explicit option pricing technique to analyze the impact of taxation on the petroleum sector in Brazil.

6 For an alternative empirical work on expropriation see Duncan (2006).

7 See mainly the chapters by Tomz and Wright (2010), Rigobón (2010) and Schwartz and Trolle (2010). In that book, Wernerfelt and Zeckhauser (2010) discuss several actions that firms can take to avoid expropriation (that may include a slower speed of production of the natural resource, as Bohn and Deacon [2000] predict). Also, Engel and Fisher (2010) analyze optimal auction design under the *threat* of expropriation. Aghion and Quesada (2010) provide a broader survey on contracts in the oil sector.

8 Decree 310/02. This decree was later complemented by several resolutions of the Secretary of Energy (Resolutions 337/04 and 394/07) introducing changes in the tax rate scale.

9 For surveys on these 1990s policies see Gadano (2006 and 2010), Roccaro and Fernandez (2006) and Scheimberg (2007). About the policy decisions after 2002 see Scheimberg (2011).

10 The data in Figure 6.8 includes quarterly estimates from the site HidrocarburosBolivia. com between 2007 and 2009 and unit values of gas imports from official data released by the Secretary of Energy. The lack of official data of gas exports from Bolivian sources force to provide such estimates (for a discussion, see Aguilar and Valdivia 2011).

11 Interestingly, this same author writes an article in 2012 arguing the necessity of adjusting tariffs upwards, neglecting in part his diagnosis made in 2005 (see Kozulj 20105 and Kozulj 2012).

12 Actually, Hancevic et al. (2016) estimate the amount of subsidies that final users received as a consequence of such tariff regulation. For example, they estimate that, in the 2008–2010, the upper decile of users received about US$102.5 million in implicit subsidies.

13 For a more complete description of tax regulation in this sector, see, e.g., Roccaro and Fernandez (2006). See also the discussion by Piffano (2003) on federal issues regarding oil and gas taxation.
14 For references on the treatment of royalties in Argentina see, e.g., Peralta et al. (2005).
15 Details on this process appear below.
16 Although historically the downstream market for gasoline and other oil-derived sources of energy presented some degree of competition (see, e.g., Serebrisky 2001), after 2003 the perception is that price is not the variable in which firms compete, given the strong degree of the intervention by the state to regulate the price. See also the empirical analysis by Petrecolla and Martínez (2008).
17 One possibly important issue is related to the way integration between downstream and upstream production is modelled. This may be important in the case of Argentina. However, the main point that the model answers does not seem to be strongly related to "transaction costs" that may arise in the relationship between the upstream and the downstream. To keep the model as simple as possible, and considering that such transaction costs problems may not be first order for this paper, the assumption is to consider two separate sectors for the upstream and the downstream.
18 Of course, there are other possible modeling options regarding the technology of resource extraction. For a more empirical approach to such technologies, see, e.g., Managi et al. (2006).
19 The definition of subsidies in equation (14) merits a warning. According to empirical evidence (see, e.g., Hancevic et al. 2016) the subsidies that gas companies receive are calculated as the difference between the import price and the domestic price of gas for final demand. In the notation of this paper, subsidies should be defined as $\tilde{s}_t \equiv \max\{0, (p_t - \pi_t)(z_t^d - y_t^L)\}$. In this case, the upstream firms would receive the final price π_t (paid by consumers) instead of p $\bar{p}_t$ This version of the model considers a slightly more general assumption of a government potentially paying a price to the resource-extracting upstream firms different from the final-demand energy price, even though the marginal productivity with respect to the resource in the downstream firm is equal to one. As it will be clear below, this seemingly more general assumption may lead to an empirically counterfactual result that prices received by upstream firms may not follow the same dynamics than the price of energy, which may be read as not realistic. The task of checking how results below may change with this adjutment in the subsidies definition is left for future research.
20 The expression "recursive" means the same as in the traditional "dynamic-programming" sense. This means that total expected discounted utilities can be written as functions of the current period state s_t. All on-equilibrium utility values mean total expected utilities from a given period on.
21 The type of game and the consequent equilibrium concept in this chapter is an extension to the well-known sustainable equilibrium developed by Chari and Kehoe (1990), Chang (1998), Phelan and Stacchetti (2001) and Fernández-Villaverde and Tsyvinski (2004), among others, based on the repeated-game-recursive framework developed by Abreu, Pierce and Stachetti (1990). In those papers the policy-maker is assumed to be benevolent, whereas in this model the policy-maker-regulator is a selfish (rent-seeking) politician. This adaptation allows studying "time-consistent regulation" within this particular framework.
22 The upperscript * is dropped for simplicity.
23 For an updated view of the uses of this rule, see, e.g., Gaudet (2007).
24 From a formal perspective, this double-threshold result is the analog of the bounds-on-the-income-tax result in Yared (2010).
25 Given that the stochastic terminal condition fore known from statement 2 of this proposition, it is possible that an iteration of the expectation on the right hand side of equation (35) would lead to the definitive answer. However, the problem is that such expression is highly non-linear, and thus such conditions can only be studied by means of numerical simulations.

26 In this multi-sector partial-equilibrium setting it is even not clear the relevant concept of Pareto efficiency, since that concept may not necessarily include the "welfare" of domestic producers.

27 However, in that type of equilibria, the price of the resource in the domestic market may become indeterminate. This issue is left for future research.

28 However, the original Engel and Fisher paper only deals with a mechanism design problem within a model of oil production much more stylized than in this paper. Thus, the possibility of extending the analysis by Engel and Fisher (2010) or even using part of the standard auction theory literature in this model may lead to a potential complexity that may not allow for analytical solutions.

29 Such extension endogenizing contracts seems important to understand recent news from the oil and gas sectors in Argentina about political declarations threatening private companies to unilaterally finish concession contracts. Such a threat is clearly absent in the model. Therefore, it would be an interesting extension of this model to introduce an assumption that the government can "kick the company out" of the concession. However, for this mechanism to become an interesting one for the model there are certain assumptions that need special consideration. For example, such an extension may need an assumption on what would be the alternative if a company is expelled from the industry. The assumption on this alternative is not obvious for the case of Argentina.

30 This problem is present in the traditional GEI literature with production.

31 A related issue is the presence of state-owned oil and gas companies. In such case the interaction between political incentives and regulation may be even more subtle. For an example of this discussion see Hartley and Medlock (2008).

32 As Osmundsen (1998) points out (an argument borrowed from Laffont and Tirole [1993]) the combination of both non-commitment and asymmetric information makes the characterization of the optimal contract less clear. This is the main reason of why Osmunden (1998) assumes perfect commitment.

33 Another information asymmetry dimension may be related to that in Acemoglu et al. (2010 and 2011). That model assumes that all politicians are identical but there are multiple types of consumers and these types are private information (to the consumer). This may become especially relevant when dealing with inequality issues, which were not covered in this paper.

References

Abreu, Dilip, David Pierce and Ennio Stacchetti. 1990. "Toward a Theory of Discounted Repeated Games With Imperfect Monitoring", *Econometrica*, 58, 1041–1063.

Acemoglu, Daron, Mikhail Golosov and Aleh Tsyvinski. 2010. "Dynamic Mirrlees Taxation Under Political Economy Constraints", *Review of Economic Studies*, 77, 841–881.

Acemoglu, Daron, Mikhail Golosov and Aleh Tsyvinski. 2011. "Political Economy of Ramsey Taxation", *Journal of Public Economics*, 95, 467–475.

Aghion, Phillippe and Luíca Quesada. 2010. "Petroleum Contracts: What Does Contract Theory Tell Us?" in Hogan, William and Federico Sturzenegger, eds., *The Natural Resources Trap: Private Investment Without Public Commitment*, pp. 47–60. MIT Press, Cambridge, MA.

Aguilar, Ruben and Daney Valdivia. 2011. *Bolivian Natural Gas Export Prices: Modeling and Forecast Pooling*, MPRA Working Paper No. 35485, Munich Personal RePEc Archive, Munich, Germany.

Ales, Laurence, Pricila Maziero and Pierre Yared. 2014. "A Theory of Political and Economic Cycles", *Journal of Economic Theory*, 153, 224–251.

Ball, Ray and John Bowers. 1983. "Distortions Created by Taxes Which Are Options on Value Creation: The Australian Resources Rent Tax Proposal", *Australian Journal of Management*, 8(2), 1–14.

Barril, Diego and Fernando Navajas. 2015. "Natural Gas Supply Behavior Under Interventionism: The case of Argentina", *The Energy Journal*, 36(4), 23–39.

Bohn, Henning and Robert Deacon. 2000. "Ownership Risk, Investment and the Use of Natural Resources", *American Economic Review*, 90, 526–549.

Campbell, H.F. and R. Lindner. 1985. "A Model of Mineral Exploration and Resource Taxation", *Economic Journal*, 95, 146–160.

Chang, Roberto. 1998. "Credible Monetary Policy in an Infinite Horizon Model: Recursive Approaches", *Journal of Economic Theory*, 81, 431–461.

Chari, V.V. and Patrick Kehoe. 1990. "Sustainable Plans", *Journal of Political Economy*, 98, 783–802.

Deacon, Robert. 1993. "Taxation, Depletion and Welfare: A Simulation Study of the U.S. Petroleum Resource", *Journal of Environmental Economics and Management*, 24, 159–187.

Duncan, Roderick. 2006. "Price or Politics? An Investigation of the Cause of Expropriation", *The Australian Journal of Agricultural and Resource Economics*, 50, 85–101.

Engel, Eduardo and Ronald Fisher. 2010. "Optimal Resource Extraction Contracts Under Threat of Expropriation", in Hogan, William and Federico Sturzenegger, eds., *The Natural Resources Trap: Private Investment Without Public Commitment*, pp. 161–196. MIT Press, Cambridge, MA.

Favaro, Orietta. 1992. "Territorio y petróleo: la intervención estatal en la industria petrolera. El caso Neuquén (1884–1955)", *Revista de Historia*, 3, 159–180.

Ferejohn, John. 1986. "Incumbent Performance and Electoral Control", *Public Choice*, 50, 5–25.

Fernandez-Villaverde, Jesus and Aleh Tsyvinski. 2002. "Optimal Fiscal Policy in a Business Cycle Model without Commitment", Working Paper, University of Pennsylvania, Philadelhpia, Pennsylvania.

Gadano, Nicolás. 2006. *Historia del Petrólea en la Argentina*, Buenos Aires, EDHASA.

Gadano, Nicolás. 2010. "Urgency and Betrayal: Three Attempts to Foster Private Investment in Argentina's Oil Industry", in Hogan, William and Federico Sturzenegger, eds., *The Natural Resources Trap: Private Investment Without Public Commitment*, pp. 369–404. MIT Press, Cambridge, MA.

Garnaut, Ross and Anthony Clunies Ross. 1975. "Uncertainty, Risk Aversion and the Taxing of Natural Resource Projects", *Economic Journal*, 85, 272–287.

Gaudet, Gérard. 2007. "Natural Resource Economics Under the Rule of Hotelling", *Canadian Journal of Economics*, 40, 1033–1059.

Gaudet, Gérard, Pierre Laserre and Ngo V. Long. 1995. "Optimal Resource Royalties With Unknown and Temporally Independent Extraction Cost Structures", *International Economic Review*, 36, 715–749.

Hancevic P., W. Cont y F. Navajas. 2016. "Energy Populism and Household Welfare", *Energy Economics*, 56, 454–474.

Hartley, Peter and Kenneth Medlock III. 2008. "A Model of Operation and Development of a National Oil Company", *Energy Economics*, 30, 2459–2485.

Heaps, Terry and John Helliwell. 1985. "The Taxation of Natural Resources", in Auerbach, Alan and Martin Feldstein, eds., *Handbook of Public Economics, Volume I*, pp. 421–472. North Holland, Amsterdam.

Hogan, William and Federico Sturzenegger. 2010. *The Natural Resources Trap: Private Investment Without Public Commitment*, MIT Press, Cambridge, MA.

Hotelling, Harold. 1931. "The Economics of Exhaustible Resources", *Journal of Political Economy*, 39, 137–175.

Kawamura, Enrique. 2016. *An Intertemporal Model of Endogenous Regulations on Energy-Related Non-Renewable Resource Sectors*, Working Paper, Universidad de San Andres, Buenos Aires, Argentina.

Kozulj, Roberto. 2002. "Balance de la privatización de la industria petrolera en Argentina y su impacto sobre las inversiones y la competencia en los mercados minoristas de combustibles", *Serie Recursos Naturales e Infraestructura No. 46*, ECLAC Santiago, Chile.

Kozulj, Roberto. 2005. "Crisis de la industria del gas natural en Argentina", *Serie Recursos Naturales e Infraestructura No. 88*, ECLAC Santiago, Chile.

Laffont, Jean-Jacques and Jean Tirole. 1993. *A Theory of Incentives in Procurement and Regulation*, Cambridge MA, MIT Press.

Leland, Hayne. 1978. "Optimal Risk Sharing and the Leasing of Natural Resources, with Application to Oil and Gas Leasing on the OCs", *Quarterly Journal of Economics*, 92, 413–438.

Lund, Diderik. 1992. "Petroleum Taxation Under Uncertainty: Contingent Claim Analysis With an Application to Norway", *Energy Economics*, 14, 23–31.

Lund, Diderik. 2010. "Rent Taxation for Non Renewable Resources", *Annual Review of Resource Economics*, 1, 287–307.

Maggi, Giovanni and Massimo Morelli. 2006. "Self-Enforcing Voting in International Organizations", *American Economic Review*, 96, 1137–1158.

Managi, Shunsuke, James J. Opaluch, Di Jin and Thomas A. Grigalunas. 2006. "Stochastic Frontier Analysis of Total Factor Productivity in the Offshore Oil and Gas Industry", *Ecological Economics*, 60, 204–215.

Manzano, Osmel. 2000. *Tax Effects Upon Oil Field Development in Venezuela*, Working Paper 2000–006, Massachusetts Institute of Technology, Center for Energy and Environmental Policy Research, Cambridge, MA.

Manzano, Osmel and Francisco Monaldi. 2008. "The Political Economy of Oil Production in Latin America", *Economía: Journal of the Latin American and Caribbean Economic Association*, 9, 59–98.

Navajas, Fernando. 2006. "'Energo Crunch' Argentino 2002–20XX", *Documento de Trabajo N° 89*, Fundación de Investigaciones Económicas Latinoamericanas, FIEL, Buenos Aires, Argentina.

Navajas, Fernando, Santiago Urbiztondo, Walter Cont and Ramiro Moya. 2005. *Inversión y eficiencia contractual: ¿Qué hace distintos a los recursos naturales? Teoría y evidencia para la Argentina*, Buenos Aires, Fundación YPF.

Osmundsen, Petter. 1998. "Dynamic Taxation of Non-Renewable Resources Under Asummetric Information About Reserves", *Canadian Journal of Economics*, 31, 933–951.

Peralta, María G., Andrea P. Abella and Juan F. Albarenque. 2005. "Tratamiento impositivo y jurídico de las regalías en la Argentina", *Petrotecnia* (Review of the *Instituto Argentino del Petróleo y Gas*), August, 62–97.

Petrecolla, Diego and Maria Fernanda Martínez. 2008. "Condiciones de competencia en el mercado de gas natural de la República Argentina: 1990–2008", *Economía*, 33, 177–199.

Phelan Christopher and Ennio Stacchetti. 2001. "Sequential Equilibria in a Ramsey Tax Model", *Econometrica*, 69, 1491–1518.

Piffano, Horacio. 2003. *Explotación de los recursos no renovables en un sistema federal de gobierno*, Documento de Trabajo, Universidad Nacional de La Plata, La Plata, Argentina.

Postali, Fernando. 2007. *The Brazilian Fiscal System and the Decision to Invest in Petroleum Reserves: A Real Options Approach*, University of Sao Paulo Working Paper.

Prado, Oscar. 2005. "Situación y perspectivas de la minería metálica Argentina", *Serie Recursos Naturales e Infraestructura No. 91*, ECLAC Santiago, Chile.

Rigobón, Roberto. 2010. "Dealing With Expropriations: General Guidelines for Oil Production Contract", in Hogan, William and Federico Stuzenegger, eds., *The Natural Resources Trap: Private Investment Without Public Commitment*, pp. 227–254. MIT Press, Cambridge, MA.

Roccaro, Isabel and Edgardo Fernández. 2006. *Aspectos tributarios del sector de hidrocarburos: El caso argentino*, Dcoumento de Trabajo, Universidad Nacional de Cuyo, Mendoza, Argentina.

Scheimberg, Sebastián. 2007. "Experiencia reciente y desafíos para la generación de renta petrolera 'aguas arriba' en la Argentina", *Documento de proyecto No. 142*, ECLAC, Santiago, Chile.

Scheimberg, Sebastián. 2011. *Desempeño del sector petrolero en la última década: Los efectos distributivos del presente marco regulatorio. Amenazas y Oportunidades a futuro*, Anales de la Asociación Argentina de Economía Política XLVI Reunion Anual, Buenos Aires, Argentina.

Schwartz, Eduardo and Anders Trolle. 2010. "Pricing Expropriation Risk in Natural Resource Contracts – a Real Options Approach", in Hogan, William and Federico Stuzenegger, eds., *The Natural Resources Trap: Private Investment Without Public Commitment*, pp. 263–288. MIT Press, Cambridge, MA.

Serebrisky, Tomás. 2001. *How Competitive Is the Argentine Gasoline Market? A Differentiated Product Model*, Anales de la Asociación Argentina de Economía Política XXXVI Reunion Anual, Buenos Aires, Argentina.

Spiller, Pablo and Mariano Tommasi. 2003. "The Institutional Determinants of Public Policy: A Transaction Approach With Application to Argentina", *Journal of Law, Economics, and Organization*, 19, 281–306.

Stroebel, Johannes and Arthur van Benthem. 2013. "Resource Extraction Contracts Under the Threat of Expropriation: Theory and Evidence", *Review of Economics and Statistics*, 95, 1622–1639.

Thomas, Jonathan and Tim Worrall. 1994. "Foreign Direct Investment and the Risk of Expropriation", *Review of Economic Studies*, 61, 81–108.

Tomz, Michael and Mark Wright. 2010. "Sovereign Theft: Theory and Evidence About Sovereign Default and Expropriation", in Hogan, William and Federico Stuzenegger, eds., *The Natural Resources Trap: Private Investment Without Public Commitment*, pp. 69–110. MIT Press, Cambridge, MA.

Vera, Juan Carlos. 2000. *Regalías óptimas en una cuenca petrolera*, Anales de la Asociación Argentina de Economía Política.

Wernerfelt, Nils and Richard Zeckhauser. 2010. "Denying the Temptation to GRAB", in Hogan, William and Federico Stuzenegger, eds., *The Natural Resources Trap: Private Investment Without Public Commitment*, pp. 197–226. MIT Press, Cambridge, MA.

Yared, Pierre. 2010. "Politicians, Taxes and Debt", *The Review of Economic Studies*, 77, 806–840.

Zhang, Lei. 1997. "Neutrality and Efficiency of Petroleum Revenue Tax: A Theoretical Assessment", *Economic Journal*, 107, 1106–1120.

7 Oil sector performance and institutions in Latin America[¥]

Lenin H. Balza[±] and Ramón Espinasa[±]

Oil producers small enough to be price-takers without barriers to investment or production should have reacted positively to the fourfold price increase after 2002 that lasted until 2014. The seven largest Latin American oil producers reacted to this permanent price signal in different ways. Based on their performance, it is possible to sort them into two groups. Three countries in effect permanently increased drilling activity and production: Brazil, Colombia and Peru. In contrast, in Mexico, Venezuela, Ecuador and Argentina, drilling activity remained stagnant and production declined over the last decade.

We shall argue in this chapter that the dissimilar behavior of these two groups of countries is related to characteristics of the institutional framework that regulates investment, activity and production. Countries in the first group have regulatory frameworks with similar features: they are open to private investment side by side and in competition with state-owned companies; they are open to public scrutiny; land assignment and operation fall under the purview of an independent regulatory agency and they have stable distributional and operational rules. Countries in the second group also have institutional features in common: production is under direct monopoly control by a state-owned company, there is some degree of discretionary government intervention in both distribution of revenue and management of the company, and the oil sector is closed to competition and public scrutiny. These different features explain the countries' dissimilar responses to market price signals.

The chapter is organized into two main parts. The first provides an analytical framework for discussing the relationship between institutions and performance in oil countries. We highlight the role of the state as owner of oil reservoirs. In the second part, we analyze empirical evidence from the seven largest Latin American oil producers with regard to investment, production and institutional changes over the last two decades. We group these countries together into two families with similar institutional features and similar reactions to market signals. We show that the different reactions to the quantum leap in prices after 2002 can be explained by the incentives to invest in response to market signals that are imbedded in the institutions governing the oil sector. Finally, we summarize the main findings of the paper.

1 Analytical framework

The analytical framework is divided into two sections. The first defines performance and institutions and highlights the state's singular role as owner of hydrocarbon reserves in oil-producing countries, with responsibility for regulating their development using two sets of interacting institutions, fiscal and operational. The second section describes the set of institutions through which the state regulates the development of its reserves. The way the state organizes the oil sector defines the industry's organization and affects the performance of the sector. In this second section of the analytical framework, we describe the main features of two sets of families that can be used to classify how the oil sector is organized worldwide. These families contain the set of seven Latin American oil countries under analysis.

1.1 Oil sector institutions: state ownership of reserves and fiscal and operational institutions

1.1.1 Defining performance and institutions

We shall define national oil sector performance very narrowly, as the extent to which and the rate at which investment and production in the oil sector respond to market signals. In a rational economic world – without frictions or barriers to investment and with producers small enough to be price-takers – there should be a causal relationship between prices and production via changes in investment in crude oil production. We therefore define good performance as a situation in which these three variables move in the same direction, whereas poor performance is defined as a situation in which investment and production show no reaction or move in a direction opposite to price movements.

The best proxy for investment in the oil sector is the number of active drilling rigs.[1] If we assume an oil-producing country small enough to be a price-taker, it should be expected that the number of active drilling rigs would fluctuate with prices. Further, assuming that a change in prices is perceived to be permanent, there will be a time lag between the price signal and a change in the number of active rigs, and after a second lag, the actual variation in the production level.

In the case of a positive price signal leading to an increase in activity, there would be a delay due to availability of rigs and/or time required to bring drilling units to selected locations and then put into place the infrastructure required for the rig to begin drilling. The drilling process can take several weeks or even months before the selected geological objective is reached. There can be an additional delay between the end of the drilling process and the point at which crude oil enters the stream if additional transportation infrastructure is needed and for the newly produced crude to reach the markets.

When a price signal is negative, some lead time is required in order for the drilling process to end. Crude oil prices will seldom be low enough that they fail to cover operational costs and lead to a shutdown in production. The fall in production following a drop in prices perceived to be permanent may be a consequence of the natural decline in production as the reservoir is exhausted and the drop in drilling activity does not compensate for pressure loss, and production comes off stream.

Response to price signals varies widely among oil countries small enough to behave as price-takers. Assuming projects with similar technical characteristics, the reasons for these diverse responses might be largely related to institutional constraints to investment in the oil sector. How societies organize themselves to develop oil-bearing lands or similar resources is a starting point for understanding their performance in this industry.

Seminal works by North (1981) and Williamson (1985), as well as many others, show why institutions are important and how institutional change affects the performance of economies.[2] We shall define institutions in the classical sense expressed in the body of work by Douglass North as "the rules of the game". North (1994, p. 360) defines institutions as "the humanly devised constraints that structure human interaction. They are made up of formal constraints (e.g, rules, laws and constitutions), informal constraints (e.g., norms of behavior, conventions and self-imposed codes of conduct) and their enforcement characteristics".

1.1.2 State ownership of reserves: production and oil fiscal revenue

With the exception of private oil-bearing lands in the United States, oil reservoirs in every country in the world are state-owned, including federal lands in the United States. Monopoly ownership of oil reserves gives the state the right to do the following: first, decide how and when such reserves are to be developed; and second, claim economic rents due to scarcity, quality, reservoir productivity and location. Such rents are not due to changes in industrial productivity but are intrinsic to the conditions of the natural resource and belong to the owner of the reserves. As such, the state has the first right to claim them.

The state has the sovereign right and obligation to administer use of the oil-bearing lands within its territory. The state can exercise its monopoly property rights on the reserves in two basic ways: first, by maintaining direct monopoly control of production through a state-owned company; and second, by maintaining indirect control through a ministry or a non-operating regulatory agency that administers the development of oil-bearing lands by private or state-owned operators.

The state also has the right to claim as specific oil revenue the rents that derive from the four sources to be developed below: scarcity, reservoir productivity, quality and location. The dual, sometimes contradictory, objectives of the state are, on the one hand, to obtain the maximum rent as owner of the natural resource and, on the other, to maximize wealth creation in the country through development of the oil reserves. At the margin, demanding too high a rent may prevent the development of the reserves, thus rendering null the achievement of both objectives, obtaining rent and creating wealth, as will be argued below.

1.2 Operational institutions and industrial organization

State ownership and how the state decides to develop its oil-bearing lands and organize production determine the structure of institutions and industrial organization of the oil sector.

To structure our analysis of the main features characterizing the organization of the industry and the institutions governing the performance of the oil sector, we have described the taxonomy of different international models, with regard to how the state as owner of the natural resource manages the development of oil reserves in its territory.

Using this taxonomy we have identified two families with similar features. In the first family type, the state develops the reserves directly through monopoly ownership of a company that retains monopoly control of oil production in the territory. There is no direct independent private investment in oil production. In the second family type, there is direct private investment in oil production, either in state-owned lands under state regulation or under free access, or in privately owned lands. This last case exists exclusively in the United States, where underground reserves belong to the private owner of the land.

Each one of these two families can in turn be divided into subfamilies depending on the degree of government intervention in oil production. The first family, in which the state retains monopoly control of production, is split into one subfamily where the government intervenes directly in the operations and financial management of the company. In the second subfamily, the relationship between the government and the state-owned company is at arm's length, with the state as sole shareholder of the oil company run as a private firm.

For the second family, wherein the state relinquishes direct monopoly control of production on state-owned lands, the first subfamily is one in which the state retains indirect control through a non-operating regulatory agency that administers the oil-bearing lands on behalf of the owner state. In the second subfamily the state gives private operators free access to potential oil-bearing lands without any restrictions other than that they must follow the same laws and regulations as any other industrial company. In the third subfamily, in which private companies operate in privately owned oil-bearing lands, these companies may be asked to pay special oil taxes in addition to the royalty paid to the private owners of the land.

Although the features of the oil production sector in most countries around the world fall into the above set of families, there are countries with features that fit into more than one. Therefore, rather than isolated categories, what we observe in real world examples is a continuum of institutional arrangements governing the oil sector, ranging from strict government control of the oil industry to freely operating companies with no governmental restrictions other than general laws.

Before we discuss the political economy of oil production within the framework described above, we need to discuss salient features of the contracting process for oil investment and production.

1.2.1 *Contracting for oil investment and production*

Whether the state develops the reserves directly, through monopoly ownership of a company with monopoly control of production, or indirectly, through a government institution such as a non-operating regulatory agency that administers the development of the reserves on behalf of the owner state, there can be different forms of private participation in oil investment.

When the state maintains direct monopoly control of production, private companies can participate in at least two ways: as service providers, producing oil for the state-owned company for a contractually fixed fee, or as equity partners, through joint ventures in companies that remain under state control.

In the case of indirect state control of production, private companies can invest directly in the development of reserves under concessionary contracts with the state. Typically the state will open up oil-bearing lands to the highest bidder under different bidding parameters. The bidding companies can be privately or state-owned, local or foreign.

In any event, investment in oil production has several idiosyncratic features that make contracting particularly complex, most of which are similar to those of other mining activities.[3] These features make investment in oil production a complex process. From a purely technical standpoint it is extremely specialized, requiring highly trained human resources, access to peak technology and significant engineering capacity. From a financial perspective, it requires access to large savings and financing, usually syndicated financing, lasting more than a single year. It is subject to geological risks and price risks and, more importantly, it is prone to political risks that can lead to sudden changes in a preset institutional framework. Whether a company is privately or state-owned, investors are bound to face a very complex set of factors when evaluating and eventually undertaking an investment to explore or develop known oil reserves.

Private companies contracting with a sovereign state for crude oil production face a complex negotiating process. Companies require contracts with a minimum set of features: long-lasting concessions to realize the full potential of large investments; fair, credible and stable distributional rules; protection against sharp price fluctuations; safeguards and protection against the possibility of expropriation and, above all, credible national institutions trusted to be neutral in case of severe disputes with the sovereign state.

With the previous considerations as a background, we discuss the theoretical determinants of performance in crude oil production under the two institutional frameworks under consideration: direct state monopoly control of production and private investment in either state or privately owned oil lands.

1.2.2 State oil company (SOC) monopoly and performance

Performance of the sector under direct state monopoly control of production through the monopoly ownership of the sole oil company operating in a country will vary depending on the degree of independence of the state oil company, whether there is significant discretionary intervention by the government or whether the relationship between the government and the company is at arm's length under a set of transparent, credible and respected rules.

STATE OIL COMPANY AS PART OF CENTRAL GOVERNMENT

An extreme case of SOC monopoly control of production under government control is when the company is in fact part of the executive branch of the state and is treated the same as any other central government entity such as a ministry. The company budget is part of the government budget, the company operations are decided in the context of government priorities, and there is no differentiation in the selection process or the compensation policy between SOC employees and other government employees. The operational and financial results of the SOC are not made explicitly public and therefore are not accountable.

STATE OIL COMPANY INDEPENDENT UNDER PRIVATE LAW

At the other end of the spectrum of SOCs under government control is the case of an arm's length relationship between the government and the SOC. In this case the SOC is a limited liability company with the state as sole shareholder. The company falls under the country's code of commerce and is a state-owned company under private law. The relationship between the parties is formalized through the shareholders meeting, where the annual budget and the company's results are approved. SOC performance indicators are made public and are subject to scrutiny, and the company is as liable as any other LLC. The SOC's management is professional, and it is run as a private company reporting periodically to a representative of the state owner in the shareholders meeting.

The real world morphology of the SOC under state monopoly will lie between these two extreme cases, and its location on that spectrum will determine its behavior and performance.[4]

As is fully explained in Balza and Espinasa (2015), the family of countries with institutional arrangements in which the state exercises full control of reserves through the monopoly control of production can be divided into two subfamilies depending on the degree of government control of the state-owned monopoly.

We have measured the degree of government intervention on the basis of four parameters: revenue distribution, management selection, commercial behavior and transparency. At one extreme, the oil company behaves as part of government, and this translates into discretionary revenue distribution, management that is appointed on the basis of political allegiances, non-commercial behavior and opacity in presenting results. At the other extreme the oil company fully owned by the state can be run under the code of commerce at arm's length. Revenue distribution takes place under preset distributional rules, the management is appointed on the basis of merits, the behavior is commercial and presentation of results is fully transparent.

For the reasons argued above, one would expect a state oil company run at arm's length to show better performance than one under direct government control.

We can plot the two subfamilies in which the state retains monopoly control of production along an axis depending on the degree of government intervention as shown in Figure 7.1, from less government interaction on the left to more government intervention on the right, according to the different parameters analyzed.

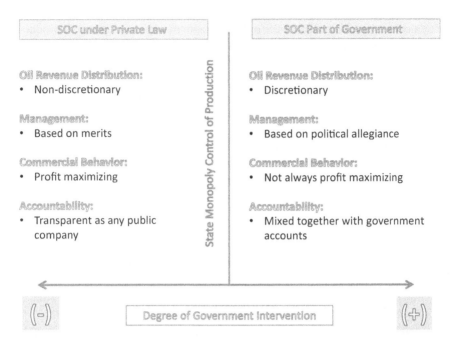

Figure 7.1 Types of government participation

Source: Authors' elaboration

1.2.3 Private direct participation competition and performance

The state may wish to hand over concessionary contracts for the development of the country's oil-bearing lands to private companies, whether or not there is a state-owned company. Performance in this circumstance also depends on the degree of independence from government regulation and control the operating companies have.

As owner of the reserves, the state may want to control and regulate the development of the reserves or leave it free for the companies to operate. As sovereign fiscal authority, the government may wish to impose specific taxes on oil activities even if they take place on private lands.

As stated above, direct private investment in oil production in state-owned oil-bearing lands takes place within two general institutional subfamilies. In the first, the state regulates production under a non-operating regulatory agency and, in the second, there is free private access to public oil-bearing lands without any specific state regulatory intervention. The case of private companies operating in private lands in the United States is very similar to the latter and will be described jointly.

PRIVATE INVESTMENT UNDER REGULATION AND CONTROL

The government, on behalf of the owner state, may want to regulate oil produc-tion for at least three basic reasons: (1) to ensure the best possible development of the reservoirs from a geological perspective, maximizing the recovery of oil and minimizing the ecological and social impact of oil exploration and production; (2) to closely control the development of the reserves to ensure that the state gets the maximum economic rent derived from the sources described above, which may include not only certification of production levels but also close scrutiny of operational costs by operating companies and (3) to maximize the productive impact on the national economy in terms of demand for goods and services and the employment of the national labor force. The latter reason may also condition private investment in the transfer of technology and expertise to national compa-nies by different means.

Regulatory agency   In the case of the state opening oil-bearing lands under direct regulation, an institution is needed to perform such a role. This could lead to the creation of a special-purpose national institution such as a national petroleum agency (NPA) or the assumption of regulatory duties by a specific department within the ministry in charge of energy and/or mining.

There are a few conditions for creating a world-class special-purpose independ-ent regulatory agency. First, the agency would require highly specialized person-nel including geologists, reservoir and petroleum engineers, petroleum financial assessment specialists and lawyers who specialize in contracting for oil produc-tion. The hiring of these personnel to essentially run the national counterpart of powerful private companies may require remuneration higher than the norm for central government employees.

Second, continuity of the staff administering the national petroleum reserves is of paramount importance to manage long-lasting contracts, and should not be sub-ject to political change. Indeed, the board directing the agency should be selected in a staggered manner not coinciding with changes in government, and should be elected by representatives of more than one branch of government, to lessen the risk of government intervention.

In this way the agency should be truly independent. The features of specialized staffing, continuity and independence make an NPA similar in its conception to a central bank, which, like an NPA, is charged with administering a national stock: the monetary base and the international reserves.

The essential roles of an NPA are the following: (1) to assess, map and store geological data about the country's oil-bearing lands; (2) to implement policies that open up prospective territories and evaluation scales for different parameters; (3) to prepare bidding packages, carry out the bidding process, select a winner, draft and sign concessionary contracts and (4) to enforce contracts on behalf of the state owner of the reserves, including auditing production, production costs and fulfillment of social and environmental safeguards.

FREE PRIVATE INVESTMENT

On the other extreme of direct private investment in oil production is the free ownership of reserves, in the case that the state relinquishes its property rights in favor of the discoverer of commercial reservoirs.

The government – on behalf of the owner state and through an indefinite contractual agreement – hands over the development of a given territory to a private company. The state rules whether the owner of the land is to be compensated and how.

In this case, the operating company is not subject to any regulation and pays specific oil taxes if necessary. Certainly the company is subject to the law of the land, as would be any other commercial firm. In the case that the oil-bearing lands are privately owned, the oil company interested in developing the underground reserves must reach a contractual agreement with the owner of the land to gain access to the reserves under concessionary conditions, paying a royalty or some other sort of rent to the private owner of the land and, if necessary, also paying specific oil taxes to the government.

The actual real world morphology of private participation in crude oil production lies between these two extreme points, free access and state regulation. Before analyzing the behavior and performance of countries with direct private investment and competition and with different degrees of government regulation and control, it is necessary to emphasize that these two arrangements do not prevent direct participation by fully or partially state-owned oil companies. As a matter of fact, this is a common arrangement and we shall pay particular attention to how operation under this type of arrangement affects the state oil company.[5]

The family of countries with institutional arrangements that allow for private direct access to reserves and control of production under competition can be divided into two subfamilies, depending on whether companies have free access to reserves that are privately or state-owned, or whether access to and development of the reserves is regulated by the state.

In the case of free access, companies pay a royalty to the private owner of the land or to the government in cases where the reserves are state-owned. Other than that, the companies are subject to the same taxes and laws as any other commercial firm. In the case of private production under state regulation, the state regulation can range from regulating access to the reserves to regulating production for geological, environmental, social or other reasons.

For the reasons argued above, one would expect companies with free access to reserves to perform better than those operating under state regulation.

In the same way that we plotted the families of countries with monopoly state control of production based on the degree of government intervention in the industry, we can plot the families of companies with private direct access and control of production along an axis depending on the degree of government intervention in the running of the oil industry in Figure 7.2, going from minimal state intervention (beyond that applicable to any commercial firm) on the left to greater state intervention (regulating access to reserves and operation) on the right.

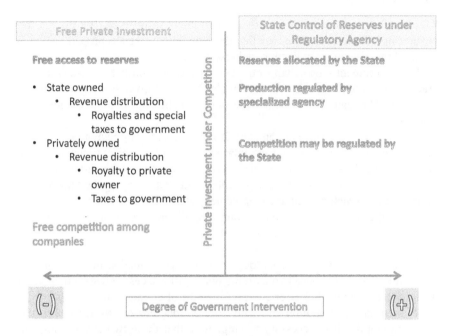

Figure 7.2 Type of firms
Source: Authors' elaboration

1.3 Summary

Finally, we can combine the set of families described above in a single Cartesian system as shown in Figure 7.3. In the upper half, we plot the family of countries where the state controls the development of reserves through monopoly ownership of a company that has monopoly control of production. As we did in Figure 7.1, we can draw these countries from left to right, from lesser to greater government intervention. Likewise, in the lower half, we can plot countries in which private companies have direct access to reserves and control production. As in Figure 7.2, we can plot the countries from left to right depending on the degree of government regulation of the activity from free access to regulated access.

Plotting the countries according to the institutional frameworks of their oil industries in this system, we could rank their performance in response to a permanent change in the price signal. Countries in the southwest quadrant should respond faster than the rest, followed by countries in the southeast quadrant, then the northwest quadrant, and finally the northeast quadrant.

Performance measured as the speed of response to change in price signals perceived to be permanent may vary according to the way each country's oil industry is set up, from free competition with free access to reserves and private control of production, to private capital access to reserves under government regulation, to state monopoly control of production at arm's length, to state monopoly control of production under direct government control.

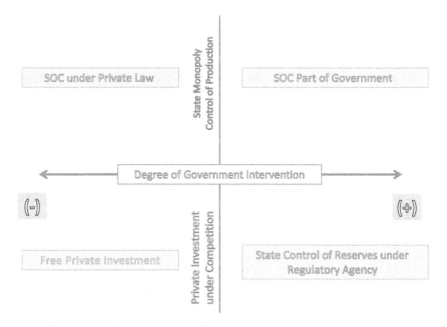

Figure 7.3 The space of firms and government intervention
Source: Authors' elaboration

Within this analytical framework we shall next analyze the evolution of the institutional framework and the performance of the oil sector of the seven largest crude oil producers in Latin America over the last 15 years.

2 Empirical evidence

It is our contention that the diverse reactions to the price signal among the largest Latin-American oil producers can be explained by differences in the institutions governing the oil sector in each country. As a matter of fact, each of the two sets of countries we grouped together according to their similar institutional frameworks and the way the oil sector is organized in each had fairly uniform responses to the price signal within the group. In this section, we explore the common institutional features of the two groups and their similar market behavior.

2.1 Market signal: upward break in price trend

Over the last 18 years, oil prices increased almost fourfold in real terms, from about 26 per barrel ($/b) in 1995 to 94 ($/b) by early 2014.[6]

Following a similar approach as in Espinasa et. al (2017), we start by identifying whether there has been a change in the real value of prices over time or if prices have remained stable over this period. That is, we estimate the time break in price trend.

To test the null hypothesis that oil prices have been stable in real terms during the period we use the following equation,[7]

$$p_t = \beta_0 + \beta_1 * t + \epsilon_t$$

The evidence against that hypothesis can be found by identifying significant changes in the time trend coefficient. The inflection point for the break in the price trend comes from minimizing the sum of square errors (SSE) using the following regression,

$$p_t = \beta_0 + \beta_1 * t + \beta_2 * t * break + \epsilon_t$$

Figure 7.4 shows the WTI marker crude monthly prices in real terms between January 1995 and January 2014. Figure 7.5 shows the same prices expressed in logs and the trend using the Hodrick–Prescott filter. It shows the quantum leap in prices and the inflection in the trend slope in July 2002.

2.2 Performance: investment and output

In a world with free access to oil-bearing lands and free capital mobility, it is expected that investment would increase in response to a quantum leap in prices, leading to higher crude oil production. However, based on evidence from the last 19 years, this has not uniformly been the case among the seven largest oil-producing countries in the Latin American region. It is possible to group these countries together according to their response to this unequivocal and sustained price signal.

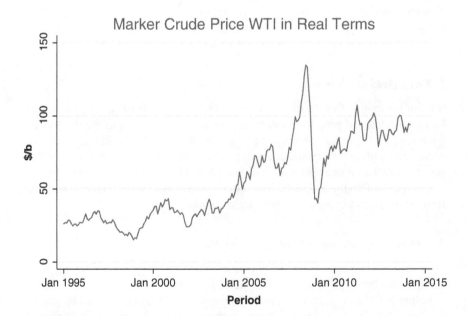

Figure 7.4 Market crude oil price WTI in real terms

Source: EIA, U.S. BLS and own calculations

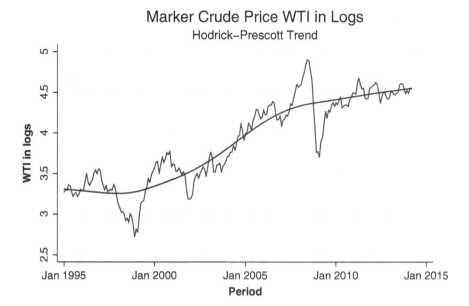

Marker Crude Price WTI in Logs
Hodrick–Prescott Trend

Figure 7.5 Market crude oil price WTI in logs

Source: EIA, U.S. BLS and own calculations

2.2.1 Group I

The first group of four countries, Mexico, Venezuela, Argentina and Ecuador, did not respond to the positive price signal, and investment as measured by drilling activity remained essentially constant, at levels too low to compensate for the natural productivity loss of the reservoirs, leading to declining production in each.

Figures 7.6, 7.7, 7.8 and 7.9 show drilling activity as the best proxy for investment, and monthly crude oil output for these four countries for the period under analysis. The price trend break date is superimposed on top of the drilling and output graphs.

It can be seen that in each individual country and for the group as a whole, there is no major drilling reaction to the price break. Given the magnitude and the duration of the transition to the new price regime, there is no sustained homogeneous investment increase in response to the quantum leap in prices. In fact, drilling activity for the group as a whole as well as for each individual country is not enough to compensate for the arrest in oil flow due to declining reservoir pressure, and output drops considerably in all four countries. Lack of investment explains the paradoxical reaction of this group of countries, with sharply declining production vis-à-vis a sharp upward movement in the price regime.

Figure 7.10 shows the index numbers for prices, drilling and output for the countries in Group I. During the period of the fourfold increase in price, drilling activity remained roughly constant, and for the group as whole production fell roughly 13% or 1 Mbd (from 7.7 down to 6.7 Mbd) between late 2002 and early 2014.

Figure 7.6 Argentina active drilling rigs/month; Argentina oil production

Source: Own elaboration based on Baker Hughes Inc.; IEA and author calculations

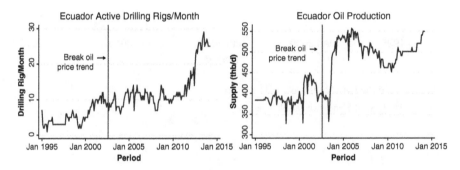

Figure 7.7 Ecuador active drilling rigs/month; Ecuador oil production

Source: Own elaboration based on Baker Hughes Inc.; IEA and author calculations

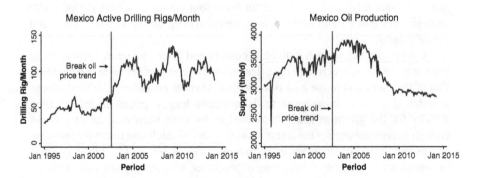

Figure 7.8 Mexico active drilling rigs/month; Mexico oil production

Source: Own elaboration based on Baker Hughes Inc.; IEA and author calculations

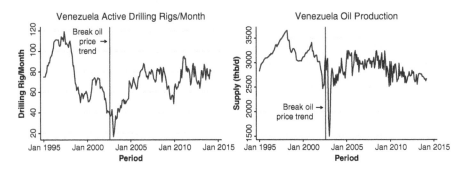

Figure 7.9 Venezuela active drilling rigs/month; Venezuela oil production

Source: Own elaboration based on Baker Hughes Inc.; IEA and author calculations

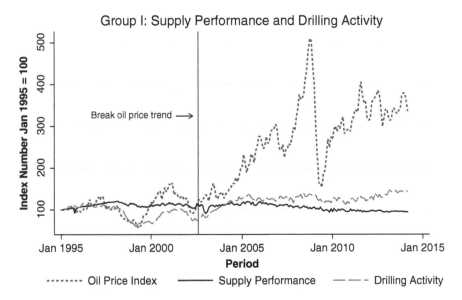

Figure 7.10 Group I supply performance and drilling activity

Source: IEA, EIA, U.S. BLS, Baker Hughes Inc. and own calculations

2.2.2 Group II

A second group of three countries, Brazil, Colombia and Peru, responded to the positive price signals by sharply increasing investment, as seen in a quantum leap in drilling activity and a subsequent increase in output. Figures 7.11, 7.12 and 7.13 show drilling activity and oil output for these three countries. There is a clear response of sharply increased drilling activity followed by booming output.

Figure 7.14 shows the index numbers for prices, drilling and output for Group II countries. The three countries all increased crude oil production. Collective production increased by 51% or 1.1 Mbd (from 2.2 up to 3.3 Mbd).

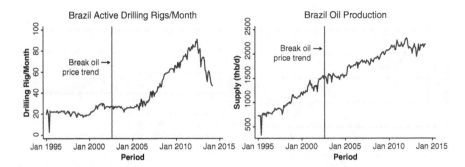

Figures 7.11 Brazil active drilling rigs/month; Brazil oil production

Source: Own elaboration based on Baker Hughes Inc.; IEA and author calculations

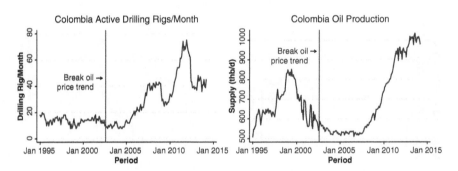

Figures 7.12 Colombia active drilling rigs/month; Colombia oil production

Source: Own elaboration based on Baker Hughes Inc.; IEA and author calculations

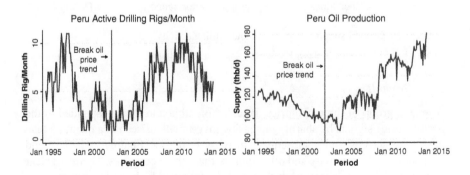

Figures 7.13 Peru active drilling rigs/month; Peru oil production

Source: Own elaboration based on Baker Hughes Inc.; IEA and author calculations

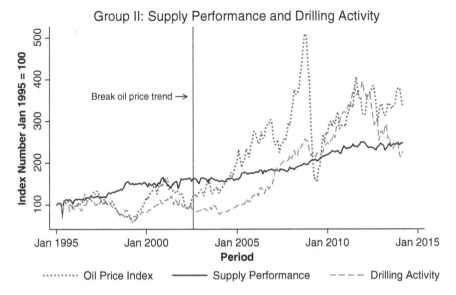

Group II: Supply Performance and Drilling Activity

Figure 7.14 Group II supply performance and drilling activity

Source: IEA, EIA, U.S. BLS, Baker Hughes Inc. and own calculations

2.3 Institutional framework and performance[8]

We will describe the evolution and present morphology of the institutional framework for the countries in each group and place them within the taxonomy we
developed in the analytical framework. We will also identify breaking points in
the evolution of the institutional framework for the countries under analysis and
discuss how these institutional changes may have altered the investment environment and thus conditioned the response.

2.3.1 Group I

The first distinctive feature of the institutional framework governing the oil sector
in Group I countries is that the government exercises a high degree of discretionary interference in the running of the oil industry in the period under analysis.
In three of the four countries in this group, the state exercises its property rights
on the natural resource through monopoly ownership of the oil company, with a
monopoly on oil production. This is the case in Mexico, Venezuela and Ecuador.
In the case of Argentina, the state took control of the largest oil company in the
country, and for several years prior, the government had directly intervened in the oil
sector through various executive orders.

The oil sectors of the countries in Group I can be classified into the first of
the two types of families described in the taxonomy. As we pointed out when
describing the taxonomy, there is not always a clear-cut relationship between the
features of a specific country's oil sector and those described for each category in

the more abstract classification. There are shades to the characterization; however, the countries in this group share the most important feature, which is state control of production through the monopoly ownership of a company that has monopoly control of production in each country. What varies is the degree of government control in the running of each company.

In the analytical framework we identified two subfamilies depending on the degree of government interference in state-owned companies, those that are run at arm's length on one extreme and those that are part of the central government on the other. For the reasons given in the analytical framework, it should be expected that the first subfamily would perform better than the second.

Argentina: In the late 1990s Argentina underwent a profound process of privatization and liberalization of public utilities.[9] This led, among other things, to the privatization of the state-owned company YPF.[10] The influx of capital, technology and engineering, together with the adoption of international prices, led to the expansion of hydrocarbon activity in Argentina at the turn of the century. The expansion of the sector was brought to a sudden end by the reversal of liberal economic policies coinciding with the swearing in of President Nestor Kirchner in May 2003, ushering in a period of growing government intervention in the oil industry. The growing tension ended with the forceful expropriation of the largest operator, YPF-Repsol, in 2012 and government takeover of oil sector operations.[11]

Ecuador: Over the decade from the mid-1990s to the mid-2000s, Ecuador carried out an oil policy oriented toward opening spaces to private capital in two ways. First it allowed private operating companies to invest in the development of marginal fields in association with the state-owned company Petroecuador. Second, the construction of a second pipeline, the OCP, built to transport heavy crude oil from the jungle fields in the east of the country across the Andes to west-coast terminals, was financed by private investment. This led to a quantum leap in oil production, since transportation infrastructure was the main bottleneck for increasing production in Ecuador. The expansion in activity and production came to an end with the change in oil policy orientation following the swearing in of Rafael Correa as president in January 2007. The reversal in oil policy orientation put a halt to growing private capital investment. However, it is important to note that since 2012, the government of Ecuador has allowed an increasing flow of foreign investment into specific projects and created a second state oil company to develop newly prolific areas.[12] This has translated into increasing activity and production in recent years that took place without a major overhaul in the institutional framework.

Ecuador's institutional framework evolved in the period under analysis, from openness to private investment to a closing of those opportunities as government control grew. In terms of our schematic framework, Ecuador moved from the northwest to the northeast quadrant.

Mexico: PEMEX is a fully state-owned company with full monopoly control of oil production in Mexico. During the period under analysis, it was run by professional management with a fair degree of operational independence from the government. Until 2007, PEMEX was able to invest well above available industry cash flow with off balance debt under the umbrella of a project financing mechanism known as Pidiregas.[13] This financing mechanism came to an end with the swearing in of President Calderon in December 2006, which put a ceiling on PIDIREGAS debt, directly affecting PEMEX investment capacity in 2007. Following this first measure, and amid concerns over the growing debt obligations of PEMEX, the Mexican Congress, in October 2008, unanimously approved amendments to the federal budget and Fiscal Responsibility Law that limited PEMEX's participation in the Deferred Impact Status Projects or PIDIREGAS.[14] The severe cuts to investment go a long way toward explaining the largest drop in PEMEX production, which began in 2005. This limiting factor came on top of other well-known PEMEX limitations related to access to technology and engineering capacity to sustain production from existing fields and to tap potential oil-bearing territories.[15]

In terms of our schematic framework, Mexico moved from the northwest quadrant to the northeast quadrant in the period under analysis. However, the sharp deterioration of the Mexican oil sector has brought about a radical institutional reform in 2013–2014 to open up the sector to private investment, technology and engineering capacity.

Venezuela: PDVSA was created as a fully state-owned company under private law. This explains part of its success from its inception in 1975 until 1998 (Espinasa 2010). The company's relationship with government was at arm's length, with shareholder meetings at least twice a year to approve the annual budget and yearly results, and no government interference on operations. On top of being a world-class state-owned company, the sustained expansion of capacity by more than 50% in the last decade of the century was supported by the opening to private investment, including the largest oil companies in the world, either as operators for PDVSA in marginal fields or in association for the development of world-class projects to develop and upgrade the country's huge heavy crude reserves base.

The success story of the Venezuelan oil sector beginning with nationalization came to a sudden end with the swearing in of President Hugo Chavez in February 1999. A number of landmarks signaled the demise of the Venezuelan oil sector starting in 1999. First, growing government interference in the operational management of PDVSA. Second, the new hydrocarbon law passed by Congress in 2002 opened the door to different forms of government intervention in management of the oil industry and reduced opportunities for private participation. Finally, a number of international companies that refused to operate under the new rules were expropriated in 2005, and a large number of national companies providing services to PDVSA were expropriated in 2007. The decimation of PDVSA and the severe constraints to private investment may well explain the sustained decline in Venezuelan oil output over the last 15 years.

During the period under analysis, the oil sector in Venezuela underwent a severe institutional transformation, though maintaining state monopoly control of production. PDVSA began as a state-owned monopoly under private law with an arm's length relationship with government, but eventually came under full government control, both operationally and financially. In terms of our schematic framework, PDVSA moved all the way from the northwest quadrant to the northeast quadrant.

GROUP I SUMMARY

During the period under analysis, all Group I countries underwent institutional changes that deepened discretional government interference in the management of the state-owned sector. We have attempted to depict the evolution of the sector during this period according to the parameters we developed in the theoretical analytical framework.

Argentina: From private direct investment and minimal government intervention to state ownership and stringent government control.

Ecuador: From state ownership and growing private participation to growing state and government control. Recent foreign selected investment.

Mexico: Permanent government financial control under full state ownership.

Venezuela: From state monopoly control with government control at arm's length and production in association with private capital to full government control of production and selected private participation.

In terms of our schematic framework, these four countries evolved toward greater government control along the period under analysis, as shown in Figure 7.15.

2.3.2 Group II

The key distinctive feature of the Group II countries in Latin America is minimal direct government interference in the running of the oil industry, with private participation in competition with state-owned companies under a regulatory agency.

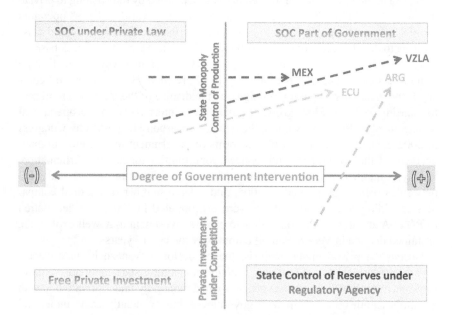

Figure 7.15 Group I transition

Source: Authors' elaboration

The countries with private direct access to production in Latin America all operate under regulatory conditions set by the state. During the period under analysis, two of the three countries in the group, Brazil and Colombia, underwent radical sector reform that had as a cornerstone the creation of an independent agency to regulate oil production and open the sector to direct private investment. In Peru similar reform took place prior to the period under analysis. In contrast to the other countries in this group, in Peru the state-owned company does not participate in the upstream-production segment of the oil industry.

The countries in Group II can be classified into the second of the two families of countries identified in the analytical framework. Within the second family, the three countries can be classified within the second subfamily. All the countries have a similar institutional framework and industrial organization and, for the reasons argued in the framework, should perform better than the countries in Group I.

Brazil: The institutional framework of Brazil's oil sector underwent a key reform in August 1997 with the creation of the National Petroleum Agency (ANP) during the term of President Fernando Henrique Cardozo, which began in January 1995. Following the Norwegian model, Brazil created an independent regulatory agency to administer oil-bearing lands and oversee hydrocarbon operations in the country. This institutional reform had several consequences that improved the oil sector's response to market signals. First, the consequences on the state own oil company, Petrobras: it freed the state-owned company from its role as administrator of the reserves, allowing the company to focus on the core oil business. This also allowed PETROBRAS to behave as a true limited liability company under private law and sell shares to private investors without putting in jeopardy the ownership of the reserves administered by the ANP on behalf of the state owner. This opened PETROBRAS to public scrutiny and made the company accountable to stakeholders that pressed for improved performance. Finally, opening PETROBRAS to private investment increased the financing sources available to the company over and above its own cash flow and public sector financing. Second, the reform opened the Brazilian oil sector to direct private investment. This second component of the reform induced competition and thus led to growing efficiency in the oil sector. In terms of our schematic framework, Brazil moved from the northeast quadrant to the southeast quadrant in the period under analysis.

Colombia: Colombia might be the most close-fitting example of the association between institutional quality and oil sector performance (Balza et al. 2014). Following the lead of Brazil and in view of the results of its new institutional framework, Colombia underwent a very similar reform in June 2003 under the presidency of Alvaro Uribe, who took office in August 2002. Colombia created the National Hydrocarbon Agency (ANH) to administer its oil-bearing territories. The results of the reform in Colombia were even more striking than in Brazil. Production had been falling for a number of years and the country was about to become a net importer, but by ten years after the reform, production had increased almost twofold, with a diverse and robust oil sector. Ecopetrol was liberated from its role as administrator of the natural resource and was able to focus on the core oil business. The reform also allowed the company to incorporate private investors as stakeholders, subjecting the company to public scrutiny that pushed it toward increased efficiency. Opening the oil sector to private investment had a greater relative impact in Colombia than in Brazil. The contribution of private companies in terms of investment, know-how and engineering capacity in relation to the state-owned company was greater in Colombia than Brazil. In terms of our schematic framework, Colombia moved from the northeast quadrant to the southeast quadrant in the period under analysis.

Peru: The creation of an independent non-operating agency to administer the hydrocarbon-bearing territories in Peru precedes the similar reforms in Brazil and Colombia. It seems that the Peruvian government did not intend to follow the Norwegian model – the Peru model had a degree of originality. The regulatory agency Perupetro was created by law when the most recent hydrocarbon law was enacted in August 1993 under the presidency of Alberto Fujimori, who was sworn in in July 1990. There are some differences from the Brazilian and Colombian models; PETROPERU remains by law fully state-owned, although it is run under private law, competing with private companies particularly in the downstream business, but recently in the upstream as well. PETROPERU as a limited liability company is open to public scrutiny. Bearing that difference, Peru's reform had the key ingredient of opening the hydrocarbon sector to private capital, both national and international. The stability of the country's institutions over the last two decades helped to boost large foreign investments in upstream oil and gas production. From being a net hydrocarbon importer, Peru has become a net exporter. Although the main success has been in gas production, the production of associated liquids has increased proportionally. In terms of our schematic framework, Peru remained in the southeast quadrant in the period under analysis.

GROUP II SUMMARY

During the period under analysis, Brazil and Colombia underwent institutional changes with two similar features: they opened the oil sector to private investment and competition, and they opened the state-owned company to private investment under public scrutiny. In the case of Peru, a similar reform took place prior to the beginning of the period under analysis, with the only difference that the state-owned company was not opened to private investment. As with the countries in Group I, we have attempted to depict the evolution of oil sector reforms for countries in Group II during the period under analysis in Figure 7.16, according to the degree of state monopoly ownership and the degree of government interference in the oil industry. Brazil and Colombia moved from the northeast to the southeast quadrant, while Peru remained in that quadrant during the period under consideration.

Brazil and Colombia: From state monopoly control of production with contractual private participation to free private participation under regulation and private investment in the state-owned company.

Peru: Production remained under private control under regulation.

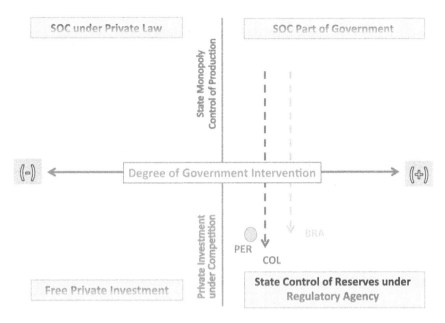

Figure 7.16 Group II transition

Source: Authors' elaboration

In terms of our schematic framework, these three countries evolved toward lesser government control and more competition along the period under analysis, as shown in Figure 7.16.

2.4 Hypothesis testing

The evolution of the oil sectors of the largest oil producers in Latin America over the last 20 years together with the break in the oil price trend give us the opportunity to formally test the hypothesis set forth about the relationship between institutional framework and performance.

With the exception of Peru, the other six largest producers underwent institutional changes associated with changes in the executive branch of government during the period beginning in 1995. In the four countries in Group I, the change brought greater government interference and/or a greater degree of state monopoly control of production. Colombia and Brazil underwent institutional changes during the same period, but toward lessening government interference and increasing direct private investment in competition with a state-owned company that was partially privatized. Peru had undergone these reforms just prior to the beginning of the period under analysis.

We should expect Group I countries' responses to price signals to become weaker or negligible, and should expect a positive response in Group II, in other words, deteriorating performance in the former and improving performance in the latter.

Group I

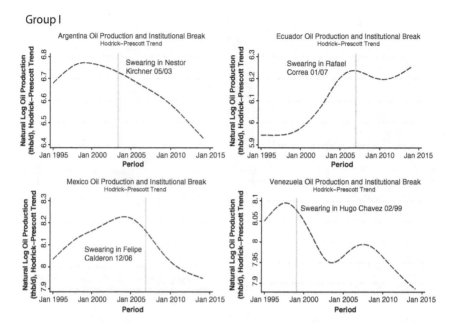

Figure 7.17 Argentina, Ecuador, Mexico, Venezuela oil production and institutional break

Source: IEA and own calculations

Figure 7.17 shows trends in production in the Group I countries between 1995 and early 2014, as well as the institutional change marked by the swearing in of the president under whose government the oil sector institutional reforms were implemented. It can be seen that production decline accelerates after the reforms in spite of accelerating prices and the break in the price regime after 2002.

Figure 7.18 shows trends in production in Group II countries and the institutional changes that took place with two landmarks: when the presidents that introduced reforms were sworn in and the date of the creation of the regulatory agency as the highlight of the reform. In the case of Peru, the reform falls before the period under analysis. It can be seen clearly that production responds to the reform in view of the positive break in prices during the period.

2.5 *Testing the relationship between institutional change and oil sector performance*

In order to test the relationship between institutional change and oil performance at the country level, we rely on the following specifications:

Group II

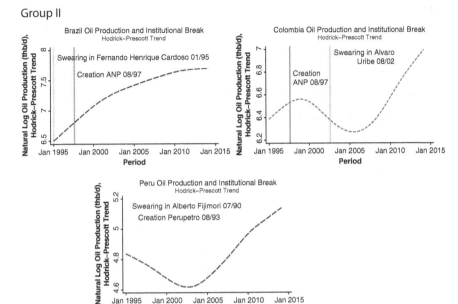

Figure 7.18 Brazil, Colombia, Peru oil production and institutional break

Source: IEA and own calculations

Before institutional change:

$$Y_t^i = \beta_0 + \beta_1^i P_t + \epsilon_t^i \qquad \forall i, \quad for\, t \in \left[0, t^*\right)$$

After institutional change:

$$Y_t^i = \beta_0 + \beta_1^i P_t + \epsilon_t^i \qquad \forall i, \quad for\, t \in \left[t^*, T\right)$$

Before and after:

$$Y_t^i = \beta_0 + \beta_1^i (I^i * P_t) + \sum_t \beta_t yr_t^i + \epsilon_t^i \qquad \forall i, t$$

Panel test:

$$Y_t^i = \beta_0 + \beta_1 (K * I^i * P_t) + \sum_t \beta_t yr_t + \epsilon_{it}$$

Where Y refers to crude oil production, P represents the real international petroleum price, I is an indicator variable taking the value of 1 when the country adopts the institutional measures, and K is also a categorical variable adopting the value of 0 when the institutional change increased the discretional government intervention or 1 when the institutional change is market-oriented. As usual, t and i

represent time and country, respectively; t^* represents the date when the country adopted the institutional change; and yr represents the year dummies. All continuous variables are detrended using the well-known Hodrick–Prescott procedure in order to account for long-term relationships only.

The sign of the correlation between price and production will be country- and period-specific. For instance, before any institutional change, it would be expected that those countries with less discretional government intervention would have a positive correlation between production (Y) and prices (P). That is, β_1 should be greater than zero. Conversely, the sign of the correlation should be negative with higher discretional government intervention. During the period under investigation, after the institutional change, those countries that increased the degree of government intervention are expected to have β_1 less than zero, or greater than zero in the opposite case.

The interaction between the institutional change and prices is expected to capture the relationship of the structural break in oil prices given the change in the institutional environment. This effect is expected to be positive when countries move in the direction of pro-market reforms (Group II) and negative when reforms are towards more government control (Group I).

The interaction between institutional type, institutional change and price break $(K*I*P)$ captures the correlation between performance and price break, given the type of institutional change. The coefficient of this interaction represents the average performance gap between those countries, with pro-market institutions outperforming those countries with a strong discretional government intervention. This gap is expected to be positive.

The drilling rigs are also expected to be a proxy of investment. However, as can be seen previously in the four countries that adopted more discretional government intervention, drilling rigs marginally increased while production sharply decreased or remained stagnant. In contrast, in those countries that adopted pro-market institutions, there was a pronounced increase in drilling rigs. This gap in performance measured by drilling rigs can be tested using a panel data regression. It is expected that those countries with pro-market institutions show a greater increase in drilling rigs than those countries with non-market institutions. The regression returns a coefficient of 0.197, statistically significant at 5%. This is consistent with the gap estimated in Table 7.1, which shows a greater gap as a consequence of clear oil production decreases in the countries with more discretional government intervention and oil production increases in the countries with a pro-market environment. Thus, oil production seems to better reflect the performance of the sector.

Finally, as a graphical test of the relationship between institutional reforms and oil sector performance, we construct average indexes representing the trends of oil production and drilling rigs by country group (Figure 7.19).[16] As expected, the oil production trend in the Group I countries decreases after the reforms, while the Group II countries increase their production. Similarly, the trend in drilling rigs shows a sharp increase in Group II, while it is practically stagnant in Group I.

3 Concluding remarks

We know that many factors play a role in successful development experiences in the oil sector worldwide. However, one element often emerges as the key variable for resource-rich countries to avoid falling behind: appropriate institutional framework.

Table 7.1 Supply performance vs. price and institutional change

| | Group I | | | | Group II | | | All |
	ARG	ECU	MEX	VEN	BRA	COL	PER	Countries 2/.
Before								
Price trend	0.0501	0.343**	0.124**	-0.783**	-5.769**	-0.398**	.	.
	(0.037)	(0.003)	(0.010)	(0.026)	(0.023)	(0.032)	.	.
Observations	85	144	143	49	32	103	.	.
Adjusted R-squared	0.01	0.987	0.51	0.95	0.999	0.6	.	.
After								
Price trend	-0.238**	-0.344**	-0.964**	-0.0649**	0.536**	0.617**	0.177**	.
	(0.01)	(0.01)	(0.01)	(0.01)	(0.01)	(0.05)	(0.02)	.
Observations	119	60	61	155	172	101	204	.
Adjusted R-squared	0.848	0.973	0.988	0.486	0.942	0.571	0.382	.
Before & After 1/.								
Price trend*institution	-0.00284**	-0.0916*	-0.00529***	-0.00487**	0.0200**	0.00042	0.228**	0.235**
	(0.001)	(0.050)	(0.002)	(0.002)	(0.004)	(0.003)	(0.032)	(0.014)
Observations	204	204	204	204	204	204	204	1428
Adjusted R-squared	0.99	1.00	0.99	0.99	1.00	0.97	0.99	0.26

Notes: Robust standard errors in parentheses
* p<0.10, ** p<0.05
1/. Year country specific effects
2/. Panel estimation

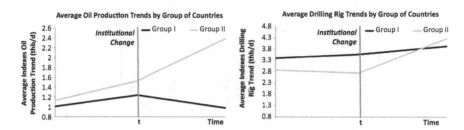

Figure 7.19 Average oil production and average drilling trends by group of countries
Source: Authors' elaboration

We argue that the success of the oil sector depends heavily on the institutions and regulatory framework that govern the extraction of natural resources. Indeed, it is possible to sort the seven largest Latin American oil-producing countries into two groups with similar oil sector frameworks, yielding similar oil sector performance over the last 19 years.

There is a first group of countries where the state exercises its monopoly property rights on the reserves by maintaining monopoly control of production through a state-owned company and through protracted government intervention in the operations of the companies, whether state-owned or private. The countries in this group are Mexico, Venezuela, Ecuador and Argentina.

In the second group of countries, the state exercises its monopoly property rights through indirect control of production by means of a National Oil Regulatory Agency which administers the oil bearing lands on behalf of the state owner. The agency opens up the territories with hydrocarbon potential for development by oil companies both national and international, and both privately and state-owned. The territories to be developed are auctioned off through a bidding process and awarded on the basis of different parameters, among others: the government take, the investment and production over and above minimum levels set up by the agency and the content of local goods and services over and above a set minimum. The countries in this group are Brazil, Colombia and Peru.

During the period under analysis, we witnessed an interesting experiment. At the beginning of the period, just one country, Peru, was open to direct private investment in the oil sector. Two other countries, Brazil and Colombia, changed their institutional framework during the period to allow for direct private participation in competition with the state-owned company under an independent regulatory agency. Finally, in four of the countries, Argentina, Ecuador, Mexico and Venezuela, the degree of government monopoly control of production increased due to different reforms associated with changes in government orientation throughout the period: Peru from the beginning, and Brazil and Colombia after their respective reforms showed positive performance. On the contrary, performance in Argentina, Ecuador, Mexico and Venezuela worsened after reforms that increased the degree of government control of production.

In a price-taker oil-producing country without barriers to investment in the sector, it would be expected that oil activity, as measured by oil output and number of drilling rigs, would increase following the permanent quantum leap in prices after 2002. However, the reaction was not positive and homogeneous in all oil-producing countries in the region. Three countries in effect permanently increased drilling activity and production: Brazil, Colombia and Peru. In contrast, in Mexico, Venezuela, Ecuador and Argentina, drilling activity remained stagnant and production declined over the last decade.

In our chapter, we have demonstrated two facts. First, in the analysis across countries, the less competitive the oil sector is, as defined by the institutional framework, the worse the performance is, as defined as the response to price signals. Second, for the same country, a change in the institutional framework leading to more government control leads to worsening performance, while reforms that produce more competitive environments improve performance.

Notes

¥ We would like to thanks Raul Jimenez and Osmel Manzano for their insightful ideas and remarks. Comments welcome to: leninb@iadb.org and ramones@iadb.org. The findings and conclusions expressed in this chapter are solely those of the authors and do not reflect the view of the IDB, its Executive Directors, or the countries they represent.

± Inter-American Development Bank/Infrastructure and Energy Sector/Office of the Manager/Extractive Sector Initiative. Ramon Espinasa, Inter-American Development Bank/General Coordinator Extractive Sector Initiative/Infrastructure and Energy Sector and Georgetown University.

1 It is a well-known industry fact that the cost of rotatory equipment for well-drilling and completion represents around two-thirds of non-wage oil production expenditures. We are particularly thankful to Mr. Juan Szabo, former head of PDVSA Exploration and Production, for this insight.

2 This literature was enriched by a good amount of empirical work across countries, which estimates the growth-promoting effects of well-run institutions.

3 See Balza and Espinasa (2015) for a complete list of the most salient features of investment in the oil sector.

4 Balza and Espinasa (2015) describe the degree of independence of the state oil company in three key aspects of the oil industry: (1) oil revenue distribution; (2) management of the oil company and (3) commercial behavior, competition and accountability.

5 Balza and Espinasa (2015) explain the variations of private participation in crude oil production along three key aspects of the oil industry: (1) oil revenue distribution; (2) management of the oil company and (3) commercial behavior, competition and accountability.

6 Growth in developing countries, especially China and India; the inability to increase oil supply to meet demand and speculation in financial markets were commonly used to explain the steep rise in global oil prices during the period of the analysis.

7 Oil prices were expressed in logs, seasonally adjusted and then filtered using the well-known Hodrick–Prescott procedure to filter short-term market fluctuations from long-term trends.

8 See Balza and Espinasa (2015) for a more detailed description of the evolution of the institutional framework for the countries under the analysis.

9 The privatization of a number of public utilities and state-owned companies was part of a series of reforms undertaken under the administration of President Carlos Menem,

oriented toward reducing the size of the state and putting public financial accounts in order. The reforms were undertaken between 1989 and 1992.

10 The privatization process began in 1992 and culminated in 1999 with Repsol owning a 51% stake in YPF-Repsol with an estimated payment of around $15 billion.

11 The expropriation took several stages. First was the forced sale of a 25% stake in YPF-Repsol to the local Group Petersen between 2007 and 2011, to be paid for out of future profits. Second, in April 2012, citing reasons of national interest, the government expropriated 51% of the capital of YPF-Repsol from a total 57% share owned by Repsol.

12 Chinese investment took place, and Petroamazonas was created.

13 On December 21, 1995, Article 18 of the Public Debt Law (Public Debt Law) and Article 30 of the abrogated Federal Public Budgetary, Accounting and Expenditures Law (FPBAEL) were amended to create a new category of long-term contingent public debt to support priority infrastructure projects that would generate revenue for their own funding, creating the Deferred Impact Status Projects or PIDIREGAS – *Proyectos de Infraestructura Productiva de Largo Plazo* (PIDIREGAS).

14 As a result of these amendments, (1) PEMEX Investment Expenditures were no longer counted for purposes of balancing the federal budget, thereby releasing additional government funds for other priority projects; (2) PEMEX's current PIDIREGAS commitments were now considered direct public debt rather than contingent debt obligations and (3) PEMEX was not permitted to undertake further PIDIREGAS authorizations and projects. "Reforms to the PEMEX-PIDIREGAS Regime" White & Case 1155 Avenue of the Americas New York, NY 10036 – February 2009.

15 The sharp drop in the Cantarell field after 2005 is explained by both mismanagement of the field and investment below the required standards.

16 Institutional changes were normalized across countries in the sample.

References

Balza, Lenin H. and Ramón Espinasa. 2015. "Oil Sector Performance and Institutions: The Case of Latin America", *Technical Note No. IDB-TN-724*, Inter-American Development Bank, Washington DC

Balza, Lenin H., Ramón Espinasa and Raul Jimenez. 2014. "Transforming Oil Abundance Into Sector Performance: Which Institutions Really Matter?" in Vieyra, Juan and Malaika Masson, eds., *Transparent Governance in an Age of Abundance: Experiences From the Extractive Industries in Latin America and the Caribbean*, pp. 351–374. Inter-American Development Bank, Washington DC.

Espinasa, Ramón. 2010. "Not Just a Distributional Matter", in Hogan, W. and F. Sturzenegger, eds., *The Natural Resource Trap: Private Investment Without Public Commitment*, pp. 467–483. MIT Press, Cambridge, MA.

Espinasa, Ramon, Sergio Guerra Reyes, Enrique ter Horst, Osmel Manzano, German Molina and Roberto Rigobon. 2017. "A Micro-Based Model for World Oil Market", *Energy Economics*, Accepted Manuscript.

Fasset, Will. 2011. *Mexican Hydrocarbons*, Georgetown University, Mimeo, Washington DC.

Manzano, O. and F. Monaldi. 2010. "The Political Economy of Oil Contract Renegotiation in Venezuela", in Hogan, W. and F. Sturzenegger, eds., *The Natural Resource Trap: Private Investment Without Public Commitment*, pp. 409–466. MIT Press, Cambridge, MA.

North, Douglas C. 1981. *Structure and Change in Economic History*, Norton, New York.

North, Douglass C. 1990. *Institutions, Institutional Change and Economic Performance*, Cambridge University Press, New York.

North, Douglass C. 1994. "Economic Performance Through Time", *American Economic Review*, 84, 359–368.

8 Transparency matters

Atanas Christev and Akram Esanov

1 Introduction

The Extractive Industry Transparency Initiative (EITI) has developed a global standard to promote revenue transparency in extractive industries. Since its inception in 2002, the EITI has been implemented by 18 compliant and 19 candidate countries. Nigeria was among the first resource-rich countries to join the EITI, while Peru blazed the trail in revenue transparency in Latin America. Moreover, most international organizations and many local NGOs pledged their support for the initiative. The EITI seeks to improve governance in resource-rich countries by disclosing full information about company payments and government revenues from oil, gas and mining. Yet, the identification and documentation of the EITI effects remain a challenge for policymakers, international organizations and civil society actors.

According to the EITI documents, the primary benefits of the EITI include improved investment climate, strengthened accountability and governance, as well as greater political stability.[1] Specifically, the existing policy relevant literature argues that the EITI might have the following direct and indirect effects:

1 strengthen/complicate macroeconomic management and economic growth;
2 improve transparency, accountability and reduce corruption;
3 reduce poverty;
4 improve investment climate/reduce borrowing costs/increase FDI;
5 improve governance;
6 mitigate conflicts.

The objective of this study is to examine the impact of the EITI membership (this includes both candidate and compliant countries) on such short-term outcomes as (1) foreign direct investment (FDI) flows, (2) investment climate, (3) corruption and (4) the cost of sovereign borrowing in resource-rich countries. This paper contends that greater transparency minimizes uncertainty in markets, boosts trust in public policies and adds predictability to government actions in the short run, leading to improvements in policies and quality of institutions. Furthermore, this study assumes that enhanced revenue transparency boosts accountability, empowers citizens, improves the allocation of resources and undermines the power of special interests in the long run.

Most existing empirical studies that examine the impact of a measure of transparency (economic, fiscal or political) are likely to suffer from a number of weaknesses due to measurement and methodological challenges. First, there is no clear consensus among researchers as to the definition and measurement of transparency. Since often studies use poor measures of transparency or weak proxies, the estimated coefficients of such regression estimations will be biased (see Glaeser et al. 2004). Second, transparency, as a component of institutional development, is highly correlated with other components of quality of institutions (Islam 2006). This fact presents a challenge when estimating the impact of transparency on other performance variables. In this case, regression analysis has to be corrected for the endogeneity problem; otherwise, the estimated results will be less robust and it becomes more difficult to establish a clear causal relationship between dependent and independent variables. Third, often researchers use multiple-country data in estimating the impact of greater transparency without paying much attention to changes that happened over time (Bellver and Kaufmann 2005). This creates omitted variable bias. Finally, many existing studies use data from all developed and developing countries with no special reference to resource-rich nations. This study attempts to addresses all these shortcomings in evaluating benefits of EITI membership.

Since the EITI is a relatively recent phenomenon, studies that attempt to measure and evaluate its benefits have to be carefully designed, taking into consideration all important information. In particular, an assessment of EITI's impact needs to focus on such short-term outcome variables as investment climate, sovereign borrowing costs, foreign direct investment and the extent of corruption that are likely to change in the short run. While the development of good institutions and an improvement in the living standards require an execution of long-term projects, an improvement in the investment climate and some dimensions of governance can be attained within a relatively short period of time. Since the start of the EITI's implementation, it is problematic to assess the EITI's long-term effects. Given data limitations, it is more appropriate to analyze the EITI's effects on the above-mentioned short-term outcomes.

Short-term outcome variables, including financial and reputation-related variables, can change within a short period of time. In contrast, changes in such long-term outcome variables as citizen empowerment, accountability and resource allocation practices will become detectable with the passage of a longer time period. Both types of variables need to be differentiated from such long-term impact variables as improvements in the quality of living standards or poverty reduction.

The remainder of the chapter is organized as follows. Section 2 surveys the evolution of the EITI. Section 3 provides a brief overview of extant research on the benefits of transparency, with special emphasis on recent studies assessing benefits of the EITI membership. Section 4 describes the data and discusses some measurement issues. Section 5 specifies the empirical model and explains the methodology. Section 6 presents the empirical findings. Section 7 is devoted to the analysis of two EITI-implementing countries to enhance our understanding of the link between fiscal transparency and its benefits. The final section summarizes major findings and provides some policy recommendations.

2 The evolution of the EITI

The EITI is a global initiative that aims to strengthen governance in resource-rich countries by improving transparency and accountability in extractive industries. This landmark initiative was announced by the British Prime Minister Tony Blair at the World Summit on Sustainable Development in South Africa in 2002. Approximately 140 delegates representing 70 governments, companies, industry groups, international organizations, investors and NGOs attended the first EITI Plenary Conference held in London in June 2003 and agreed upon a set of principles to increase transparency over payments and revenues in the extractive sector. These 12 principles became known as the EITI Principles and laid the foundation for the formulation of the EITI standard. In particular, the tenth principle states that "a broadly consistent and workable approach to the disclosure of payments and revenues is required".[2] Informed by these principles, the EITI rules spell out the requirements for implementing the EITI. The EITI Board elected at the EITI biennial conference plays a major role in championing the EITI principles and reviewing EITI validation reports.

This initiative is grounded in the belief that "the prudent use of natural resource wealth has the potential to provide the basis for sustainable economic growth and development".[3] Although the EITI began as a civil society campaign for publication of payments by extractive companies, within a few years it grew into a multi-stakeholder organization with comprehensive rules and a well-established governing structure. The development of a work plan agreed upon by all the stakeholders is a main sign-up requirement for achieving the EITI candidate status. A candidate country needs to meet all the EITI requirements and go through the validation process within two and a half years to become designated as EITI compliant.

The rapid growth of the EITI membership attests to the global support for the EITI principles. As shown in Table 8.1, the number of EITI-compliant countries increased from two in 2009 to 12 in 2011. Azerbaijan was the first country to gain the status of EITI compliant. In addition, the number of implementing countries, including compliant and candidate ones, doubled from 15 in 2007 to 37 in 2012. A parallel trend was the growing number of supporting companies, increasing from 37 in 2007 to 61 in 2011. Moreover, several countries indicated the

Table 8.1 The evolution of the EITI

	2007	2008	2009	2010	2011	2012
Compliant countries	N/A	N/A	2	5	12	18
Implementing countries	15	23	29	33	35	37
Supporting companies	37	37	41	52	60	68
Supporting investors	N/A	$14trm	$16trm	84	90	90
Supporting countries	10	12	16	17	18	18
Countries that have submitted final validation reports	N/A	N/A	2	17	27	29

Note: The number of supporting investors is measured in assets under management in 2007–2009. Target estimates are reported in parenthesis for year 2011.

Source: *EITI International Secretariat 2011 Report*, p. 11.

Table 8.2 List of candidate, compliant and intending countries (as of Dec. 2012)

Intent to implement	Candidate status	EITI compliant
Australia	Afghanistan	Azerbaijan
Brazil	Albania	Central African Republic
Colombia	Burkina Faso	Ghana
Myanmar	Cameroon	Iraq
Philippines	Chad	Kyrgyz Republic
Senegal	Cote d'Ivoire	Liberia
South Sudan	DRC	Mali
United States	Gabon	Mauritania
Vietnam	Guatemala	Mongolia
	Guinea	Mozambique
	Indonesia	Niger
	Kazakhstan	Nigeria
	Madagascar (suspended)	Norway
	Republic of the Congo	Peru
	Sierra Leone	Tanzania
	Sao Tome and Principe	Timor–Leste
	Solomon Islands	Yemen
	Togo	Zambia
	Trinidad and Tobago	

Source: EITI website http://eiti.org/countries and http://eiti.org/news

willingness to join the initiative in the near future. Table 8.2 provides a list of candidate, complaint and intending countries. A number of resource-rich developed countries are also willing to implement the EITI.

Critics of the EITI identify several weaknesses in this global standard. A major criticism of the EITI is that it lacks enforcement procedures (Aaronson 2011; McGee and Gaventa 2010). There are few real disincentives for non-compliance with the EITI standards. Another perceived weakness of the EITI is its narrow focus on revenues and payments in the extractive sector, which does not entail substantial reforms in the public sector and leaves resource-rich countries vulnerable to corruption (Kolstad and Wiig 2009; Scanteam 2011).

In turn, the EITI declares that compliance with its principles has multiple benefits for implementing countries, companies, investors and civil society actors.[4] The implementation of the EITI rules may improve an investment climate and promote greater political stability. The reduction of these political and economic risks is beneficial to business because it may attract more investment in the extractive industry. Moreover, the implementation of the EITI may benefit multiple civil society actors because the supply of information about payments and revenues is likely to make governments more accountable to citizens. Nonetheless, it is challenging to clearly demonstrate the effects of compliance with the EITI standard on implementing countries.[5]

3 Prior research

Voluminous empirical work documents that countries endowed with substantial natural resources tend to perform worse in terms of economic growth than their resource-poor counterparts. This negative impact is particularly pronounced in the case of oil, gas and mineral resources. Social scientists have defined this puzzling phenomenon as a "resource curse" and have attempted to identify potential mechanisms through which resource dependence negatively affects the long-term growth prospects of resource-dependent countries (Auty 1993; Ross 1999).

This literature generally finds that resource abundance could affect the level of output and economic growth through crowding out the manufacturing sector (Dutch disease phenomenon), creating opportunities for rent-seeking (corruption), reducing incentives for human capital accumulation and lessening government accountability and incentives for reform. Most recent studies demonstrate that poor institutional quality in resource-rich countries is the primary cause of sluggish economic growth in these countries (Kolstad 2009; Robinson et al. 2006). A major contention in this literature is that fragile institutions in resource-dependent countries create good conditions for corruption, reduce government accountability, deteriorate fiscal discipline and distort allocation of public funds (Acemoglu and Johnson 2005; Mehlum et al. 2006).

In light of these findings, international organizations and local NGOs championed transparency as a tool for improving the quality of institutions in resource-rich countries. Most of these countries are among the most corrupt and underdeveloped in the world despite the fact that natural resource wealth has a potential to benefit the poor and generate economic growth. In countries where democracy is weakly rooted and the state is predatory, improved transparency empowers citizens, makes governments more accountable and boosts efficiency in the provision of public services (Bellver and Kaufmann 2005; Hameed 2005). In general, the growing policy consensus is that increasing transparency in managing natural resource wealth is an important step towards a more responsible and efficient management of natural resource wealth. Yet, most empirical research failed to register significant positive changes in EITI-implementing countries (Ölcer 2009; Scanteam 2011).

The literature on the benefits of greater transparency can be divided into three distinct groups: (1) theoretical studies, (2) micro-level empirical analysis and (3) the strand of literature that examines the impact of greater transparency on macroeconomic and development indicators. The theoretical studies have convincingly demonstrated that accurate and timely information enhances market efficiency and leads to better resource allocation (Stigler 1961; Stiglitz and Weiss 1981). This literature argues that improvements in information play an important role in bringing down adverse consequences associated with principal-agent problems.

At the firm level, increasing corporate transparency can help firms to reduce their cost of capital. Even though a link between enhanced transparency and the cost of equity capital seems fairly intuitive, there has been little empirical research on the topic. Leuz and Hail (2003) found a correlation between the cost of equity capital and the level of disclosure and securities regulation in 40 countries, controlling for country differences and risk variations between countries. Gelos and Wei (2005) find that international investment funds tend to hold more assets in more transparent countries and international investors prefer to hold fewer assets in opaque countries during crisis.

At the macro-level, this literature investigates the impact of greater transparency on monetary policy making, fiscal outcomes, financial market stability, corruption and economic development. Numerous studies that explore the relationship between central bank transparency and efficiency of monetary policy conclude that more transparent central banks tend to more effectively communicate with the markets and serve as a mechanism for democratic accountability. Along these lines, Fracasso et al. (2003) assess inflation reports of 19 inflation-targeting countries and conclude that more transparent central banks are more predictable and achieve consistently high ratings. Based upon the analysis of data from 100 central banks, Dincer and Eichengreen (2009) illustrate that countries with more advanced and stable institutions are more likely to have transparent monetary policy arrangements, which, in turn, lead to less inflation variability. Moreover, Hameed (2005) finds that countries with more transparent fiscal practices tend to have higher credit ratings, less corruption and better fiscal discipline. Along similar lines, Christofides et al. (2003) provide empirical support for the argument that adherence to different international governance standards such as data dissemination, financial sector and market integrity standards improves credit ratings and lowers the cost of capital measured by spreads on foreign currency-denominated sovereign bonds. In addition, numerous multiple-country studies report at least some link between releasing more macroeconomic data and lower fiscal deficits, lower inflation and increased inflow of foreign direct investment. We also argue that the disclosure of payments and revenues in oil, gas and mineral sectors will impact on FDI flows, investment climate, corruption and the cost of capital.

Unlike corporations, countries are not bound by disclosure requirements, and it is much harder to measure and estimate the causal relationship between increased transparency and the cost of sovereign borrowing. Yet, the IMF generated unique country-level data when it suggested that governments make public the IMF's assessment of their policies. This policy reform initiative was intended to promote transparency, and it has been considered as an episode comparable to mandatory disclosure regulations faced by corporations, even if releasing assessments were not obligatory. Using data from 23 emerging economies, Glennerster and Shin (2008) demonstrate that the credit spread of countries that chose to publish the IMF's assessments declined, on average, by 11%, and the benefits of increased transparency are likely to be greater if a country is less transparent at the start of the reform.

There have been several attempts to evaluate the impact of the EITI such as the Scanteam evaluation (2011) and the Independent Evaluation Group evaluation of the Multi-Donor Trust Fund (2011). The Scanteam report failed to detect any statistically significant relationship between EITI membership and big-picture indicators such as economic growth, poverty, investment climate and governance. Along similar lines, the IEG evaluation finds that the MDTF-EITI program is an important tool in promoting transparency in resource-rich countries, although the review provides no evidence to support the argument that revenue transparency, measured by EITI membership, improves governance and reduces corruption in resource-dependent countries. Methodological deficiencies and data limitations in these documents reduced the validity of the findings, and robust assessment of the EITI effects still remain a challenge for policymakers, governments and civil society groups.

In addition, two recent studies specifically analyze the impact of the EITI on corruption and other economic variables. Ölcer (2009) finds that EITI has no significant impact on corruption in implementing countries. Similarly, David-Barrett and Okamura (2010) demonstrate that joining the EITI decreases the level of perceived corruption. By the same token, the gap between perceived corruption and actual corruption has narrowed after countries joined the EITI. Furthermore, this study shows that there are some tangible benefits of implementing the EITI. Countries that join the EITI receive more foreign aid and debt forgiveness from donor countries. Both studies differ from the current study in terms of their objectives, time-span, country coverage and methodology.

Furthermore, this paper differs from earlier studies in terms of data employed in the empirical analysis, the estimation methodology and the sample size. The next section discusses these issues in detail.

4 Data and measurement issues

The empirical analysis covers 60 resource-rich countries implementing EITI or intending to do so from 2003 to 2010,[6] according to the IMF definition of "resource dependence". Descriptive statistics and definitions of all the variables are reported in Appendices 2 and 3, respectively.

4.1 Dependent variables

4.1.1 Foreign direct investment

There is a strong belief among policymakers that foreign direct investment (FDI) enhances the productivity in host countries and promotes economic development. Most recent research demonstrates that FDI increases economic growth under certain conditions.[7] Notably, countries that have better institutions and prudent macroeconomic management attract more foreign direct investment. It is reasonable to argue that enhanced transparency improves the quality of institutions and macroeconomic policies. For our purpose, the inflow of FDI as a share of nominal GDP is used. More precisely, this is net foreign direct investment inflows divided by nominal GDP. Net inflows are new investment flows less disinvestments as reported in the balance of payments.

4.1.2 Investment climate

In recent years, policymakers and international organizations have championed the idea that investment climate plays an important role in generating economic growth in developing countries. Broadly speaking, the investment climate includes sound macroeconomic policies, governance and institutions and physical infrastructure. Guided by the existing literature,[8] we assume that transparency improves macroeconomic policies, quality of institutions and allocation of fiscal revenues leading to improvements in investment climate. We use two proxies to measure investment climate. These measures relate to country credit risk and business environment. The OECD country risk measure is composed of two components: (1) transfer and currency convertibility risk and (2) cases of force majeure. The values of this measure run from zero to seven, zero indicating no country risk. The second measure of investment climate is the Business Freedom Index of the Heritage Foundation and it measures an "individual's right to establish and run an enterprise without undue interference from the state".[9] The values of the Business Freedom Index run on a scale from 0 to 100, where the value of 100 indicates the maximum freedom. These two variables measure two different aspects of country risk: the first variable measures risk from inept economic policies while the second variable deals with business freedom from excessive state interference.

4.1.3 Corruption

A widely used definition of corruption is the use of public office for private gain. Corruption can increase transaction costs and raise uncertainty, impeding domestic and foreign investment. Recent evidence from a number of developing and emerging economies has demonstrated that strong political will and good government policies can contain corruption (Kaufmann et al. 2009). In this study, we argue that governments improve accountability by disclosing information on resource revenues, thus reducing the level of corruption. As a measure of corruption, we use the World Bank's Control of Corruption Index. This index captures "perceptions of the extent to which public power is exercised for private gain, including both petty and grand forms of corruption, as well as 'capture' of the state by elites and private interests".[10] The rescaled value of the index ranges from 1 (most corrupt) to 6 (least corrupt).

4.1.4 Cost of capital

The paper uses country risk premiums as a measure of the cost of capital. The data are taken from the data set generated by Aswath Damodaran.[11] A country risk premium refers to an increment in interest rates (long term or short term) that would have to be paid for loans and investment projects in a particular country above some standard. Usually the US is used as a benchmark country and the other countries are compared to this benchmark. Data on the sovereign risk ratings are easily available for a large set of countries. The data can be used as a proxy for the cost of capital since there is a strong statistical correlation between sovereign cost of capital and country risk ratings.

4.2 Independent variables

4.2.1 Fiscal transparency

Existing transparency measures lack temporal dimension and any causal relationship between transparency and other variables can only be obtained using panel data estimation techniques. This paper develops a new measure of fiscal transparency that measures transparency over time across different resource-rich countries.[12] EITI membership is used as a proxy for revenue transparency in resource-rich countries. We rank all resource-dependent countries (IMF definition and EITI implementation) based on their support of the EITI: non-member countries, candidate countries, early compliant countries and advanced compliant countries (if compliant more than two years).[13] We attach values to these qualitative statements to get quantitative data usable in the regression analysis and track progress over time. These values help to quantify the status of a country with regard to EITI and capture the progress (or regress) over time. Obtaining a compliant status is a complicated two-stage process and simply using a dummy variable does not capture dynamics of the entire process. Furthermore, retaining a compliant status over time also requires additional efforts from EITI-implementing countries, which justifies our approach of giving higher points for advanced compliant countries. Appendix 4 discusses the details of this process. Our measure of fiscal transparency has a mean of 0.49 and a standard deviation of 0.84.

4.2.2 Other control variables

Additional *right hand* variables include measures of the macroeconomic fundamentals, governance indicators and political accountability. The regression analyses also account for the impact of the size of the country's oil/mineral reserves or production on selected dependent variables. In light of previous research, one set of control variables is used to explain FDI flows, while another set of control variables is included in models explaining multiple-country differences in corruption, credit risk and sovereign premium risk.

Prior research shows that such macroeconomic variables as growth potential, economic stability, income level and resource wealth are significant predictors of FDI (see Asiedu 2006). Furthermore, scores of studies demonstrate that the political regime and the quality of institutions are important for attracting FDI (e.g. Schneider and Frey 1985; Wei 2000). In view of these studies, we include economic growth, executive constraints, current account balance, fiscal balance, per capita GDP and an indicator of resource dependence as explanatory variables when we examine the relationship between FDI and EITI membership.

In addition, social scientists have identified numerous factors to account for multiple-country differences in credit risk and sovereign premium risk (Gupta et al. 2008). In our analysis, we use variables that measure the quality of institutions (EITI membership, measures of monetary policy, political regime and fiscal balance) and variables that gauge the solvency and vulnerabilities to external shocks. Broadly speaking, the following variables were included in the estimations as the explanatory variables:

Fiscal Balance: central government's fiscal balance as a percentage of GDP is used to capture the fiscal strength of a country. The conventional wisdom is that a strong fiscal stance lowers default likelihood and lowers the bond spread and country risk premiums. In addition, we use government consumption to measure the size of the government.

Monetary Policy: a stable monetary policy and strong macroeconomic conditions are expected to narrow bond spread or sovereign risk premiums. Inflation is used to account for changes in the macroeconomic fundamentals when we examine the association between the country risk premium and fiscal transparency.

Vulnerabilities to External Shocks: the current account balance as a percentage of GDP is used in the regression estimations to measure a country's solvency and vulnerabilities to external shocks. It is expected that the surplus of current account balance lowers credit risk and credit spreads. Finally, resource rent, per executive constraint and rule of law are used to explain variations in the country risk premium, while per capita GDP is also included in regressions analyzing the relationship between the country credit risk and fiscal transparency.

An alternative measure of investment climate – the Business Freedom Index – is also used as a dependent variable to check robustness of our results. In these regressions, we augmented the previous empirical model of credit risk by adding new variables such as resource rents (abundance), per capita GDP and property rights.

Various strands of the literature examine empirical regularities between corruption and various economic, institutional and political variables (Olken and Pande 2011). Since there is no widely agreed-upon theoretical model to be used as a basis for building an empirical model, most studies examine the causes of corruption by including different explanatory variables in an ad hoc manner (Alt and Lassen 2003). In our regression analysis, we include institutional and economic variables to investigate the link between corruption and fiscal transparency (EITI). In particular, fiscal transparency, political competition, current account balance, per capita GDP, government consumption, fiscal balance and inflation have been included in our empirical model to examine the causes of corruption.

5 Empirical model and estimation methodology

In our empirical analysis, we run panel data regressions to estimate and analyze the impact of EITI on five dependent variables, namely foreign direct investment, level of corruption, investment climate (two measures) and sovereign risk premiums. The baseline model for the panel data framework can be written as follows:

$$Y_{it} = \alpha_i + \beta_1 EITI_{it} + \beta_2 X_{it} + u_{it}, i = 1,....N; t = 1,....T \qquad (1)$$

where Y_{it} is the selected dependent variable for each country and each year in the sample. EITI is a measure for fiscal transparency and X_{it} represents the explanatory variables used in the regressions while u_{it} is the error term and β represents estimated coefficients. However, simple panel estimations fail to take into consideration the fact that dependent variables are also affected by their own past values and estimating the model without a lagged dependent variable term yields biased estimations. A more rigorous (statistical) approach will be to run a dynamic panel model which accounts for various institutional inertia present at the time of EITI implementation. For our purpose, we need to specify the basic econometric model as follows:

$$Y_{it} = \alpha Y_{it-1} + \beta_1 EITI_{it} + \beta_2 X_{it} + \upsilon_t + e_{it}, \, i = 1,....N; \, t = 1,....T \qquad (2)$$

where Y_{it} is a dependent variable, Y_{it-1} is a one period lag of the dependent variable, $EITI_{it}$ is the measure of transparency and X_{it} is a range of explanatory variables that are important in explaining variations in the dependent variable.

The primary objective of fitting this model to the data is to examine whether the measure of transparency (EITI implementation) has a significant impact with the expected sign on the selected dependent variables. Estimation of these types of models is challenging due to a number of statistical issues.[14] In simple dynamic models, regular fixed effect models are inconsistent when the time span is short as in our case (Nickell 1981). Furthermore, the lagged dependent variable is endogenous (or highly correlated) to the fixed effects in the error term and leads to biased results. There are two possible solutions to this problem.

The first approach is to difference the data to remove the fixed effects and estimate the model. However, this approach is not fully successful in addressing the problem. This allows us to instrument the lagged dependent variable or other endogenous variables in the model with past values of the variable to remove the potential correlation with the fixed effects. The model based on differencing and using past values of endogenous variables as instruments can be estimated utilizing the instrumental variables (IV) estimator (Anderson and Hsiao 1981) or generalized method of moments (GMM) estimator (Arellano and Bond 1991). However, both estimators suffer from a weak instrument problem when the dynamic panel autoregressive coefficient approaches unity. To correct this problem Blundell and Bond (1998) developed the "system GMM" estimator that suggests differencing the instruments themselves and using the levels of the variables with the first differenced instruments in the estimation process.

The system GMM estimator is designed for situations with few time periods (short T) and large number of individual units (large N). The estimator can be used to treat models where not all independent variables are exogenous, a linear functional relationship exists among the regressors, there are fixed individual effects and the dependent variable is dynamic. We control for potential heteroscedasticity and autocorrelation in the error structure of the model (Roodman 2009), and report (country-specific) clustered errors. In our empirical model, dependent variables are persistent and some of the explanatory variables are endogenous. These deficiencies warrant employing the GMM-system estimator to retrieve our coefficient estimates.

The following section empirically investigates whether fiscal transparency measured by EITI membership is significant in explaining investment climate and institutional quality. In addition, to strengthen the validity of empirical findings derived from statistical analysis, the study utilizes a case-study approach. The qualitative analysis focuses on two specific countries: Nigeria and Peru. These countries are selected because they were among the first countries in Africa and Latin America to achieve an EITI-compliant status. The analysis traces how the government's efforts to enhance transparency led to improvements in governance. The results of the case study analysis will not only help us to establish and understand the link between enhanced transparency and the above-mentioned dependent variables but also will inform the policy debate regarding the promotion of fiscal transparency.

6 Findings

The regression analysis is performed using five different dependent variables: foreign direct investment, country risk (proxy for investment climate), an alternative measure of country risk (business freedom), corruption and sovereign cost of capital. Each model seeks to identify whether fiscal transparency in resource-rich countries – measured by EITI membership – affects investment climate and the quality of institutions. Broadly, the empirical results lend support for the argument that the EITI strengthens investor confidence and assists establishing good governance.

The empirical analysis begins with estimating effects of the EITI on foreign direct investment flows. To reiterate, the level of foreign direct investment at a certain point in time is usually affected by the level of foreign direct investment at an earlier time point. Consistent with this argument, the results show that the estimated coefficient for lagged foreign direct investment is significant and positively correlated with the current value of the dependent variable. The new measure (developed in this study) of fiscal transparency (EITI membership) is also positively correlated with the dependent variable and this relationship is statistically significant. This finding signifies that becoming an EITI-implementing country increases foreign direct investment flows into the country. This result also provides empirical support for the argument that governments are likely to raise the confidence of international investors and financial institutions by sending accurate information about their fiscal activities, commitment to greater transparency and economic policies.

In Table 8.3, the level of executive constraints is positively correlated with the flow of foreign direct investment in the country. When we change the model specification, the effect of executive constraints on foreign direct investment remains statistically significant. This finding implies that foreign investors seek markets where executive constraints are strong and the system of checks and balances is in place. In contrast, current account balance is negatively associated with foreign direct investment. Arguably, foreign investors assume that a positive current account balance is a sign of economic controls – either trade or currency – and not favorable for doing business. In addition, government fiscal balance is not correlated with foreign direct investment flows. The findings presented in Table 8.3 also illustrate that a measure of resource abundance is positively associated with FDI and statistically significant. It must also be noted that resource abundance is significantly correlated with a measure of per capita income in our sample. This finding implies that foreign direct investment flows benefit not only resource-rich countries, but also relatively wealthy economies. There is a positive statistical

Table 8.3 The effects of the EITI membership on FDI

Variables	(1)	(2)	(3)	(4)
	FDI	FDI	FDI	FDI
FDI (t–1)	0.526***	0.450***	0.446***	0.428***
	(0.101)	(0.127)	(0.124)	(0.134)
EITI	1.776***	1.105**	1.140**	1.048**
	(0.521)	(0.540)	(0.528)	(0.473)
Resource abundance		0.0299**	0.0251*	0.0253**
		(0.0146)	(0.0134)	(0.0129)
Executive constraints		0.289***	0.240***	0.250***
		(0.0782)	(0.0741)	(0.0798)
Fiscal balance		0.0404	0.0296	0.0455
		(0.0560)	(0.0573)	(0.0565)
Current account balance		–0.0970**	–0.116**	–0.118**
		(0.0412)	(0.0483)	(0.0494)
GDP per capita			4.07e–05**	3.93e–05**
			(1.78e–05)	(1.74e–05)
Inflation				0.00512
				(0.0288)
Observations	418	411	411	411
Number of country	60	59	59	59
Number of instruments	15	19	20	21
Hansen test	0.49	0.23	0.25	0.31
AR(1)	0.009	0.009	0.008	0.011
AR(2)	0.45	0.49	0.47	0.49
Diff–in–Hansen test	0.43	0.49	0.63	0.81

Note: The estimation method is a two-step system GMM. In all regressions the measure of fiscal transparency is treated as potentially exogenous. All *p*-values are calculated using the robust standard errors and the Windmeijer (2005) correction. Standard errors in parentheses.
*** $p<0.01$, ** $p<0.05$, * $p<0.1$

association between GDP per capita and foreign direct investment. Finally, inflation is not associated with the foreign direct investment flows into the country. The last decade has seen dramatic decline in the inflation rates across the globe, and for many investors high inflation posed no threat. It is very likely that the regressions are capturing this phenomenon.

Next, the estimates show the effect of fiscal transparency on country risk. As with foreign direct investment, the present value of country risk is strongly correlated with its lagged value. This finding suggests a significant part of the changes in the dependent variable can be explained by the past values of the dependent variable. In Table 8.4, EITI membership is not associated with country risk while executive constraint is negatively related to country risk (column 3 and 4), indicating that country risk is small when a country has a strong checks and balances or the executive level of government has less power in its hands. Although the coefficient of current account balance is negative, its correlation with country risk is insignificant in our fuller model. Finally, both fiscal balance and property

Table 8.4 The effects of the EITI membership on country risk (CRISK)

Variables	(1)	(2)	(3)	(4)
	CRISK	CRISK	CRISK	CRISK
CRISK (t–1)	1.265***	1.293***	1.254***	1.399***
	(0.250)	(0.145)	(0.146)	(0.0718)
CRISK (t–2)	–0.381	–0.312**	–0.293	–0.532***
	(0.271)	(0.141)	(0.207)	(0.101)
CRISK (t–3)	0.109	0.0164	0.0231	0.123**
	(0.0887)	(0.0991)	(0.0778)	(0.0623)
EITI	0.00685	–0.00743	–0.00426	0.00204
	(0.0278)	(0.0330)	(0.0184)	(0.0146)
Executive constraints		0.00452	–0.0131**	–0.0185***
		(0.0196)	(0.00610)	(0.00613)
Property rights			–0.000264	
			(0.00148)	
Current account balance			–0.00337**	–0.00107
			(0.00139)	(0.00279)
GDP per capita			0.0167	0.0127
			(0.0127)	(0.0108)
Resource abundance		–1.74e–05		
		(0.00121)		
Economic growth		–0.0123*		0.00399
		(0.00680)		(0.00443)
Fiscal balance				–0.00653
				(0.00551)
Observations	295	288	279	288
Number of country	59	58	57	58
Number of instruments	20	32	29	36
Hansen test	0.33	0.46	0.31	0.33
AR(1)	0.122	0.017	0.051	0.001
AR(2)	0.894	0.478	0.441	0.902
Diff–in–Hansen test	0.21	0.52	0.46	0.26

Note: The estimation method is two-step system GMM. Standard errors in parentheses.
*** $p<0.01$, ** $p<0.05$, * $p<0.1$
See Note to Table 8.3

rights have no statistically significant association with country risk while the esti-mated coefficient of economic growth becomes statistically insignificant when we change slightly the model specification.

The finding that fiscal transparency measured by EITI membership is quite weakly associated with country risk is somewhat unexpected. In the results presented in Table 8.4, the correlation between these two variables is statistically insignificant across all models. This finding might emerge due to the OECD measurement of the country risk used in these regressions gauging risk from currency convertibility, capital controls and force majeure situations and omitting the measurement of sovereign risk. While the OECD measure of country risk is widely used in empirical studies as a measure of country risk, this variable is too narrow to capture changes in business environment and poorly serves for our purpose. Given this rationale, we used another variable to examine the relationship between EITI membership and investment climate.

When we run regressions using a broader measure of investment climate, we find that there is a positive association between EITI implementation and the dependent variable measured by the Business Freedom Index of the World Economic forum. Since higher values of this index indicate better investment climate, the positive relationship between the Business Freedom Index and EITI membership suggests that fiscal transparency tends to improve investment climate. The results are presented in Table 8.5. Different model specifications and the inclusion of additional explanatory variables left unchanged the initial results that fiscal transparency improves business freedom. The results also indicate that the quality of institutions and political regime, measured by the rule of law and executive

Table 8.5 The effects of the EITI membership on business environment

Variables	(1)	(2)	(3)	(4)
	CRISK2	CRISK2	CRISK2	CRISK2
CRISK2 (t–1)	0.96***	0.92***	0.84***	0.79***
	(0.0162)	(0.0473)	(0.0645)	(0.0632)
EITI	1.991***	0.887**	0.660*	0.668**
	(0.562)	(0.378)	(0.355)	(0.297)
Fiscal balance		–0.0931	–0.133*	–0.136*
		(0.0578)	(0.0752)	(0.0738)
Rule of law		0.809		1.566***
		(0.493)		(0.525)
Resource abundance		0.0392		–0.00133
		(0.0311)		(0.0146)
Executive constraints		0.793*	0.401*	0.479*
		(0.463)	(0.236)	(0.248)
Inflation		–0.0485	–0.114**	
		(0.0528)	(0.0515)	
Property rights			0.00408	
			(0.0342)	
GDP per capita			0.988**	1.236***
			(0.394)	(0.385)
Observations	387	380	380	380
Number of country	56	55	55	55
Number of instruments	15	20	23	23
Hansen test	0.12	0.17	0.22	0.31
AR(1)	0.00	0.00	0.00	0.00
AR(2)	0.41	0.53	0.64	0.62
Diff–in–Hansen test	0.86	0.37	0.45	0.76

Note: The estimation method is two-step system GMM. Standard errors in parentheses.
*** p<0.01, ** p<0.05, * p<0.1
See note to Table 8.3

constraints respectively are positively correlated with business freedom, and these correlations are statistically significant. In contrast, property rights and resource abundance are not correlated to the Business Freedom Index. In addition, two measures of economic stability, namely fiscal balance and inflation, are negatively associated with the dependent variable, at least in one model specification. Finally, GDP per capita – a measure of economic development – is positively correlated with the Business Freedom Index. This finding suggests that more developed countries tend to have better business environments. In sum, across the different model specifications the relationship between fiscal transparency and the Business Freedom Index remain positive and statistically significant.

The regression results presented in Table 8.6 demonstrate the effect of fiscal transparency on corruption. Again, the current value of the dependent variable

Table 8.6 The effects of the EITI membership on corruption

Variables	(1)	(2)	(3)	(4)
	Corrup	Corrup	Corrup	Corrup
Corrupt (t–1)	0.942***	0.941***	0.940***	0.937***
	(0.0276)	(0.0274)	(0.0250)	(0.0253)
EITI	0.0143**	0.0144**	0.0143**	0.0133*
	(0.00691)	(0.00708)	(0.00707)	(0.00702)
Political competition	0.0166***	0.0168***	0.0176***	0.0181***
	(0.00424)	(0.00430)	(0.00412)	(0.00395)
GDP per capita	0.0173*	0.0176*	0.0174*	0.0183**
	(0.0102)	(0.0101)	(0.00934)	(0.00919)
Inflation	–0.000694	–0.000689		
	(0.00132)	(0.00131)		
Current account balance	0.000701	0.000791	0.000992	0.00101
	(0.000779)	(0.000859)	(0.000828)	(0.000775)
Government consumption	–0.00927***	–0.00932***	–0.0100***	–0.0101***
	(0.00359)	(0.00360)	(0.00363)	(0.00340)
Fiscal balance		–0.000315	–0.000436	–0.000479
		(0.00134)	(0.00121)	(0.00126)
Resource abundance				3.28e–05
				(0.000287)
Observations	404	404	404	404
Number of country	58	58	58	58
Number of instruments	38	39	38	39
Hansen test	0.446	0.442	0.544	0.554
AR(1)	0.00	0.00	0.00	0.00
AR(2)	0.998	0.982	0.978	0.974
Diff–in–Hansen test	0.78	0.78	0.77	0.80

Note: The estimation method is two-step system GMM. Standard errors in parentheses.
*** $p<0.01$, ** $p<0.05$, * $p<0.1$
See Note to Table 8.3

is strongly correlated with the lagged value of the dependent variable, and this relationship is statistically significant. EITI membership is positively correlated with corruption and this association is statistically significant. Across different model specifications, the estimated coefficient of fiscal transparency is highly stable. Since higher values of the corruption index indicate less corruption, the positive relationship suggests that EITI-implementing countries tend to have less corruption. This finding presents a rare case when the link between EITI membership and corruption is empirically established using a sound econometric technique. This is a welcome finding for the EITI community, since it affirms the significance of transparency in extractive industries in reducing corruption in EITI-implementing countries.

The regression analysis also indicates that political competition is positively associated with corruption indicating that more democratic countries suffer less from corruption. The present analysis does not find a stable statistically significant relationship between corruption and resource abundance. This finding is consistent with a number of existing studies. We also find that corruption is not related to fiscal balance and inflation. Table 8.6 also reports that government consumption is negatively related to corruption. This finding suggests that higher government expenditures provide more opportunities for corruption. Finally, we find that the relationship between GDP per capita and corruption is positive and this relationship remains stable across different model specifications. The sign and the value of the estimated coefficient of income do not change across different models. This finding implies that more developed countries or countries with high per capita income tend to suffer less from the incidence of corruption compared to less developed countries.

The estimation results reported in Table 8.7 demonstrate the impact of a number of economic and governance variables on sovereign risk premium. Except in column 4, the measure of fiscal transparency or EITI membership is not related to sovereign risk premium in a statistically meaningful way. This suggests that this

Table 8.7 The effects of the EITI membership on risk premium

Variables	(1)	(2)	(3)	(4)
	Riskprem	Riskprem	Riskprem	Riskprem
Riskprem (t–1)	0.346***	0.345***	0.307***	0.348***
	(0.0942)	(0.0928)	(0.0738)	(0.101)
EITI	–0.00246	–0.00250	–0.00183	–0.00278*
	(0.00191)	(0.00192)	(0.00205)	(0.00155)
GDP per capita	–0.00275**	–0.00270**		–0.00293***
	(0.00111)	(0.00109)		(0.000942)
Inflation	0.00113***	0.00113***	0.00118***	0.00104***
	(0.000294)	(0.000295)	(0.000275)	(0.000257)
Trade openness	0.000509***	0.000505***	0.000489***	0.000444***
	(0.000156)	(0.000154)	(7.73e–05)	(0.000134)
Rule of law	–0.0102***	–0.0102***		–0.00965***
	(0.00249)	(0.00253)		(0.00237)

(Continued)

Table 8.7 (Continued)

Variables	(1)	(2)	(3)	(4)
	Riskprem	Riskprem	Riskprem	Riskprem
Fiscal balance		−1.31e−05		
		(9.35e−05)		
Resource abundance			1.96e−05	0.000118*
			(5.13e−05)	(6.52e−05)
Property rights			−0.000474***	
			(7.81e−05)	
Current account balance			−0.000291**	−0.000170
			(0.000143)	(0.000111)
Executive constraints				0.00131
				(0.000854)
Observations	195	195	195	195
Number of country	30	30	30	30
Number of instruments	19	20	20	22
Hansen test	0.37	0.36	0.39	0.30
AR(1)	0.043	0.043	0.033	0.051
AR(2)	0.70	0.70	0.68	0.90
Diff−in−Hansen test	0.64	0.71	0.54	0.58

Note: The estimation method is two-step system GMM. Standard errors in parentheses.
*** p<0.01, ** p<0.05, * p<0.1
See note to Table 8.3

relationship is not statistically robust, since it changes with model specification. As expected, the current value of sovereign risk premium is strongly correlated with its past value, and this relationship is statistically significant. Across different model specifications, the quality of institutions, gauged by rule of law and property rights, is negatively associated with sovereign risk premium and this relationship is statistically significant. This finding suggests that sovereign risk premiums tend to be lower in countries with well-functioning institutions.

Wealthier countries also tend to lower sovereign risk premium, since there is a negative association between risk premium and GDP per capita. A measure of sound macroeconomic management – inflation – is positively related to sovereign risk premiums, indicating that countries with high inflation face high cost of capital if they decided to borrow in the international financial markets. This trend has profound repercussions for a country's long-run development prospects. Trade openness is also positively related to the dependent variable suggesting that international financial markets consider openness to international trade as an indicator of a greater risk. We also find that the estimated coefficient of current account balance is marginally significant, while fiscal balance and executive constraints are not associated with the dependent variable.

Another important finding presented in Table 8.7 is that in our fuller model, resource abundance is positively correlated with sovereign risk premium. While this relationship is statistically significant, the value of the estimated coefficient for resource abundance is quite small. This implies that countries with substantial rents from the natural resource sector tend to have somewhat high risk premiums if they borrow. This finding can be explained by the very nature of revenues generated in oil, gas and mining industries. It is well documented that the extractive sector rents are finite and highly volatile, which increases uncertainty and leads to higher sovereign risk premiums.

The lower part of all the tables present some diagnostic results on the various statistical tests to determine whether the regression estimates are statistically robust and well specified. The AR1, AR2 and the Hansen tests indicate that there is no serial correlation in these regression models and the over-identifying restrictions are not rejected. The results do confirm that the models fit the data well and the coefficient estimates are consistent. In addition, tables provide information about the number of instruments, number of countries and observations included in the regression analysis. It must be noted that we follow Roodman's methodological approach (2009) and in several occasions "collapsed" the instrument set to improve the robustness of the results.

7 Case studies: Nigeria and Peru

7.1 Nigeria

Nigeria is the most populous African state endowed with abundant natural resources. The country ranks among the top ten oil producers in the world, and it is a leading producer of oil in Africa. The oil sector alone accounts for 90% of government revenues. Furthermore, Nigeria stands out as one of the first resource-rich countries that gained EITI-compliant status. The former Army General Olusegun Obasanjo who led the country out of the dictatorship and served as the president from 1999 to 2007 implemented a series of economic reforms to improve the macroeconomic environment. Nonetheless, the African state remains crippled with corruption, and the national government needs to take additional steps to take full advantage of abundant oil wealth and boost economic development.

The government's decision to join the EITI was an important part of a larger state effort to curb corruption and improve efficiency of public policies. As a sign of his support for the Nigerian EITI (NEITI), President Obasanjo declared in November 2003 that the government would disclose its revenues from the petroleum sector and charged one of his top advisors with the responsibility to oversee the implementation of this initiative. Within a few months after this bold statement, on February 19, 2004, the president initiated the establishment of the National Stakeholder Working Group (NSWG) to act as NEITI's board. In 2007 the National Assembly passed the NEITI Act to provide a legal basis for participation in and implementation of the EITI (Scanteam Report 2011). In the course of this presidency, President Obasanjo sought to galvanize mass support for the initiative and send a strong message to the private sector and, in particular, extractive companies. Despite some skepticism in the international community, Nigeria fulfilled the EITI requirements and obtained a compliant country status in 2010.

A combination of political and economic factors influenced the president's commitment to the EITI. The president's first term was marked with the high incidence of civilian deaths and the increasing level of economic hardship, which dampened his popularity on the eve of elections. There was growing public discontent with the incumbent government. In addition, international organizations stepped up pressures on the incumbent president to improve the country's public image and combat flagrant mismanagement of oil revenues and rampant corruption. These internal and external pressures provided an incentive for the government's compliance with the EITI requirements.

Furthermore, civil society organizations and extractive companies significantly contributed to the success of NEITI. Civil society groups and the mass media closely followed the reform process and endorsed the government's push for greater transparency. By that time, Nigeria had a relatively vibrant civil society, but civic activists were unable to expose corruption in the extractive industry due to the lack of access to relevant economic data. The adoption of the EITI standard enabled local civic activists and journalists to gain access to public finance data and critically assess state policies towards the petroleum industry. Compared to civil society, the private sector showed a weaker interest in supporting NEITI. Still, petroleum companies cooperated with the government to achieve greater transparency in the sector.

As a result of the government's reforms, Nigeria achieved a dramatic decline in the incidence of corruption. The country's score on the International Transparency's Corruption Perceptions Index climbed up, indicating a drop in perceived corruption. Enhanced transparency was a pivotal factor explaining an improvement in public perceptions of corruption. In 2003 the Nigerian government embarked upon an ambitious reform program known as the National Economic Empowerment and Development Strategy. These reforms aimed to devise and implement a long-term economic development strategy, curtail public expenditure volatility, privatize inefficient state-owned enterprises, reform the banking sector, and reduce Nigeria's massive international debt. President Obasanjo and the Finance Minister Ngozi Okonjo-Iweala closely cooperated with the World Bank and other international organizations to implement a number of structural and macroeconomic programs.

The Nigerian government took a wide range of measures to enhance transparency. First, the government expressed its intent to comply with the EITI standards and made public data on government revenues paid by oil companies. Second, the government developed a clear formula for delinking public expenditure from oil prices, which increased the predictability of the Nigerian budgeting process by removing price fluctuations. Third, state authorities began to release information about the allocation of public funds to the federal, state and local governments. This state initiative enabled the general public and policymakers to gain a better understanding of the size and the distribution of government revenues in Nigeria. Fourth, the Nigerian government set up such anti-corruption bodies as the Economic and Financial Crimes Commission (EFCC) and the Independent Corrupt Practices and Other Related Offenses Commission (ICPC) to investigate and prosecute corruption among public officials. Moreover, the government introduced greater transparency in the procurement process by publishing a journal of public tender and supplying information about government officials responsible for procurement. Though these state measures failed to fully eradicate corruption and allay international concerns about political instability, especially in the oil-producing Niger Delta, the government did bring about some positive change.

Figure 8.1 displays the change in Nigeria's score of the Corruption Perceptions Index over time. The score increased from 1.4 in 2003 to 2.4 in 2010, signifying a decrease in the level of perceived corruption. These improvements in corruption perceptions were hailed by international analysts as a significant step towards the reduction of corruption in the poverty-stricken country.

The transparency initiatives were closely connected with broader economic reforms in Nigeria. The IMF's Policy Support Instrument (PSI) approved for Nigeria in October 2005 made provisions for greater transparency. In January 2006 the Nigerian government released a preliminary report of the 2003 and 2004 oil and gas accounts of both the government and oil companies. In light of the country's compliance with the IMF's PSI, Nigeria reached a concessional debt agreement with the Paris Club and creditors cancelled 33% of the country's outstanding debt. In turn, the debt write-off was a key factor driving Fitch and Standard & Poor's decision to award Nigeria with its first-ever credit ratings in

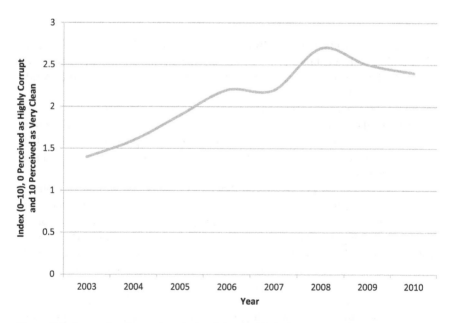

Figure 8.1 Corruption Perceptions Index, Nigeria, 2003–2010

Source: Transparency International

2006. The Finance Minister Okonjo-Iweala has repeatedly stressed transparency as a crucial component of the package:

> The oil-price-based fiscal rule and the adoption of the EITI both underscored Nigeria's determination to make a clean break with the past by fighting corruption and improving governance. In a revolutionary move, Nigeria went beyond the petroleum sector by publishing revenues from all sources at all tiers of government. The credibility boost facilitated Nigeria's debt cancellation by the Paris Club and lifted its profile in the eyes of investors. Standard & Poor's and Fitch Ratings assigned Nigeria a sovereign credit rating of BB – for 2007, affirming earlier results. The improved rating led to sizable increases in foreign direct investment in both the oil sector (about $6 billion a year) and non-oil sectors (about $3 billion a year).
>
> (Okonjo-Iweala 2008, p. 43)

In assigning the initial BB- rating, Fitch cited the oil-price-based expenditure rule, the introduction of key financial responsibility legislation, the participation in EITI, and the government's stated commitment to "improving transparency and governance" as elements of its decision (Fitch Ratings 2006). Standard & Poor's has also cited the influence of transparency in its decisions to award credit ratings to Nigeria and other African governments, citing it as one of the important factors influencing its rating decisions (Standard & Poor's 2006).

7.2 Peru

Peru is endowed with significant mineral resources, including copper, gold, zinc, silver and iron. The country also possesses some oil and natural gas. Peru ranks second in the world on copper, zinc and silver production, and it is the world's sixth largest producer of gold. While the fiscal revenue from the extractive sector represents a relatively small fraction of the total government revenues (17.4% in 2010), mineral exports constitute more than 60% of the country's export earnings. The Peruvian economy grew at an average rate of 5.3% per year in 2003–2010, reflecting improvements in economic fundamentals and an accelerated political decentralization process launched in 2002.

Peru launched the EITI process in 2005 and became a compliant country in early 2012. Compared to Nigeria, the EITI process in Peru has received weak state backing, and not all mining companies participated in the process. Seven years since joining the EITI, the national parliament failed to pass the EITI Law. Instead, the presidential decrees offer the legal basis for the fulfillment of the EITI requirements. The absence of strong political will and the fragmentation of civil society significantly diminished the visibility of the EITI process in Peru.

Notably, the fragmentation of civil society undermines the capacity of NGOs to press for transparency in the extractive sector. The presence of multiple social cleavages has resulted in the emergence of NGOs that serve different constituencies. In particular, the high level of poverty and economic disparities between urban and rural areas keep such issues as social conflict, health and environmental problems in mining areas at the top of the public agenda. Compared to Nigeria, much fewer Peruvian NGOs focused on the issue of transparency in the extractive sector, while some mining companies declined to participate in the EITI progress altogether.

Despite the slow pace of reforms, Peru is the only EITI-compliant country in Latin America. The Fiscal Responsibility and Transparency Law (FRTL) adopted in 1999 tightened fiscal discipline and made the budgeting process more credible, predictable and transparent. In 2003 the *Fiscal Management Responsibility Act* supplemented the FRTL and stated clear objectives to consolidate the public debt. The EITI membership was another major step towards establishing transparency and making the government accountable to its citizens. So far, Peru performs much better than most resource-dependent countries in terms of revenue and expenditure transparency.

The government's commitment to strengthen transparency in the mining sector sent a powerful signal to foreign investors and financial markets. Specifically, transparency improvements combined with widespread pro-market macro-economic reforms represented a critical component of the country's increased attractiveness in the eyes of investors. Figure 8.2 illustrates improvements in the business environment in Peru in 2003–2010. The level of business freedom increased by approximately ten points during this period.

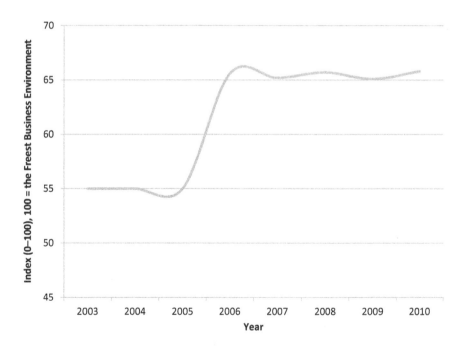

Figure 8.2 Business freedom, Peru, 2003–2010

Source: The Heritage Foundation

Furthermore, improvements in the quality of institutions and macroeconomic stability substantially increased net foreign direct investment into the country. As demonstrated in Figure 8.3, foreign direct investments increased from 2.18% of GDP in 2003 to nearly 5% of GDP in 2010. Overall, government efforts to enhance fiscal transparency combined with good macroeconomic policies improved the investment climate and made the country more attractive for foreign direct investments.

Despite all these positive changes, local NGOs and many observers of EITI implementation in Peru felt that the society as a whole gained little from the EITI. While poverty and income inequality significantly declined due to solid economic performance throughout the last decade, social conflicts around the mining industry steadily rose. The main reason for increase in social unrest is that the gains from the mining sector were unevenly distributed across Peruvian regions. Approximately one-third of the Peruvian population lives in rural areas, yet 60.2% of the poor inhabited the rural areas in 2010. Many impoverished rural communities felt that they were left behind. Different natural resource endowments, unfocused social programs, the structure of regional economies and the decentralization process are among the potential factors that might account for the existing regional disparities. Another contributing factor for increased social tension is that the EITI is not designed to address environmental issues. The impact

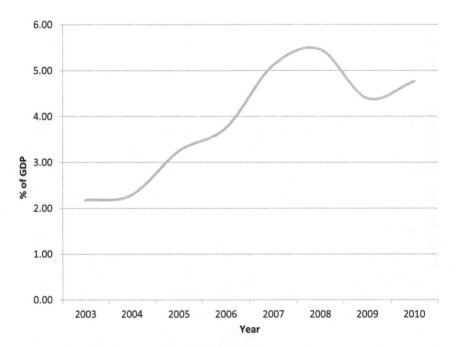

Figure 8.3 Foreign direct investment, Peru, 2003–2010

Source: The World Bank

of the extractive industry on the environment and the population is a salient issue in many mining communities.

The administrative division of Peru has significant implications for the implementation of the EITI. The country is divided into 25 regions (departments), 195 provinces and 1,834 districts. The main responsibilities of regional governments include planning regional development, implementing public investment projects, managing public property and promoting economic activity. Since the regions are highly heterogeneous in terms of geography, population and the level of economic development, the EITI needs to be implemented with great care at the sub-national level to strengthen the impact of the initiative. Another issue is enhancing transparency of public spending and social programs at both national and sub-national levels. Finally, Peru needs to improve its fiscal regime in the mining sector and generate more revenues to finance social and infrastructure projects in the rural areas.

8 Concluding remarks

Using data from 60 resource-abundant countries, this chapter has analyzed the impact of EITI membership on foreign direct investment, investment climate, corruption and cost of sovereign borrowing. The regression results clearly demonstrate that greater fiscal transparency, measured by EITI membership, tends to increase foreign direct investment flows into the country and reduce the incidence of corruption. We also find that EITI membership has a negligible impact on country risk premiums and investment climate in resource-abundant countries. When we use the Business Freedom Index as a broader measure of investment climate, we find that EITI membership significantly improves the country's business environment. Moreover, the two case studies shed some light on how the government's commitment to the improvement of fiscal transparency leads to a drop in the incidence of corruption and an increase in the flow of foreign direct investment.

These results have important policy implications for governments, investors and civil society groups. In particular, natural-resource-rich countries interested in eradicating corruption and attracting more direct investments from foreign countries ought to enhance fiscal transparency and establish policies in line with economic fundamentals. If governments are interested in attracting more foreign direct investment and reducing the level of corruption, then an effective policy option for governments may include introduction of a more transparent budgeting process, support of the EITI, regular publication of good quality economic data and the promotion of greater transparency in the public sector. Civil society can play an important role in advocating such policies and monitoring their enforcement.

Appendix 1

The list of countries included in the regression analysis (60)

Albania	Guatemala	Peru
Algeria	Guinea	Philippines
Angola	Indonesia	Qatar
Azerbaijan	Iran	Russia
Bahrain	Jordan	Saudi Arabia
Bolivia	Kazakhstan	Senegal
Botswana	Kuwait	Sierra Leone
Brazil	Kyrgyzstan	South Africa
Burkina Faso	Libya	Sudan
Cameroon	Mali	Syria
Chad	Mauritania	Tanzania
Chile	Mexico	Timor-Leste
Colombia	Mongolia	Togo
Congo Dem	Mozambique	Trinidad & Tobago
Congo Rep	Namibia	Turkmenistan
Cote d'Ivoire	Niger	UAE
Ecuador	Nigeria	Venezuela
Equatorial Guinea	Norway	Vietnam
Gabon	Oman	Yemen
Ghana	Papua New Guinea	Zambia

Appendix 2

Data summary

Variable	Mean	St. dev	Min	Max
	(1)	*(2)*	*(3)*	*(4)*
FDI	4.54	5.73	−14.37	45.15
EITI	.492	.84	0	3
Economic growth	3.35	5.16	−11.99	35.44
Executive constraints	4.14	1.98	1	7
Rule of law	−.55	.74	−1.76	1.99
Property rights	36.45	17.80	0	90
Current account Balance	2.15	13.87	−48.99	66.66
Inflation	7.43	7.71	−7.44	98.34
Fiscal balance	.66	7.64	−15.1	39.12
Government consumption	10.44	7.79	.9	55.25
Resource abundance	23.86	25.60	0	206.51
Log GDP per capita	8.40	1.26	5.54	11.21
Country risk	5.22	1.93	0	7
Country risk 2	57.62	12.79	20	91.4
Corruption	3.01	.74	1.82	5.63
Political competition	6.04	3.03	1	10
Risk premium	.04	.03	0	.15

Appendix 3

List of variables, definitions and sources

Variables	Definition	Source
Foreign Direct Investment	Foreign direct investment are the net inflows of investment to acquire a lasting management interest (10 percent or more of voting stock) in an enterprise operating in an economy other than that of the investor (% of GDP),	*World Development Indicators*, The World Bank
EITI	This study ranks all resource dependent countries (IMF definition and EITI implementation) based on their support of the EITI: non–member countries, candidate countries, early compliant countries and advanced compliant countries (if compliant more than two years). This variable takes four different values. Higher values indicate more transparency.	EITI web site
Economic Growth	Annual percentage growth rate of GDP at market prices based on constant local currency. Aggregates are based on constant 2000 U.S. dollars.	*World Development Indicators*, The World Bank
Executive Constraints	A measure of the extent of institutionalized constraints on the decision making powers of chief executives. The variable takes seven different values.	Polity IV Data Set www.systemicpeace. org/polity/polity4. htm
Political Competition	This variable combines development of institutional structures for political expression and extent to which non–elites are able to access institutional structures for political expression. Higher values indicate more competition.	Polity IV Data Set www.systemicpeace. org/polity/polity4. htm

Variables	Definition	Source
Government Consumption	Government consumption share of PPP converted GDP per capita at current prices (%).	The Penn World Table, https://pwt.sas. upenn.edu/php_site/ pwt_index.php
Rule of Law	Indicates perceptions of the extent to which agents have confidence in and abide by the rules of society, and in particular the quality of contract enforcement, property rights, the police, and the courts, as well as the likelihood of crime and violence. The value of the index ranges from –2.5 (weak) to 2.5 (strong).	*The Worldwide Governance Indicators* (WGI), The World Bank
Property Rights	An assessment of the ability of individuals to accumulate private property, secured by clear laws that are fully enforced by the state. It measures the degree to which a country's laws protect private property rights and the degree to which its government enforces those laws. The values of the property rights index range from 0 to 100, where 100 indicates the maximum protection.	The Heritage Foundation
Current Account Balance	Current account balance is the sum of net exports of goods, services, net income, and net current transfers (% of GDP).	*World Development Indicators,* The World Bank
Inflation	Inflation as measured by the consumer price index reflects the annual percentage change in the cost to the average consumer of acquiring a basket of goods and services (annual %).	*World Development Indicators,* The World Bank
Fiscal Balance	Central government receipts minus central government outlays, as a percentage of GDP.	Economic Intelligent Unit Data
Trade Openness	Trade freedom is a composite measure of the absence of tariff and non–tariff barriers that affect imports and exports of goods and services.	The Heritage Foundation
Resource Abundance	Total natural resources rents are the sum of oil rents, natural gas rents, metals and mineral rents (% of GDP).	*World Development Indicators,* The World Bank

(Continued)

(Continued)

Variables	Definition	Source
GDP Per Capita	GDP per capita is gross domestic product divided by midyear population. GDP is the sum of gross value added by all resident producers in the economy plus any product taxes and minus any subsidies not included in the value of the products.	*World Development Indicators*, The World Bank
Country Risk	OECD country risk classifications. The OECD country risk measure is composed of two components: a) transfer and currency convertibility risk and b) cases of force majeure. The values of this measure runs from zero to seven, zero indicating no country risk.	The OECD Webpage
Country Risk 2	The Business Freedom Index. This variable measures "individual's right to establish and run an enterprise without undue interference from the state". The values of the Business Freedom Index uses a scale from 0 to 100, where 100 indicates the maximum freedom.	The Heritage Foundation
Corruption	The World Bank's Control of Corruption Index (rescaled to run from 1 to 6). This index captures "perceptions of the extent to which public power is exercised for private gain, including both petty and grand forms of corruption, as well as "capture" of the state by elites and private interests". The value of the index ranges from 1 (most corrupt) to 6 (least corrupt).	*The World Bank Governance Indicators*, The World Bank
Risk Premium	A country risk premium refers to an increment in interest rates that would have to be paid for loans and investment projects in a particular country above some standard.	Country Risk Premiums, http://pages.stern. nyu.edu/~adamodar/

Notes

1 See EITI International Secretariat, "Benefits from Implementing EITI," http://eiti.org/eiti/benefits.
2 For a full list of the EITI principles, see EITI International Secretariat, "The EITI Principles," http://eiti.org/eiti/principles.
3 *EITI: Statement of Principles and Agreed Actions.* London Conference, 17 June 2003. Retrieved from http://webarchive.nationalarchives.gov.uk/+/www.dfid.gov.uk/pubs/files/eitidraftreportstatement.pdf.
4 For an overview of EITI benefits, see http://eiti.org/eiti/benefits.
5 We do not include the private sector in our analysis. Benefits of transparency at the micro-level are well documented, while studies that examine this issue at the country level are rare and their findings are mixed at best.
6 See Appendix 1 for a list of countries included in the regression analysis.
7 At least one study finds that foreign direct investment crowds out local entrepreneurship in the short run, although this effect is moderate in the long run. See: http://faculty.utep.edu/Portals/167/16%20Does%20Foreign%20Direct%20Investment%20Crowd%20Out%20Domestic%20Entrepreneurship.pdf.
8 Further discussion of the framework which underpins this study is found in the literature review section.
9 See Heritage Foundation, "The 2017 Index of Economic Freedom," Chapter 7, www.heritage.org/index/book/chapter-7.
10 See World Bank, "Worldwide Governance Indicators," http://info.worldbank.org/governance/wgi/resources.htm.
11 See Aswath Damodaran, "Country Default Spreads and Risk Premiums," http://pages.stern.nyu.edu/~adamodar/New_Home_Page/datafile/ctryprem.html.
12 EITI membership and fiscal transparency will be used interchangeably in the text.
13 This is a very narrow measure of fiscal transparency. The existing measures of fiscal transparency such as open budget index gauge a number of aspects of fiscal transparency.
14 See Technische Universität Wien, http://web.student.tuwien.ac.at/~e0301345/texte/dynamic_panel.pdf.

References

Aaronson, Susan A. 2011. "Limited Partnership: Business, Government, Civil Society, and the Public in the Extractive Industries Transparency Initiative (EITI)", *Public Administration and Development*, 31(1), 50–63.

Acemoglu, Daron and Simon Johnson. 2005. "Unbundling Institutions", *Journal of Political Economy*, 113(5), 949–995.

Alt, James E. and David D. Lassen. 2003. "The Political Economy of Corruption in American States", *Journal of Theoretical Politics*, 15(3), 341–365.

Anderson, T. W. and Cheng Hsiao. 1981. "Estimation of Dynamic Models With Error Components", *Journal of American Statistical Association*, 76(375), 598–606.

Arellano, Manuel and Stephen Bond. 1991. "Some Tests of Specification for Panel Data: Monte Carlo Evidence and an Application to Employment Equations", *Review of Economic Studies*, 58, 277–297.

Asiedu, Elizabeth. 2006. "Foreign Direct Investment in Africa: The Role of Natural Resources, Market Size, Government Policy, Institutions and Political Instability", *The World Economy*, 29(1), 63–77.

Auty, Richard M. 1993. *Sustaining Development in Mineral Economies: The Resource Curse Thesis*, Psychology Press, Hove, UK.

Bellver, Ana and Daniel Kaufmann. 2005. *Transparenting Transparency: Initial Empirics and Policy Applications*, World Bank Policy Research Working Paper, The World Bank, Washington DC.

Blundell, Richard and Stephen Bond. 1998. "Initial Conditions and Moment Restrictions in Dynamic Panel Data Models", *Journal of Econometrics*, 87(1), 115–143.

Christofides, Charis, Christian Mulder and Andrew Tiffin. 2003. *The Link Between Adherence to International Standards of Good Practice, Foreign Exchange Spreads, and Ratings*, IMF Working Paper No. 03/74, International Monetary Fund, Washington DC.

David-Barrett, Elizabeth, and Ken Okamura. 2010. "Transparency as a Tool for Reputation Building? Evidence From the Extractive Industries Transparency Initiative", available here www.transparencyconference.nl/wp-content/uploads/2012/05/DavidBarrett-Okamura.pdf

Dincer, Nergiz and Barry Eichengreen. 2009. *Central Bank Transparency: Causes, Consequences and Updates*, NBER Working Paper No. 14791, National Bureau of Economic Research, Cambridge, MA.

Fitch Ratings. 2006. "Fitch Assigns Nigeria 'BB-' Rating; Outlook Stable", available here www.dawodu.com/fitch2006.pdf

Fracasso, Andrea, Hans Genberg, and Charles Wyplosz. 2003. "How Does Central Banks Write? An Evaluation of Inflation Reports by Inflation Targeting Central Banks", Geneva Reports on the World Economy Special Report 2, International Center for Monetary and Banking Studies, Centre for Economic Policy Research and Norges Bank.

Gelos, R. Gaston and Shang-Jin Wei. 2005. "Transparency and International Portfolio Holdings", *Journal of Finance*, 60(6), 2987–3020.

Glaeser, Edward L., Rafael La Porta, Florencio Lopez-de-Silanes and Andrei Shleifer. 2004. "'Do Institutions Cause Growth", *Journal of Economic Growth*, 9, September, 271–303.

Glennerster, Rachel and Shin Yongseok. 2008. "Does Transparency Pay?" *IMF Staff Papers*, 55(1). International Monetary Fund, Washington DC.

Gupta, Sanjeev, Amine Mati, and Emanuele Baldacci. 2008. *Is It (Still) Mostly Fiscal? Determinants of Sovereign Spreads in Emerging Markets*, IMF Working Paper No. 08/259, International Monetary Fund, Washington DC.

Hameed, Farhan. 2005. *Fiscal Transparency and Economic Outcomes*, IMF Working Paper, pp. 1–45, International Monetary Fund, Washington DC.

IEG Evaluation of the Multi-Donor Trust Fund. 2011. "The World Bank", http://sitere sources.worldbank.org/EXTGLOREGPARPROG/Resources/GPR_EITI.pdf

Islam, Roumeen. 2006. "Does More Transparency Go Along With Better Governance?" *Economics & Politics*, 18(2), 121–167.

Kaufmann, Daniel, Aart Kraay and Massimo Mastruzzi. 2009. *Governance Matters VIII: Aggregate and Individual Governance Indicators, 1996–2008*, World Bank Policy Research Working Paper 4978, World Bank, Washington DC.

Kolstad, Ivar. 2009. "The Resource Curse: Which Institutions Matter?", *Applied Economics Letters*, 16(4), 439–442.

Kolstad, Ivar and Arne Wiig. 2009. "Is Transparency the Key to Reducing Corruption in Resource-Rich Countries?" *World Development*, 37(3), 521–532.

McGee, Rosemary and John Gaventa. 2010. *Review of Impact and Effectiveness of Transparency and Accountability Initiatives*, Institute of Development Studies, Brighton, UK.

Mehlum, Halvor, Karl Moene and Ragnar Torvik. 2006. "Institutions and the Resource Curse", *Economic Journal*, 116(508), 1–20.

Okonjo-Iweala, Ngozi. 2008. *Point of View: Nigeria's Shot at Redemption*, IMF Finance and Development, Washington DC.

Ölcer, Dilan. 2009. *Extracting the Maximum From EITI*, OECD Development Centre Working Paper No. 276, OECD, Paris.

Olken, Benjamin and Rohini Pande. 2011. *Corruption in Developing Countries*, Working Paper No 17398, National Bureau of Economic Research, Cambridge, MA.

Robinson, James A., Ragnar Torvik and Thierry Verdier. 2006. "Political Foundations of the Resource Curse", *Journal of Development Economics*, 79(2), 447–468.

Roodman, David. 2009. "How to Do xtabond2: An Introduction to Difference and System GMM in Stata", *Stata Journal*, StataCorp LP, 9(1), 86–136.

Ross, Michael. 1999. "The Political Economy of the Resource Curse", *World Politics*, 51, 297–322.

Scanteam. 2011. "Achievements and Strategic Options: Evaluation of the EITI", http://eiti.org/files/2011-EITI-evaluation-report.pdf.

Schneider, Friedrich and Bruno Frey. 1985. "Economic and Political Determinants of Foreign Direct Investment", *World Development*, 13(2), 161–175.

Standard & Poor's. 2006. "Credit FAQ: The Future of Sovereign Credit Ratings", September 5, 2006, http://www2.standardandpoors.com/spf/pdf/fixedincome/KR_sovereign_CreditFAQ.pdf

Stigler, George. 1961. "The Economics of Information", *Journal of Political Economy*, 69(3), 213–225.

Stiglitz, Joseph and Andrew Weiss. 1981. "Credit Rationing in Markets With Imperfect Information", *American Economics Review*, 71(3), 393–410.

Wei, Shang-Jin. 2000. "Local Corruption and Global Capital Flows", *Brookings Papers on Economic Activity*, 31(2), 303–354.

Index

Notes: Page numbers in *italics* indicate a figure and page numbers in **bold** indicate a table on the corresponding page.